United Nations Conference on Trade and Development

Investment Policy Review

Nigeria

UNITED NATIONS
New York and Geneva, 2009

NOTE

UNCTAD serves as the focal point within the United Nations Secretariat for all matters related to foreign direct investment. This function was formerly carried out by the United Nations Centre on Transnational Corporations (1975-1992). UNCTAD's work is carried out through intergovernmental deliberations, research and analysis, technical assistance activities, seminars, workshops and conferences.

The term "country" as used in this study also refers, as appropriate, to territories or areas; the designations employed and the presentation of the material do not imply the expression of any opinion whatsoever on the part of the Secretariat of the United Nations concerning the legal status of any country, territory, city or area or of its authorities, or concerning the delimitation of its frontiers or boundaries. In addition, the designations of country groups are intended solely for statistical or analytical convenience and do not necessarily express a judgement about the stage of development reached by a particular country or area in the development process.

The following symbols have been used in the tables:

Two dots (..) indicate that date are not available or not separately reported. Rows in tables have been omitted in those cases where no data are available for any of the elements in the row.

A dash (-) indicates that the item is equal to zero or its value is negligible.

A blank in a table indicates that the item is not applicable.

A slash (/) between dates representing years – for example, 2004/05, indicates a financial year.

Use of a dash (–) between dates representing years – for example 2004–2005 signifies the full period involved, including the beginning and end years.

Reference to the "dollars" ($) means United States dollars, unless otherwise indicated.

Annual rates of growth or change, unless otherwise stated, refer to annual compound rates.

Details and percentages in tables do not necessarily add to totals because of rounding.

The material contained in this study may be freely quoted with appropriate acknowledgement.

UNCTAD/DIAE/PCB/2008/1

UNITED NATIONS PUBLICATION
Sales E.08.II.D.11
ISBN 978-91-1-112743-0

PREFACE

The UNCTAD Investment Policy Reviews (IPRs) are intended to help countries improve their investment policies and familiarize Governments and the international private sector with an individual country's investment environment. The reviews are considered at the UNCTAD Commission on Investment, Enterprise and Development.

The Investment Policy Review of Nigeria, initiated at the request of the Government, was carried out through a fact-finding mission in October 2005. The mission received the full cooperation of the relevant ministries and agencies, in particular the Nigerian Investment Promotion Commission (NIPC). The mission also benefited from the views of the private sector, foreign and domestic, civil society and the resident international community, particularly bilateral donors and development agencies.

The report was presented at a national stakeholders' workshop held in Abuja in July 2008, and organized in collaboration with the Office of the Chief Economic Adviser to the President, the NIPC and the United Nations Development Programme (UNDP) office in Nigeria. After the workshop, the Secretary-General of UNCTAD presented the key recommendations of the IPR to the President of Nigeria and cabinet ministers. The President fully endorsed the IPR and its recommendations, and committed to send a high-level delegation to Geneva for the presentation of the IPR at UNCTAD's intergovernmental meeting.

This report was prepared by Rory Allan, Stephen Young, Massimo Meloni and Nana Adu Ampofo under the supervision of Fiorina Mugione and Chantal Dupasquier, and overall direction of Khalil Hamdani and James Zhan. Collaborators included Suraj Yakubu, Cécile Leque, Daniel Gay and Noelia Garcia Nebra. Lang Dinh provided research assistance and Elisabeth Anodeau-Mareschal provided production support. This report received the financial and logistical support of the UNDP office in Nigeria.

It is hoped that the analysis and recommendations of this review will contribute to improved policies, promote dialogue among stakeholders and catalyse investment and beneficial impact in Nigeria.

Geneva, December 2008

CONTENTS

TABLES

FIGURES

BOXES

ABBREVIATIONS

AGOA	African Growth and Opportunity Act (United States)
ASYCUDA	Automated System for Customs Data Entry
BIT	bilateral investment treaty
BOT	build–operate–transfer
BP	business permit
BPE	Bureau of Public Enterprises
CAC	Corporate Affairs Commission
CBN	Central Bank of Nigeria
CERPAC	Combined Expatriate Residence Permit and Alien Card
CET	common external tariff
DAS	Dutch Auction System
DFID	Department for International Development (of the United Kingdom Government)
DTT	double tax treaty
ECOWAS	Economic Community of West African Countries
EFCC	Economic and Financial Crimes Commission
EIA	Energy Information Administration
EIA	environmental impact assessment
EITI	Extractive Industries Transparency Initiative
EIU	Economist Intelligence Unit
EPZ	export processing zone
EQ	expatriate quota
FDI	foreign direct investment
FEPA	Federal Environmental Protection Agency
FGN	Federal Government of Nigeria
FIAS	Foreign Investment Advisory Service
FIRS	Federal Inland Revenue Service
FTZ	free trade zone
GDP	gross domestic product
GSM	Global System for Mobile
ICPC	Independent Corrupt Practices and other related offences Commission
ICSID	International Centre for Settlement of Investment Disputes
IDCC	Industrial Development Coordination Committee
IFC	International Finance Corporation
IFCTU	International Confederation of Free Trade Unions
ILO	International Labour Organization
IMF	International Monetary Fund
IPA	investment promotion agency
IPP	independent power producer
IPR	Investment Policy Review
LEEDS	Local Economic Empowerment and Development Strategies
M&A	mergers and acquisitions
MFN	most favoured nation
NAFDAC	National Agency for Food and Drug Administration and Control
NCC	Nigerian Copyright Commission
NCCA	National Commission for Conciliation and Arbitration
NCS	Nigeria Customs Service
NEEDS	National Economic Empowerment and Development Strategy
NEPA	National Electric Power Authority

NEPAD	New Partnership for Africa's Development
NEPD	Nigerian Investment Promotion Decree
NEPZA	Nigerian Export Processing Zones Authority
NIDO	Nigerians in the Diaspora Organization
NIPC	Nigerian Investment Promotion Commission
NIS	Nigeria Immigration Service
NITEL	Nigeria Telecommunications Limited
NNPC	Nigerian National Petroleum Corporation
NOIP	National Office of Industrial Property
NOSCP	National Oil Spill Contingency Plan
NOSDRA	National Oil Spill Detection and Response Agency
NOTAP	Nigerian Office for Technology Acquisition and Promotion
NOUN	National Open University of Nigeria
NPC	National Planning Commission
NT	national treatment
NTB	non-tariff barrier
OAU	Organization of African Unity
OECD	Organization for Economic Cooperation and Development
OPEC	Organization of the Petroleum Exporting Countries
OSIC	One-Stop Investment Centre
PIDC	Patent Information and Documentation Centre
PPP	public–private partnership
PUR	Permanent Until Reviewed Visa
R&D	research and development
SAP	structural adjustment programme
SEEDS	State Economic Empowerment and Development Strategy
SME	small and medium-sized enterprise
SMEDAN	Small–Medium Enterprise Development Agency Nigeria
SON	Standards Organization of Nigeria
STR	Subject to Regularization Visa
STRAP	Strategic Action against Piracy
TI	Transparency International
TNC	transnational corporation
TRIPS	Trade-Related Aspects of Intellectual Property Rights
UNDP	United Nations Development Programme
UNESCO	United Nations Educational, Scientific and Cultural Organization
UNIDO	United Nations Industrial Development Organization
VAT	value added tax
WACIP	West African Common Industrial Policy
WAEMU	West African Economic and Monetary Union
WB	World Bank
WBES	World Business Environment Survey
WDAS	Wholesale Dutch Auction System
WIPO	World Intellectual Property Organization
WTO	World Trade Organization

NIGERIA

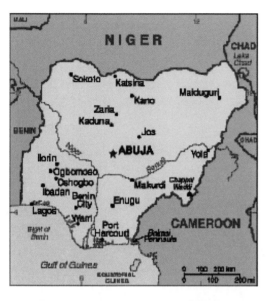

Business indicators 2007&2008

	Nigeria	Egypt	South Africa	ECOWAS
Starting a business (# of days)	9.0	7.0	8.0	11.0
Cost of registering property (% of property value)	22.2	1.0	8.8	13.0
Investor protection index	5.7	5.0	8.0	4.0
Rigidity of employment index	7.0	27.0	42.0	44.0
Cost of hiring (% of salary)	7.5	26.0	2.6	19.1
Firing cost (weeks of wages)	50.0	132.0	24.0	64.6
Enforcing contracts cost (% of debt)	32.0	25.3	33.2	51.0
Inter telecom cost ($/3 min call to US, 2004)	1.5	1.5	0.8	2.5
Time for export (days)	26.0	15.0	30.0	29.9
Time for import (days)	46.0	18.0	35.0	36.5
Domestic investment (% of GDP)	22.0	18.7	20.5	20.3

NIGERIA	1987-96 average	1997-06 average	2006	ECOWAS 2006
Key economic and social indicators				
Population (millions)	98.9	129.8	144.7	276.3
GDP at market prices (billion dollars)	26.7	58.8	115.3	185
GDP per capita (dollars)	270.0	453.1	797.0	669.7
Real GDP growth (per cent)	4.1	4.5	5.2	4.7
Inflation (annual %)	39.7	11.9	8.2	4.2
GDP by sector (%)				
Agriculture	31.1	29.3	23.3	8.5
Industry	45.7	46.8	56.8	7.8
Services	23.2	23.9	19.9	14.7
Trade (billions dollars):				
Merchandise exports	11	24	52	70.7
Services exports	0.7	2.2	4.2	2.7
Merchandise imports	6.4	12.3	21.8	45.1
Services imports	2.4	4.9	7.3	4.2
Exports of goods and services (% GDP)	38.9	46.8	56.3	46.4
Imports of goods and services (% GDP)	33.3	37.2	34.7	35.9
Capital flows (billions dollars) :				
Net FDI flows	1.4	2.2	5.5	6.8
FDI inflows (% GDP)	3.3	3.7	4.7	3.7
Net flows from private creditors	8.8	13.1	18.4	28.6
Net flows from official creditors	0.1	-0.2	2.5	7.1
Grants	0.2	0.8	6.1	10.6
Life expectancy at birth (years)	47.3	46.9	46.8	50.5
Infant mortality rate (per thousand)	120.0	101.9	98.6	99.8
Literacy rate, adult (per cent)	55.4	69.1	69.1	54.6
Literacy rate, youth (per cent)	71.2	84.2	84.2	67.6
Human development index (HDI) rank			158	159

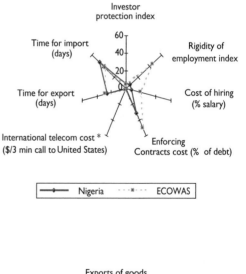

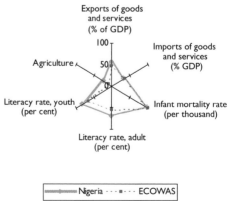

Sources: UNCTAD, FDI/TNC database, World Bank (Doing Business 2007&2008).

World Development Indicators and Global Development Finance. UNDP, Human Development Report 2007/2008.

INTRODUCTION

Nigeria is well known as a major oil producer. However, oil wealth has not been converted into a comparable improvement in living standards, due to decades of economic mismanagement. Compared to the early 1960s, agriculture, manufacturing and even services have all shrunk as a proportion of gross domestic product (GDP). For example, manufacturing exports per capita have halved. Furthermore, while foreign direct investment (FDI) has been prominent in oil and gas development, it has remained low in other sectors and of marginal developmental value.

The return to democracy in 1999 was accompanied by a fundamental reorientation of economic policy, expressed in Nigeria's "home-grown" National Economic Empowerment and Development Strategy (NEEDS). Following this new approach, the Government is gradually withdrawing from direct conduct of commercial activity to embrace a private sector-led growth strategy. Foreign investors are therefore fully welcome to participate in the process. Although their response has so far been most evident in the utilities sector, there are signs of increased foreign interest throughout the economy.

As a result of the measures taken by the Government, Nigeria is today more open and corruption is being tackled. Against this background, high growth rates, together with favourable oil prices and unprecedented fiscal responsibility, create a unique opportunity for lifting millions of people out of poverty in a sustainable manner. In manufacturing, the strategic focus of this report a more robust presence of transnational corporations (TNCs) can help to bridge capital, management, skills and technology gaps where they are most severe, and to support the competence of local companies and the workforce towards world standards. This would enable Nigerian manufactures and services companies, foreign and national alike, to stand with the best in supplying local and global markets.

For this to happen, however, sustained policy action and appropriate strategies are required. In this regard, this report examines how to obtain a more significant contribution of investment, including FDI. In addition to reviewing the investment framework needed to regulate and facilitate FDI, the report focuses on the strategic importance of FDI beyond the oil sector. Thus, given its importance for broad-based development, the report proposes a strategy to foster a flourishing manufacturing sector, including in the agro-allied industries. While FDI in the hydrocarbon sector, including downstream activity, is historically prominent in terms of flows, this report does not elaborate on a strategic orientation for the oil sector. Furthermore, the role of State and local administrations, in spite of its importance for shaping the investment environment in Nigeria, is not covered in this review.

The report is structured as follows. *Chapter I* provides an overview of FDI trends and performance. Once a dynamic player in all sectors of the economy, FDI has been largely concentrated in oil extraction since the 1970s due to the sector's profitability, successive indigenization policies affecting the non-oil sectors and the overall poor infrastructure in the country. As a result, Nigeria has significantly underperformed compared to other large African countries in attracting FDI beyond the oil sector. In addition, foreign operations in the country are generally at very early stages of firm-level development and their impact on wider industrial development has been low.

Chapter II analyzes the investment framework. Since 1995, Nigeria has been open to FDI in virtually all sectors of the economy, and foreign and domestic investors receive the same treatment in most respects. An impressive number of modernizing reforms, ranging from the design of a competition regime to the restructuring of the labour and tax regimes, are currently reshaping the investment environment. However, a series of regulatory impediments – relating primarily to the registration of foreign investors, their access to land, the status and conditions for the entry of expatriate workers and to some aspects of the taxation regime – still need to be addressed. Some of these measures represent a quite recent turnaround from policies that thwarted FDI for decades and have not yet affected investor sentiment. In this regard, issues of insecurity, instability and corruption are candidly acknowledged by the Government, which is showing resolve in tackling them.

Chapter III outlines a strategy of "supported market forces" to induce and support foreign affiliates in manufacturing to increase their presence in the country and in so doing their contribution to Nigeria's development. Improving the investment climate will certainly provide the conditions to attract more FDI to Nigeria's large market. However, globalization has changed the world of manufacturing, and Nigeria needs a strategy that reflects contemporary realities. Important new institutions are therefore proposed, along with an upgrading of the Nigerian Investment Promotion Commission (NIPC) to address the challenges brought about by the new global environment. In this regard, good strategic policy, combined with improved management of its growing oil wealth, give Nigeria opportunities available to few other developing countries.

Chapter IV summarizes the main findings of the report and the proposed policy recommendations.

I. FDI TRENDS AND PERFORMANCE

Today, the FDI story of Nigeria is dominated by the oil industry. It was not always so. At independence, in 1960, there was a widespread FDI presence in the economy. Policy design thereafter narrowed the scope for FDI and decades of political instability, economic mismanagement and endemic corruption further reduced Nigeria's ability to attract and retain FDI. This was compounded by a relentless deterioration of the country's social conditions and physical infrastructure, in spite of increased public revenues generated by the oil sector.

While oil has played an important role in Nigeria, data show that over 70 per cent of the population lives on less than one dollar a day (this represents a quarter of all Africans living in this condition). The manufacturing sector, the focus of the FDI strategy of this report, has hardly progressed and only 3 per cent of agriculture is mechanized.

The return to democracy in 1999 has created the opportunity for economic renewal and an associated broader base of FDI. To reap the benefits from FDI, the Government of Nigeria undertook ambitious measures with a view to improve the investment climate. The reform process also takes into account the potential role that could play the Diaspora (close to 5 million Nigerians live abroad). The policy changes have started bearing fruits and if sustained, they will certainly provide an environment more conducive to private investment and contribute to enhance the attractiveness to FDI of Nigeria's large and growing market.

A. Economic backdrop

At independence, in addition to being a leading exporter of groundnut, Nigeria accounted for 16 and 43 per cent of world cocoa and oil palm production respectively.[1] The country was largely self-sufficient in terms of domestic food production (85 per cent) and Nigerian agriculture contributed to over 60 per cent of GDP and 90 per cent of exports. Conversely, manufacturing was less than 3 per cent of GDP and 1 per cent of exports, while the oil sector represented only 0.2 per cent of GDP.

At that time, the foreign presence in the economy was significant. More than 25 per cent of companies registered in Nigeria in 1956 were foreign-owned while in 1963 as much as 70 per cent of investment in the manufacturing sector was from foreign sources (Ohiorhenuan, 1990). Most FDI was from the Middle East and Europe (the United Kingdom especially) and concentrated in commerce and cash crops.

The first National Development Plan (1962–1968) sought to broaden the base of the economy and limit the risk of over-dependence on foreign trade (Okigbo, 1989). In keeping with the developmental rhetoric of that era, the tariff structure was formulated with industrialization and import substitution in mind. Manufacturing initially responded positively to the new policy but with foreign exchange and import licensing controls introduced in 1971–1972, the progress halted.

In addition to industrialization, removing the dominance of foreign entities in Nigerian economic and political life was a preoccupation of popular discourse. Legislation embodying goals of economic nationalism and State-led growth was adopted.

The second National Development Plan (1970–1974) accelerated indigenization on grounds that it was "vital for Government...to acquire, by law if necessary, the greater proportion of the productive assets of the economy" (p. 289). Restrictions were therefore imposed on the activities of foreign investors with the

---

[1] By 1997, Nigeria's share of world oil palm production had dropped to 7 per cent.

first "indigenization decree" adopted in 1972.[2] The zenith of the indigenization policy, however, was the second indigenization decree in 1977.[3] The result has been described as amongst the most comprehensive joint venture schemes in Africa and the developing world at large (Biersteker, 1987). The number of activities reserved exclusively for Nigerians was expanded to include a wide range of basic manufactures. Foreign firms were compelled to enter into joint ventures with local capitals or the State (box I.1). Many foreign investors – such as IBM, Chase Manhattan Bank and Citigroup – divested during this period.[4]

Box I.1. FDI policies in Nigeria before and after 1995

The indigenization policy started in 1972 with "the Nigerian Enterprises Promotion Decree" (NEPD). The decree imposed several restrictions on FDI entry. As a result, some 22 business activities were exclusively reserved for Nigerians, including advertising, gaming, electronics manufacturing, basic manufacturing, road transport, bus and taxi services, the media and retailing and personal services. Foreign investment was permitted up to 60 per cent ownership and provided that the proposed enterprise had, based on 1972 data, share capital of ₦200,000 ($300,000) or turnover of ₦500,000 ($760,000).

The second indigenization decree, the Nigerian Enterprises Promotion Decree of 1977, tightened restrictions on FDI entry in three ways: (a) by expanding the list of activities exclusively reserved to Nigerian investors (e.g. bus services, travel agencies, the wholesaling of home products, film distribution, newspapers, radio and television and hairdressing); (b) by lowering permitted foreign participation in the FDI-restricted activities from 60 to 40 per cent and adding new activities restricted to 40 per cent foreign ownership such as fish-trawling and processing, plastic and chemicals manufacturing, banking and insurance; and (c) by creating a second list of activities where permitted foreign investment was reduced from 100 to 60 per cent ownership, including manufacturing of drugs, some metals, glass, hotels and oil services companies.

Relaxation of these restrictions began in 1989. The NEPD was amended so as to leave a single group of 40 business activities in which foreign participation was completely prohibited unless the value of the enterprise exceeded ₦20 million ($2.7 million in 1989). In addition, foreign investors could hold only a share of up to 40 per cent in insurance, banking, oil production and mining.

Finally, in 1995, the Nigerian Investment Promotion Commission Act opened all sectors to foreign participation except for a short negative list (including drugs and arms) and allowed for 100 per cent foreign ownership in all sectors, with the exception of the petroleum sector (where FDI is limited to joint ventures or production sharing). For more details on the current FDI regime, see chapter II.

Sources: NIPC and UNCTAD.

The third National Development Plan (1975–1980) was framed after the world price of crude oil quadrupled (1973) and the share of oil in total exports reached 90 per cent. In this setting, exchange controls were reduced and restrictions on import payments abandoned. Public expenditure increased sharply and the Naira appreciated, further eroding agricultural competitiveness. Additional incentives for industrialization were adopted, including pioneer status and fast depreciation allowance on capital goods. These incentives produced a temporary increase in manufacturing output, which grew on average 14 per cent per annum between 1975 and 1980, compared to 6 per cent in services. On the other hand, agriculture production shrank by 2 per cent annually over the same period.

---

[2] The first decree did not cause the large multinationals to quit Nigeria although the smaller firms of Levantine origin were affected and FDI inflows did fall.
[3] 1977 Nigerian Enterprise Promotion Decree, which imposed restrictions on FDI in several economic sectors. More details in chapter II.
[4] The three of them have since returned, although Chase Manhattan Bank closed its branch in 1996–1997.

Following the major decline of oil prices in the early 1980s, the shortcomings of past economic planning were exposed. Agriculture accounted for less than 10 per cent of exports and the country had become a net food importer. Manufacturing output started falling at about 2 per cent per annum between 1982 and 1986 while GDP stagnated, with less than 1 per cent growth annually. Furthermore, by 1986, there were about 1,500 State-owned enterprises, of which 600 were under the control of the federal Government and the remainder under State and local Governments. The evidence suggests that many made no contribution to Nigeria's productive capacities and many enterprises were not financially viable (Mahmoud, 2004).

Figure I.1. Economic structure and manufacturing output in Nigeria and selected comparator countries, 1965–2003*

(Percentages, millions of dollars)

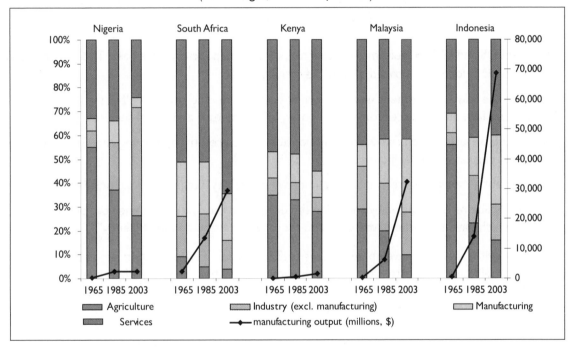

Source: World Bank, World Development Indicators Database.
Notes: Oil production is accounted for in "industry".
* 2003 is the most recent available data for comparing the manufacturing sector performance.

The cumulative effect of these policies is that Nigeria has not undergone the structural transformation experienced by other developing countries in the last 40 years (figure I.1). Manufacturing still represents only around 4 per cent of GDP, compared with 14 per cent on average throughout sub-Saharan Africa.[5] Furthermore, the comparative growth of manufacturing and services in Malaysia (also a leading oil palm producer at independence in 1957) and in Indonesia (a large country with significant oil production) are clear examples of how Nigeria has fallen behind.[6] Hence, nearly 40 years of misallocation of public finances have taken a heavy toll on the state of basic infrastructures. Maintenance spending at levels close to zero led to the sharp deterioration in the water supply, sewerage, sanitation, drainage, roads and electricity infrastructure (Central Bank of Nigeria, 2004a; and World Bank, 1996).

---

[5] World Bank, World Development Indicators 2007. The figure refers to 2005, latest available.
[6] Of course, there are also bright spots, such as Nigeria's vibrant film industry, better known throughout Africa as "Nollywood". The film industry has been growing consistently since the mid-1990s and is today Nigeria's second biggest employer after agriculture (see: Economist, 2006).

In order to restore economic prosperity and address external shocks such as the global recession of the early 1980s, the Government initiated a series of austerity measures and stabilization initiatives in 1981–1982. These, however, proved unsuccessful and a structural adjustment programme (SAP) followed. The SAP (1986–1988), which emphasized privatization, market liberalization and agricultural exports orientation, was not implemented consistently and was at odds with other facets of policy, e.g. tariff increases. But an economic reform process, which continues to the present, has it origins in this period.

Following the return to democracy in May 1999, the reform process was re-energized, mainly through Nigeria's home-grown poverty reduction strategy. The National Economic Empowerment and Development Strategy (NEEDS), adopted in 2003, was meant to guide public policies until 2007. The preparation of NEEDS followed a highly participatory process. Associated poverty reduction strategies were developed at the State and local levels – State Economic Empowerment and Development Strategies (SEEDS) and Local Economic Empowerment and Development Strategies (LEEDS).

NEEDS, SEEDS and LEEDS were major departures from the policies of the past. Their broad agenda of social and economic reforms was based on four key strategies to:

(a) Reform the way Government works in order to improve efficiency in delivering services, eliminate waste and free up resources for investment in infrastructure and social services;

(b) Make the private sector the main driver of economic growth, by turning the Government into a business regulator and facilitator;

(c) Implement a "social charter", including improving security, welfare and participation; and

(d) Push a "value re-orientation by shrinking the domain of the State and hence the pie of distributable rents which have been the haven of public sector corruption and inefficiency".

In contrast with previous development plans, NEEDS made FDI attraction an explicit goal for the Government and paid particular attention to drawing investment from wealthy Nigerians abroad and from Africans in the Diaspora. In this context, both current President Yar'Adua and his predecessor President Obasanjo have consistently expressed commitment to removing barriers to FDI in non-oil sectors. Though most FDI is still destined for the oil industry, the steps being taken under the reform agenda are bearing fruit. Average GDP growth, which was 2.8 per cent per annum between 2000 and 2003, had reached 6 per cent in 2006 (9.4 per cent in the non-oil sector). The Government has now set a two-digit growth target for the short-to-medium term.[7] According to NEEDS, Nigeria would have to achieve 30 per cent annual investment and 7 to 8 per cent growth to successfully halve poverty by 2015 in line with the Millennium Development Goals. However, growth alone will not automatically translate into poverty reduction. To achieve this objective, Nigeria will need to implement socially-oriented policy reforms.

The reform drive informed by NEEDS also allowed Nigeria to become the first African country to settle its official debt through an agreed-upon programme of debt forgiveness and repayment in October 2005. This achievement, together with a banking sector reform initiated by the Central Bank of Nigeria in 2004, aimed at fostering consolidation in the sector, helped the country improve its financial environment. As a result, Nigeria received a BB- credit rating from Fitch and Standard and Poor's Ratings Agencies in early 2006, the same rating of countries such as Brazil and Ukraine.

NEEDS is currently under review, and will be harmonized with the policy platform of the new administration which took office in mid-2007. President Yar'Adua has indicated that the new development strategy will not abandon the focus on private sector-led development and will rely on a "seven-point agenda": (1) wealth creation; (2) development of physical infrastructure (power, energy and transportation); (3) human capital development (education and health); (4) security, law and order; (5) land tenure changes

---

[7] "FG Targets Two-Digit GDP Growth Rate", in *Daily Trust*, 24 October 2007.

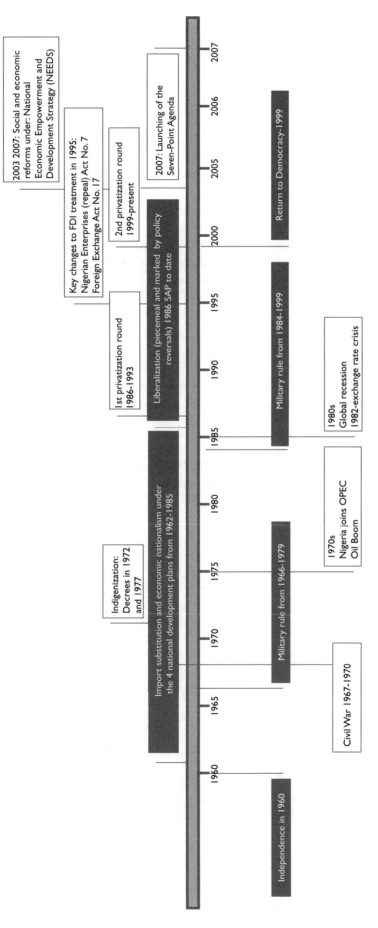

Figure I.2. Timeline of major economic and policy events in Nigeria since independence

Source: UNCTAD.

and home ownership; (6) regional development (Niger Delta); and (7) food security. The ultimate goal is to make Nigeria one of the 20 largest economies in the world by 2020.[8]

B. FDI trends

1. FDI size and growth

FDI inflows to Nigeria have been profoundly affected by the development of the oil sector, its world price and the Government's policies in this area.

In 1970, one year before Nigeria joined the Organization for the Petroleum Exporting Countries (OPEC), FDI inflows stood at $205 million. By 1975, they had reached $470 million. As figure 1.3 shows, FDI inflows also reacted positively to more attractive fiscal terms for private sector participation in oil and gas that were introduced in 1986. The reduction of the Nigerian National Petroleum Corporation (NNPC) stake in Shell Nigeria and other oil companies from 80 to 60 per cent, which took place in 1989 (mergers and acquisition (M&A) data shows $1 billion worth of such transactions in 1989, after which FDI inflows to Nigeria have never decreased below $1 billion per year) also had a positive impact.

In the same way, although there are indications that non-oil FDI is rising (section B.3), the correlation between the level of world oil prices and the FDI inflows to Nigeria is particularly strong. This is especially the case since the early 2000s, when the rise in oil prices undoubtedly explains most of the sharp increase in FDI (figure 1.3).

Figure 1.3. FDI inflows to Nigeria, 1970 - 2007
(Millions of dollars)

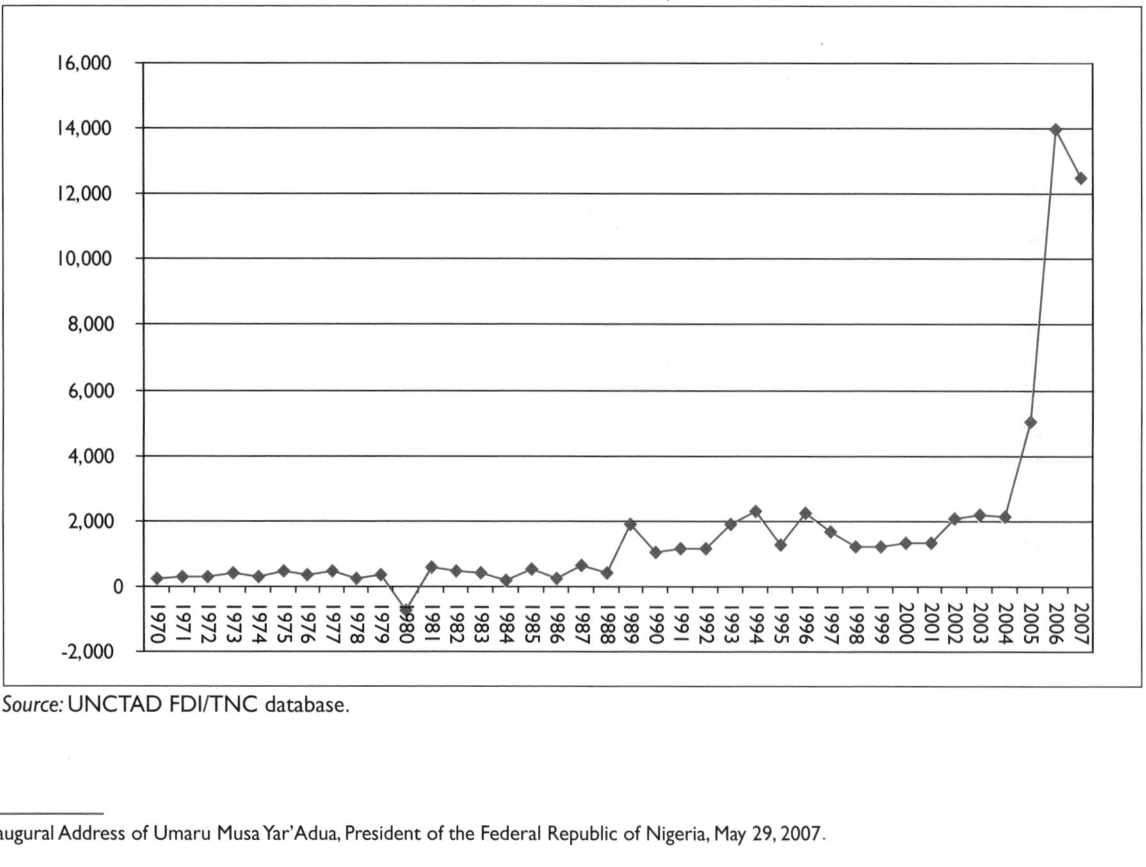

Source: UNCTAD FDI/TNC database.

---

[8] Inaugural Address of Umaru Musa Yar'Adua, President of the Federal Republic of Nigeria, May 29, 2007.

FDI inflows in sectors other than oil were directly affected by the various private sector policies adopted since the early 1970s. For instance, figure I.3 shows clearly that FDI inflows fell in the immediate aftermath of the Second Indigenization Decree, which pushed many TNCs to divest. Among those were Citigroup, IBM and Barclays Bank in 1979.

Restrictions on the entry of non-oil FDI continued until the late 1980s. In 1989, they were partially reversed (box I.1), which contributed to the shift in the levels of FDI after that year. However, it was not until 1995 that the National Investment Promotion Act opened virtually all areas of the economy to foreign investors. This was accompanied by the Foreign Exchange Decree, which eased access to foreign exchange for business purposes. More recently, the improved macroeconomic environment and the reforms to the business environment explain the increase in non-oil FDI.

Between 1970 and the mid-1990s, Nigeria – as the primary destination of FDI inflows to Africa – accounted for more than 30 per cent of all FDI inflows to the continent. This is largely a result of its oil attractiveness. However, in 2007, notwithstanding the booming oil industry, Nigeria accounted for only about 16 per cent of total FDI inflows to Africa. Its leading role in terms of attracting FDI started eroding due to the surge of FDI inflows to other oil-rich countries, such as Angola and Sudan. Another factor is the improved FDI performance of other large African countries such as Egypt and South Africa, which were successful in attracting FDI in diverse sectors of their economies (table I.1).

Given its population, Nigeria's recent underperformance in FDI attraction within Africa is becoming more pronounced. In the first half of the 1990s, per capita FDI inflows were higher in Nigeria than in any other African country in the table I.1 sample, with the exception of Angola and Equatorial Guinea. Thereafter, other African countries began to catch up. In the most recent period (2001–2007), the average per capita FDI inflows to other large African countries and other oil producers in the continent all exceeded those to Nigeria. This indicates that Nigeria is not sharing fully the growing non-oil FDI to the continent.

Nigeria is the dominant recipient of FDI within the Economic Community of West African Countries (ECOWAS) group, accounting for more than 70 per cent of group inflows since 2001. In the 1970s, Nigeria attracted about half of the FDI inflows to the region. The increased Nigerian share since then reflects both the less restrictive conditions for oil FDI and the growing foreign interest for the sector.

In terms of absolute FDI stock, Nigeria remains second only to South Africa in the continent with $63 billion and $93 billion respectively. In per capita terms, however, its relative underperformance is evident, and while its stock ($424) is at par with the African average ($405), it is much smaller than that of other oil-producing countries, and of South Africa and Egypt.

FDI to Nigeria is nonetheless a key contributor to the country's capital accumulation. During 2001–2007, FDI accounted for more than half the gross fixed capital formation (GFCF), compared to an average of around 15 per cent in the rest of Africa, and 12 per cent for developing countries as a group.

2.   Nigerian privatization and FDI

In many developing countries, privatization has been a very important source of FDI over the last two decades. Nigeria has implemented two rounds of privatization since the 1980s – the first one (1968–1993) as part of the structural adjustment programme (SAP) and the second one since return to democracy in 1999.

Table 1.1. Comparative performance of Nigeria with selected countries, 1971-2006

(Dollars and percentage)

| | ABSOLUTE PERFORMANCE | | | | | | RELATIVE PERFORMANCE | | | | | | | | | | | | | | | | |
| | FDI inflows (Millions dollars) | | | | | FDI stocks (Millions dollars) | Per capita (Dollars) | | | | | Per $1000 GDP | | | | | As per cent of GFCF (%) | | | | | FDI Stock | |
Country name	1971-1980	1981-1990	1991-1995	1996-2000	2001-2007	2007	1971-1980	1981-1990	1991-1995	1996-2000	2001-2007	1971-1980	1981-1990	1991-1995	1996-2000	2001-2007	1971-1980	1981-1990	1991-1995	1996-2000	2001-2007	Per capita ($) 2007	% GDP 2007
Nigeria	**225**	**608**	**1,543**	**1,506**	**5,572**	**62,791**	**4**	**7.4**	**15.6**	**13.5**	**39.5**	**13**	**21.8**	**32.3**	**29.4**	**47.7**	**5.5**	**17.1**	**35.7**	**43.9**	**51.4**	**424.0**	**41.5**
Large Regionals																							
South Africa	58	7	377	1,517	2,984	93,474	2.7	0.4	9.2	34.4	63.0	3	0	2.6	10.7	16.9	1.2	-0.1	1.7	6.6	10.6	1,924.3	34.3
Egypt	226	878	729	980	4,364	50,503	5.3	17.3	12.3	15.1	58.9	12.5	25.9	13.1	10.8	39.0	4.4	5.6	7.9	6.1	21.3	668.9	39.6
Oil Producers																							
Angola	6	96	379	1,011	847	12,207	0.9	10.7	33.1	75.4	60.1	2	18	41.3	150.1	93.9	..	10.3	18.9	57.7	71.9	717.0	19.9
Sudan	3	3	22	246	1,776	13,828	0.2	0.1	0.8	7.7	48.4	0.4	0.3	1.7	23.9	71.8	0.4	0.2	1.7	16.3	34.8	358.6	30
Equatorial Guinea	0	3	30	191	1,373	10,745	-0.1	7.6	78.5	447.8	2,814.3	-0.4	24.1	202.4	420	301.3	..	14.4	36.9	44	67	21,172.5	102.5
Indonesia	453	418	2,342	843	2,664	58,955	3.4	2.4	12.2	4.5	11.5	17.2	4.4	12.8	0.5	6.7	9.8	1.7	4.7	-1.1	2.5	254.5	13.6
ECOWAS	**439**	**870**	**1,900**	**2,378**	**6,756**	**81,267**	**3.9**	**5.4**	**9.8**	**10.9**	**25**	**12.3**	**13.9**	**22.5**	**25.6**	**37.9**	**5.1**	**8.1**	**19**	**22.7**	**22.1**	**287.1**	**32.7**
ECOWAS excluding Nigeria	213	262	357	872	1,184	18,476	3.7	3.3	3.8	8.1	9.3	11.9	8	9.3	21.4	19.8	7.5	5.6	6.4	12.6	11.4	136.9	22.7
Côte d'Ivoire	50	45	118	325	285	5,702	7	4.2	8.3	20.4	15.6	10.9	5.1	11.3	27.1	18.5	4.8	4	11.7	19.7	19.1	296	27.9
Ghana	17	9	101	133	294	3,634	1.6	0.6	5.9	7		5.9	1.8	17.3	20.3	26.5	4	1.1	8.1	9.2	10.2	154.8	24.5
Africa excluding Nigeria	**812**	**1,798**	**3,373**	**8,203**	**22,776**	**330,638**	**2.2**	**3.7**	**5.7**	**12.4**	**29.5**	**5.1**	**5**	**7.3**	**15.7**	**29.5**	**2.4**	**2.1**	**4.1**	**8.6**	**14.6**	**405.2**	**30**
Developing countries and territories	6,825	24,058	78,047	202,362	295,606	4,246,739	3.1	6.5	18.1	43	57.1	6.3	8.6	16	32.1	30.7	2.6	3.4	6.4	13.2	11.9	792.5	29.8

Source: UNCTAD, FDI/TNC Database, Globstat.

During the first privatization wave, foreign investors were excluded from bidding in all sectors except oil. This was effectively the last major expression of the indigenization policy. The sale of oil interests to Elf Aquitaine for $500 million in 1992, however, represented almost two thirds of the total proceeds from privatization ($740 million). Before the process stalled due to lack of investor interest, 88 of the 111 companies slated for privatization were privatized, including those in the financial, agriculture, food manufacturing, tourism and transport (railroad) industries.

In contrast, the second privatization wave, originally scheduled to last from 1999 to the end of 2003, focused on attracting foreign investment. By then, the 1995 landmark NIPC decree was in place. Almost 100 enterprises were targeted for privatization or commercialization in three phases.[9]

- Phase I – Full divestiture of Government ownership in banks, oil marketing and cement;

- Phase II – Full divestiture in hotels, insurance companies, vehicle assembly and parts, and other enterprises in competitive markets; and

- Phase III – Partial divestiture of Government ownership in major public enterprises in backbone services, e.g. electric power, telecommunications, ports and rails, oil and gas.

All 14 enterprises intended for the first phase of the current round of privatization have been fully divested. Sale proceeds totalled approximately N28 billion ($261 million), of which about N4 billion ($36 million) was from foreign sources. Another 14 enterprises falling under phase two had been privatized by April 2005 and N8 billion ($62.4 million) was raised for the federal Government as a result. Foreign investors included Blue Circle Industries of the United Kingdom (71 per cent of Ashaka Cement Co. Plc. and 58 per cent of the West African Portland Company – WAPCO), Scancem of Norway (87 per cent of Cement Company of Northern Nigeria) and Global Infrastructure of India (80 per cent stake of Delta Steel Company).

Progress in the privatization of Nigeria's public utilities (phase III) has been slower due to the need to develop an adequate regulatory and institutional environment for private sector participation. Privatization in the power sector has proceeded so far as the restructuring of the industry but divestiture is as yet to be realized. Nevertheless, there have been some successes in the drive to draw FDI into Nigeria's third phase industries, particularly in aviation and ports (chapter II reviews the regulatory environment for the backbone services in more detail).

3. FDI by sector and country of origin

Any accurate analysis of the distribution, role and impact of FDI inflows in a host economy should be based on reliable statistics. In Nigeria, such analysis is made difficult by concerns about data quality and availability issues (annex I). In the absence of reliable official data as to the sector composition of FDI, estimates have largely been made from alternative sources.[10] Prior to the 1970s, oil FDI was estimated to amount to only 10 per cent of total inflows. FDI was significant in commerce and what were then Nigeria's principal exports, e.g. palm oil (World Bank, 1974; and Central Bank of Nigeria, 2004b). Since then, FDI inflows have concentrated in the oil sector.[11] This is despite the opening of the economy to FDI started in the 1990s and the efforts to attract investment in other sectors, including via the establishment of free trade zones (FTZs). Nevertheless, more recently, an incipient diversification of FDI inflows is observed (see below in this section). It is attributable to the positive effect of the improvements in macroeconomic management and in the business environment on investors' confidence, as reflected in the favourable country rating

---

[9] Note that the phases refer to the planned sequencing of privatization; the actual privatization timetable varied. For example, bank privatizations were taking place as late as October 2002, whilst phase II began in January of the same year.

[10] Indeed, the two official sources of FDI statistics provide starkly contrasting views, both of which are likely to be inaccurate. For example, Central Bank statistics suggest that non-oil FDI is actually lower now that in the 1990s. Annex I to this chapter presents these statistics and measures needed to provide more credible information.

[11] Some official comments suggest that oil FDI accounts for 90 per cent ot total FDI inflows.

by international rating agencies, and in the de-listing of the country by the Financial Action Task Force (Chapter II).[12]

Prospects for the continued attraction of oil FDI in the near future remain positive, due to the commodity's high price. Exxon Mobil Corporation, for instance, plans to invest $11 billion in the country's oil sector through 2011 and the Total Oil group has announced plans to invest approximately $10 billion in the industry over the years 2005–2011.

There are some indications that FDI inflows to sectors other than oil and gas are reacting positively to the various reforms to the investment climate carried out since 1999 (many of which will be addressed in chapter II of this report). Several established non-fuel-sector TNCs have recently expanded production in Nigeria. For example, Heineken invested €250 million (about $390 million) in purchasing and expanding Nigerian Breweries in 2004.[13] The South African telecommunication company MTN, now the largest mobile telephony operator in Nigeria, has invested over $3 billion in the sector between 2001 and 2006, and has expressed commitment to ongoing expansion.

The Nigerian authorities are also renewing their efforts to attract FDI to the FTZs. Between 2001 and 2007, four new zones became operational and 10 more were under construction. At present, of the nine operational zones, three are reserved for services to the oil sector. The remaining zones have so far attracted some FDI. Calabar, the most advanced zone, reported total foreign investment of about $230 million as of the end of 2005 (more details on the FTZs and their performance are given in chapter III).

Nigeria's underperformance in FDI attraction outside the oil sector can nonetheless be illustrated by reference to prominent TNCs that are *not* present in Nigeria but have invested in its peers. Table 1.2 shows that in 2003, only 18 of the top 100 world's largest non-oil TNCs (as measured by assets held abroad) had affiliates in Nigeria, compared with 42 in South Africa, 25 in Egypt, and 17 in Kenya. In total, 41 of the top 100 were present in at least one of these countries but not in Nigeria. These 41 TNCs represent a wide range of sectors, with pharmaceuticals and motor vehicles prominent, as shown in table 1.3.

An important challenge for the diversification of future FDI flows into the Nigerian economy will be the attraction of world-class TNCs. As discussed later in chapter III, continued growth in Nigeria's internal market, matched with accelerated regional integration within ECOWAS, would contribute to Nigeria's FDI attractiveness, including for the world's top TNCs.

Table 1.2. Presence of World's 100 Largest TNCs in major African economies

	Nigeria	**Kenya**	**Egypt**	**South Africa**
TNCs present	24	19	26	45
Oil	6	2	1	3
Non-oil	18	17	25	42

Source: UNCTAD (2005c).

However, their decisions will be heavily influenced by concerns about insecurity and instability. Poor perceptions are fed by the frequent disruptions of oil production and incidents involving foreign personnel and assets in the Niger Delta oil region. Objectively, these issues are less problematical outside the oil sector and need to be more firmly differentiated in investors' perceptions. For example, in 2007, the World Economic Forum's index of business perceptions of costs of crime and violence ranks Nigeria 120th of 130 countries – but ahead of Brazil, Kenya and South Africa. Chapter III of this report notes the need to formalize an approach to improving perceptions of Nigeria in the international investment community.

---

[12] Central Bank of Nigeria, *Annual Report & Statement of Accounts for the Year Ended 31st December 2007,* Abuja 2007.
[13] Agreement for increase in stake from 24 per cent to 50.05 per cent, 29th November 2004.

Table I.3. Global top-100 non-oil TNCs present in Africa but absent from Nigeria

Home country	Number
Total	41
Australia	2
Canada	1
Finland	1
France	8
Germany	8
Japan	5
Norway	1
Spain	1
Switzerland	2
Sweden	1
United Kingdom	2
United States	9

Sector	Number
Total	41
Chemicals	2
Diversified	3
Electronic & electric equipment	3
Food & beverages	-
Machinery & equipment	1
Media	2
Metal products	2
Mining	2
Motor vehicles	8
Non-metallic mineral products	2
Pharmaceuticals	4
Telecommunications	6
Textiles	1
Tobacco	1
Transport	1
Wholesale	1
Utilities	2

Source: UNCTAD (2005c).

In light of the oil industry's prominence, it is not surprising that the countries of origin of FDI to Nigeria have traditionally been the host countries of the oil majors. Topping the list of the largest foreign investors in Nigeria are the United States, present through Chevron Texaco and ExxonMobil; the Netherlands with Shell; France with Total; and Italy with ENI. While Western Europe and the United States remain dominant as sources of FDI, Nigeria's home country relationships are broadening. Chinese firms are becoming increasingly involved in the Nigerian oil sector. In late 2004, the Chinese companies Funsho Kupolokum and Sinopec have both signed agreements with the Nigerian National Petroleum Corporation for the exploration of new oil fields and the construction of new refineries. There is also evidence of more interest in non-oil investment from China and India.

An upsurge in FDI from South Africa is one of the most significant trends of the last decade. Nigeria is South Africa's third-largest trading partner on the continent after Zimbabwe and Mozambique (which benefit from regional trade agreements), and the largest in West Africa (Business in Africa, 2005). More than 20 South African companies are today present in Nigeria, in segments ranging from construction, telecommunications and entertainment, to revenue collection and aviation.

C. Impact of FDI

Oil extraction has been the dominant target of FDI for the last 30 years and its impact on the Nigerian economy has been large. Understandably, the oil industry story attracts the most attention in international commentary on FDI in Nigeria.

Beyond the oil industry, and in manufacturing in particular, foreign affiliates are few and have had no significant developmental impact. However, opportunities for FDI have opened up in the "backbone" services and the impact of FDI in this area, though recent, is promising. A more extensive analysis on the impact of FDI on the overall economy, based on employment and poverty reduction, is not possible due to data deficiencies.

Taking this into account, this chapter reviews the impact of FDI in three areas – oil, manufacturing and services – with a particular focus on manufacturing as background to the extended review of this sector in chapter III.

1. FDI impact in oil

Foreign investors have been instrumental in the development of oil extraction to a point where Nigeria is now the 11th largest oil producer in the world and the largest in Africa. TNCs have been able to deploy capital and technology on a scale beyond Nigeria's domestic resources. They have been especially important in exploration and extraction from difficult areas, such as deepwater reserves in the Gulf of Guinea. Nigeria plans to increase oil production to 10 million barrels a day by 2010 from today's level of 1 million to 2 million. To achieve this, the involvement of TNCs in deepwater areas will be essential.[14]

FDI has not, however, been prominent in the downstream side of the oil industry. For example, Nigeria's imports of refined products account for 21 per cent of total imports. In response, the Government is attempting to privatize four State-owned refineries, along with other plants and pipelines. Recently, the Government has been pursuing negotiations with Libyan, Indian, and Chinese investors. In April 2006, the Chinese National Petroleum Corporation won licences in four exploration blocks and committed to invest $2 billion in the Kaduna refinery in northern Nigeria and as of March 2007, Mittal Steel of India was looking to purchase a controlling stake in the Port Harcourt Refinery Company.

Figure I.4. Share of non-oil exports in total exports from Nigeria, 1962–2006

(Percentage)

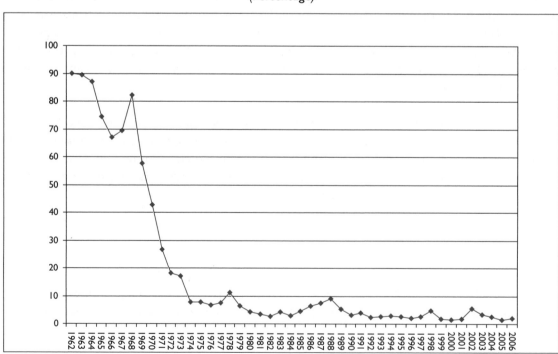

Sources: United Nations Comtrade database, Central Bank of Nigeria (CBN).

---

[14] The Energy Information Administration's Nigeria Country Analysis Brief, Environmental Issues, available online at www.eia.doe.gov/emeu/cabs/nigenv.html.

While oil contributes to around 98 per cent per cent of national exports (i.e. $56.3 billion in 2006) and 87 per cent of consolidated fiscal revenue (figure I.4 shows how the dominance of oil exports has evolved), the oil bounty has not been well managed. As a result, the booming oil sector is yet to contribute to lifting people out of poverty in Nigeria. There are, in this regard, mounting pressures to adopt representative and participatory processes to address issues related to the exploitation of oil resources (UNCTAD, 2007). Furthermore, the conduct of oil TNCs has been questioned. With respect to the environmental impact of their operations, the practice of gas flaring is gradually being phased out and a specialized agency has recently been created to regulate oil spillages. Regarding the lack of transparency in the payments of TNCs to the Government and other agents, Nigeria has committed to implement the principles of the Extractive Industries Transparency Initiative (EITI). Nigeria is among very few countries that have made the most progress in implementing this initiative. As a result, in March 2007, it became the first country to adopt a law making revenue disclosure mandatory.

2.   FDI impact in manufacturing

FDI has not had a meaningful impact on the development of Nigeria's manufacturing sector. This is an inescapable conclusion from figure I.1, which shows the manufacturing industry as a whole has stagnated for over 30 years. Of course, for much of this period, FDI was on a low scale, either because it was unwelcome or because general business conditions were inhospitable for those foreign investors who remained during the indigenization period.

As mentioned, chapter III describes the development ladder in which foreign affiliates progress from simple sale and assembly functions to manufacturing capacity. In doing so, they seek to enhance their domestic competitive position by product adaptation and development, and by encouraging linkages with local suppliers. They progress further by developing an export capability, initially to regional markets and, ultimately, in the case of many products, by participating in the global supply chains of their parent groups. The higher the position of foreign affiliates on the development ladder, the stronger their contribution to a country's economic development. In Nigeria, it is likely that foreign affiliates, including those that have been long established, have made only a few tentative steps along the development ladder (figure III.1).[15]

In relation to *export capability*, a recent survey identified the top non-oil sector exporters in 2006 (Central Bank of Nigeria, 2004b). Of the top 50 exporters, 13 appear to be foreign enterprises, contributing 36 per cent of export value. This is a moderate impact by foreign investors. In Brazil, for example, foreign affiliates accounted for about 50 per cent of national secondary sector exports in 2000 (Central Bank of Brazil, 2001). Overall, Nigeria's manufactured exports performance is very weak. Figure I.5 presents the long-term performance of the bulk of Nigeria's manufactured exports.[16] Manufacturing exports have revived since the 1990s. But they are not appreciably greater now (2005) than in 1965 (in constant United States dollars) and have halved on a per capita basis. In comparative terms, exports per capita in 2003 were $493 in South Africa, $59 in Egypt, $24 in Kenya and $3 in Nigeria for the same group of manufactures.

---

[15] The evidence is not systematic due to data and survey constraints.
[16] Transport equipment is excluded.

To provide more direct insight into foreign affiliates' export performance, box I.2 shows Nigeria's exports across a number of industry categories compared with the prevalence of foreign investors in these industries. Food and beverages and rubber products have a strong foreign investor presence and exports have increased in recent years. But export values are low (less than $15 million in 2005 in both cases). The strongest export industry is leather products (exports in excess of $160 million in 2005) yet here foreign investor presence appears to be minor. The footwear and textiles industry has an important foreign presence (up to 50 per cent of the industry may be foreign owned) and has clearly struggled in the last 10 years to retain export competitiveness (despite the potential boost from the United States African Growth and Opportunity Act (AGOA)). The building materials, pulp and paper and chemicals industries have been largely in the hands of State- or nationally-owned enterprises. This is changing as the most recent round of privatization has been open to foreign investors and foreign acquisitions have taken place (e.g. in cement and aluminium).

Figure I.5. Total manufactured exports, 1965–2005

(2005 constant dollars, millions)

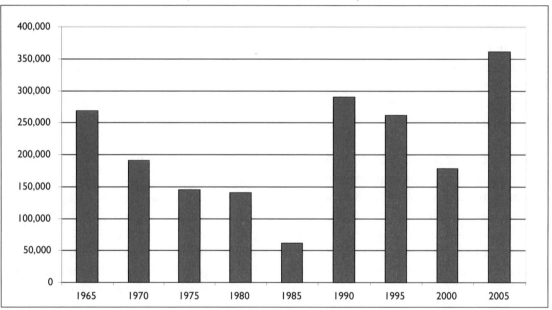

Source: WITS_Comtrade, classification SITC Rev. I
Notes: Mirror data (world imports from Nigeria) including costs, insurance and freight. When data was not available for the chosen year, data for adjacent years has been used instead.

In relation to *developing supplier capacity*, the limited presence of foreign investors in manufacturing suggests that they have had little impact on the development of a local supplier base. This is confirmed by UNCTAD's interviews, which revealed little sustained integration of foreign operations with local suppliers. Companies reported that mandatory local content rules in the past had been ineffective. This is consistent with UNCTAD's international experience of mandatory local content requirements, which have in most cases shown disappointing results (UNCTAD, 2000a). Foreign affiliates in Nigeria report problems relating to local suppliers inability to meet cost and quality standards or supply in sufficient volume and to maintain consistent pricing policies.

Although no comprehensive study on the linkages between TNCs and local suppliers in Nigeria is available, a survey conducted by UNCTAD as part of the research for this report of some of the largest TNCs in manufacturing found that linkages have largely been established in low or medium technology or intermediate products. Only one out of six large TNCs present in Nigeria for more that 40 years (on average) reported having established a network of internationally competitive local suppliers, while the majority only resorts to a few local suppliers of low/medium technology inputs (table I.4).

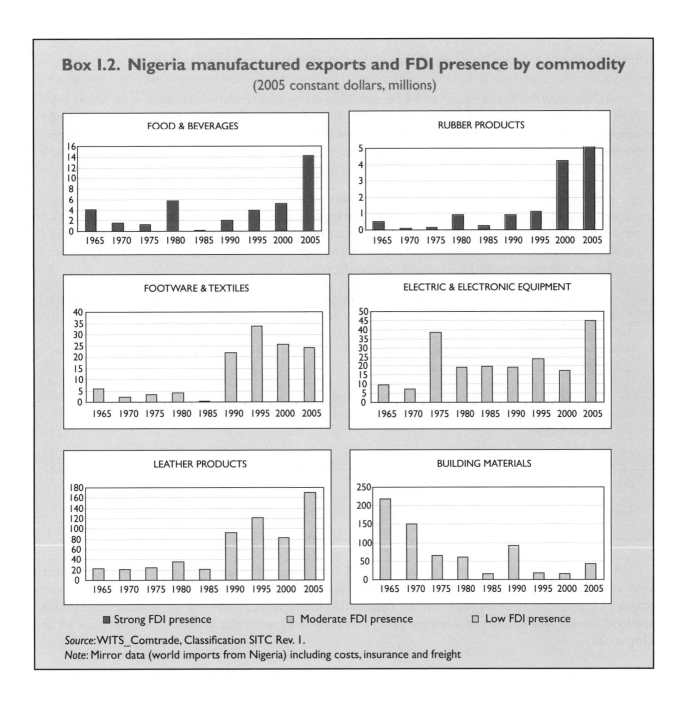

Box I.2. Nigeria manufactured exports and FDI presence by commodity
(2005 constant dollars, millions)

Source: WITS_Comtrade, Classification SITC Rev. I.
Note: Mirror data (world imports from Nigeria) including costs, insurance and freight

Table I.4. Major TNCs in manufacturing and supplier linkages in Nigeria
(Number of firms with local suppliers)

Period / Local suppliers, type	Few and very basic	In low or medium tech/ cost-intensive sectors	In higher-tech intermediate products	Regionally/ globally competitive supplier firms
Arrival in Nigeria	5	1		
Now		4	1	1

Source: UNCTAD's survey of major TNCs in manufacturing in Nigeria.

Box I.3. Non-fuel sector FDI and innovation

Company A: The company has 5-6 core people working part-time in R&D to analyse the properties and quality of materials' supply. The company started registering patents after a design problem (leaking packaging) which they solved for a TNC was registered by a competitor. Now they have registered a large number of patents for both domestic and international markets. R&D is viewed as essential to support their objective of being a quality and innovative producer if not the largest packaging company in the country.

Company B: R&D for the global group is located in Europe. In Nigeria, there is a development department employing three people at the management level. Its role concerns the transfer of technology, and especially formulations, which is highly challenging because of the difficulties of availability, cost and quality of raw materials. The department is currently involved in a packaging localization programme, highlighting the link between local sourcing and product development.

Company C: The affiliate has a small but focused development department of six people, directly supporting the businesses in respect of local development and innovation. One process is patented (in India and United Kingdom). The global science and technology facility is in Europe. All businesses across Africa have access to each other's development results through a computer-integrated tool for innovation called "Integrated Product Management".

Company D: 10-15 people work in development, principally to support the main R&D operations in Japan and South Africa. The role is principally that of testing and providing feedback on performance of the final product.

Company E: Around 30 people work in adaptation and product testing, although there is no R&D unit as such.

Sources: Company interviews and UNCTAD's survey of major TNCs in Nigeria, 2006.

In relation to *product adaptation and design,* UNCTAD's interviews with TNCs in Nigeria suggest that, with very few exceptions, their research and development (R&D) operations are typically at the early stages of sophistication. Small departments, responsible for technology transfer or product adaptation to the local market, are maintained in support of main research departments in home countries (box I.3 and chapter 3).

On average, only 20 patent applications per annum are filed with the Patent Registry, compared with 63,009 and 1,527 in South Africa and Egypt, respectively.[17]

3.   FDI impact in the backbone services

a. Telecommunications

FDI has had a notable impact on the expansion of mobile telephony in Nigeria since the launch of Global System for Mobile (GSM) licensing in January 2001. Two of the three licences issued went to foreign companies – MTN of South Africa and Econet Wireless (at the time a Zimbabwean–South African firm and now Celtel Nigeria, further to the entry in 2006 of the Zain Group of Kuwait) – for $285 million each.[18]

---

[17] Nigerian Office for Technology Acquisition and Promotion (NOTAP), World Bank Development Indicators and WIPO.
[18] A fourth licence was issued to domestically owned Globacom in 2002.

Within two years, Econet and MTN had signed up 2.2 million subscribers. MTN alone claims to have invested more than $3 billion to date in Nigeria and the Zain Group has pledged another $2 billion investment.

The impact of FDI under competitive conditions in mobile telephony has been remarkable. In the sector as a whole, subscriber numbers have grown from 35,000 to over 16 million by September 2005,[19] while prices are being driven below those in comparator countries (figure 1.6).

Competition in the fixed-line sector is provided by nationally-owned Globacom, which was issued the second national operator licence in 2002. After various failed attempts to privatize the State-owned operator, 51 per cent of Nigeria Telecommunications Limited (NITEL) was eventually acquired by Transnational Corporation (Transcorp) of Nigeria, a local company, in November 2006. However, the Government reversed the privatization in February 2008, on grounds that Transcorp failed to achieve the objectives of the privatization guidelines, and is now looking for a new core investor.

Figure I.6. Cost of local cellular phone calls in Nigeria and comparator countries
(Peak rate, $/3 minutes)

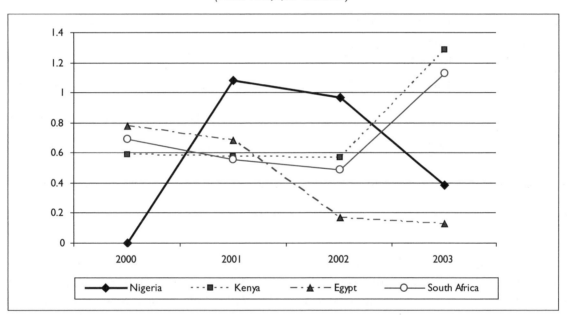

Source: ITU World Telecommunications indicator 2006.
Note: Nigeria communications Commission.

b. Power

Power provision has long been a thorn in the side of Nigerian competitiveness and quality of life. The erratic and costly provision of electricity hurts businesses generally but especially the energy intensive manufacturing sector. According to NEEDS, up to 25 per cent of business start-up costs are accounted for by expenditure on private power generators and privately generated electricity can be up to 2.5 times as costly as that from the national infrastructure.[20] According to the 2001 World Bank Investment Climate Assessment, 97 per cent of firms in Nigeria "own or share a generator" compared with 9 per cent in South Africa and 19 per cent in Egypt, while some manufacturers operate independently of the national infrastructure.

---

[19] Nigeria Communications Commission.

[20] In 2003, MTN reported that unforeseen problems with power and environment resulted in an additional $100 million in the cost of telecoms infrastructure rollout.

Traditionally, the power sector has been run by the State monopoly, the Nigerian Electric Power Authority (NEPA). Over the last few years, there have been various attempts at liberalizing the sector and NEPA has already been broken up for privatization, changing its name to Power Holding Company of Nigeria. No private investment has been attracted so far, however, due to the deteriorated state of the energy infrastructure. Finally, in May 2008 President Yar'Adua indicated that the Government will invest to repair the nation's power stations and transmission lines before proceeding with its sale.[21]

Table I.5. Independent power producers in Nigeria

Commencement date*	Location	Company	Ownership	Proposed capacity	Initiating Government
July 2000	Lagos	AES and Y.F. Power	US/Nigeria	270 MW	Lagos State Government
N.A.	Abuja	ABB Group	Swiss	30 MW (Energy) 450 MW	Federal Government
August 2000	P-Harcourt	Siemens	Germany	276 MW	Federal Government
April 2000	Kwale, Delta State	ENI/Agip	Italy	450 MW	Federal Government
N.A.	Bonny	Exxon/Mobil	United States	388 MW	Federal Government
N.A.	Enugu	Eskom	South Africa	2000 MW	Federal Government
March 2001	3 locations in River State	N.A.	N.A.	180 MW	Rivers State

Sources: Energy Information Administration (EIA) and Heinrich Boll Stiftung: *Utility Privatization and the Poor Nigeria in Focus*, by Ademola Ariyo (2004).

* Agreement signed.

Pending privatization of the respective business units, foreign participation in the sector is limited to a number of independent power producers (IPPs). For example, in June 2000, the federal Government signed an agreement with Enron for the construction of a 270 MW IPP in Lagos State. Ownership has since been transferred to AES Corporation and Nigerian firm, Y.F. Power. It is not clear to what extent the IPPs listed in Table I.5. are as yet operational. The commercial prospects for IPPs have been complicated by the financial frailty of NEPA and its successor businesses, which would be the principal buyers of independently generated power.

c. Transport sector

FDI in the transport sector is at the emergent stages as liberalization and privatization have only just begun to make private investment opportunities available. Ports sector concessioning is well underway, with 20 long-term concession agreements fully executed by the end of 2006 and six more in progress, and concessions have recently been announced for airport services. A.P. Moller of the Maersk Group has acquired the Apapa container terminal concession and the ENL consortium has emerged as preferred bidder for Apapa terminals A and C. Although these investments are too recent to judge their impact on the cost and quality of port services, some benefits are already visible, and include increased competition in

---

[21] *Nigeria power shortage to persist*, BBC News, 30 May 2008.

port services and the removal of concession charges (normally $300 per container) by some shipping lines, as operations and ship turnaround times improve (Leigland and Pallson, 2007).

In September 2004, Virgin Atlantic was named as technical partner in the new national flag carrier. Initial capitalization for Virgin Nigeria was $50 million, of which Virgin Atlantic provided approximately $24.5 million.

D. Summary

The oil industry has dominated FDI flows to Nigeria since the 1970s. FDI in the non-oil economy was held back by overt restrictions in favour of national enterprises until the 1990s and by poor business conditions. Although by 1995 Nigeria had relaxed virtually all restrictions on the entry of FDI, other countries moved faster to attract non-oil FDI including through privatization. Taking oil and non-oil FDI together, Nigeria now accounts for only 15 per cent of all FDI inflows to Africa compared with 30 per cent in the 1970s. However, it still accounts for 73 per cent of inflows to all ECOWAS countries.

Outside the oil-based economy, Nigeria is a country of widespread poverty. The commercial agriculture sector has declined and there has been no structural transformation into manufacturing. FDI in manufacturing (the focus of this report) has not been the dynamic force it might have been in a more favourable climate. Major reforms to improve the investment climate and infrastructure for business are underway. More FDI outside the oil industry is forthcoming as a result. The challenge will be to position this FDI to make the greatest contribution to Nigeria's development.

II. THE INVESTMENT FRAMEWORK

This chapter reviews Nigeria's policy framework and provides recommendations to improve the investment climate. This should contribute to attaining Nigeria's development objectives through increased investment, including FDI inflows.

After placing considerable restrictions on FDI in the past, in 1995 Nigeria opened its economy to foreign investment in almost all business activities. In a liberalization effort, sweeping reforms have been carried out in most policy domains affecting business activities, ranging from privatization of backbone services, labour regulations and environmental protection to, more recently, competition policy and taxation. An important effort to combat corruption at all levels is also taking place.

Although much has been accomplished, reminiscences of the old regulatory approach, in areas such as land policy or technology transfers agreements, continue to constrain private sector development. Hence, the current reform drive needs to persist not only to remove the remaining bottlenecks, but also to ensure effective implementation of the new regulations.

A. Specific FDI measures

1. Entry and establishment of FDI

In 1995, Nigeria adopted one of the most liberal regimes in Africa for the entry of foreign investors, virtually opening all its economy to FDI and reversing the severe restrictions on FDI imposed by the "indigenization" policy of the 1970s and 1980s.

The indigenization policy proposed to promote the participation of Nigerians to the economy by the transfer of foreign holdings to Nigerians. As mentioned in chapter I, the policy was also conceived as a method for pushing foreign investment into intermediate and capital goods, and to dilute foreign concentration in consumer non-durable goods (Ogbuagu, 1983). Foreign investors affected by the indigenization decrees reacted either by issuing shares on the Nigerian stock market (e.g. Metal Box Ltd., The United Africa Company, Lever Bros and Dunlop) or by pulling out of the Nigerian market altogether (as in the case of Chase Manhattan Bank, Citigroup and IBM, among others).

Initial steps to open the economy were taken in the late 1980s. In 1988, the Industrial Coordination Committee (IDCC), the forerunner of today's Nigerian Investment Promotion Commission (NIPC), was established to coordinate the grant of all approvals (business permits, expatriate quotas and incentives) in respect of establishing new businesses with foreign interests. The major amendment was introduced in 1989. Many sectors were partially re-opened to FDI and foreigners were allowed to invest in a list of activities provided they complied with a total project investment of ₦20 million ($2.7 million in 1989) and a citizens' ownership of at least 40 per cent.

Finally, in 1995, the Nigerian Enterprises (repeal) Act abolished restrictions on limits to foreign shareholding while the Nigerian Investment Promotion Commission Act established the NIPC as a successor to the IDCC, to become the agency in charge of promoting and facilitating foreign investment in Nigeria.

The NIPC Act is Nigeria's investment law and governs the entry of FDI. It allows for 100 per cent foreign ownership of firms in all but the petroleum sector, where investment is limited to existing joint ventures or new production-sharing agreements, and in a short negative list. The last refers to investment in industries considered crucial to national security, which are precluded to both Nigerian and foreign investors. These include the production of:

- Arms and ammunition;
- Narcotic drugs and psychotropic substances; and
- Military, paramilitary disciplined services uniforms.

The Federal Executive Council may, from time to time, determine what other items enter the negative list. No changes to the list have, however, been adopted since its introduction in 1995.

Companies are incorporated via the Corporate Affairs Commission (CAC), prior to registration with the NIPC. The CAC, present with offices in 32 of the 36 States of Nigeria, provides clients with an excellent way of incorporating companies. A new online system for incorporation was established in 2003 and is now replacing manual paper in the processing of registration. The record-keeping system is also efficient and CAC is proceeding to electronic recording of all former paper registrations. An e-payment system was established and the average duration of the incorporation process was brought down to three working days (starting from the date all payments of fees are received), from up to three months before the introduction of the electronic system (World Bank, 2002).[22]

Under the current system, no investment approval is needed, but it is required that all investments with foreign participation be registered with the NIPC to be covered by the treatment and protection clauses of the act (sections 17 and 27). In practice, however, the NIPC has been limiting the registration to companies investing a minimum share capital of ₦10 million (about $80,000). Registration with NIPC is not necessary for companies establishing in the Export Processing Zones (EPZs), or obtaining the "Export Processing Factory" status. In those cases, investment approval and licensing is the responsibility of the Nigerian Export Processing Zones Authority – NEPZA (box II.1).

The minimum investment threshold for registration introduced by the NIPC appeared to derive from its administrative involvement in the process of enabling investors to bring in foreign employees. Statutory responsibility for this rests with the Ministry of Internal Affairs, which requires investors seeking to hire foreign employees to obtain a "Business Permit" (BP) and an Expatriate Quota (EQ).[23] The minimum investment requirement for a Business Permit is set at ₦10 million ($80,000).

Previous analyses of the Nigerian investment climate by the Foreign Investment Advisory Service (FIAS)[24] and others have recommended the elimination of the NIPC Business Permitting process. NEEDS has reflected such concerns and calls for "eliminating the registration process for foreign direct investment" altogether and transforming "the NIPC into a promoter, facilitator and advocate". A first step in that direction was taken with the opening, in March 2006, of a One-Stop-Shop Investment Centre (OSIC) within the NIPC premises (box II.2). The NIPC reports that, since the introduction of the OSIC, the steps necessary to obtain a Business Permit have been reduced from nine to three and that business permits are issued fairly automatically (in 10 minutes).

---

[22] Same-day incorporation is also possible, for a higher fee. Another benefit of CAC's systems is that the Federal Inland Revenue System is proposing to create stamp duties offices in all CAC offices to further improve its services to the investors.

[23] *Handbook on Expatriate Quota Administration*, Federal Ministry of Internal Affairs – Citizenship and Business Department, 2004 revision.

[24] FIAS, 2000 and *The Nigeria Investors' Roadmap*, 2002.

Box II.1. Entry and protection regime in Nigerian export free zones

The regime for entry and protection of FDI in Nigeria's Free Zones (Export Processing Zones before 2001) differs significantly from that of the customs territory. The Nigeria Export Processing Zones Act of 1992, which provides the legal framework for the establishment and operation of the zones in Nigeria, is also the legal foundation of the Nigerian Export Processing Zones Authority (NEPZA). Apart from the management of all Free Zones, responsibilities of NEPZA include:

- Granting and removal of all requisite permits and licences;
- Establishment of customs, police, immigration and similar posts;
- Resolution of trade disputes between employers and employees and between public and private organizations;
- Investment promotion strategies (including opening of oversees promotion offices); and
- Budget approval functions in respect of the zones' annual budgets.

Investors are allowed to enter the zones only for a list of approved activities. These are:
- Manufacturing of goods for export;
- Warehousing, freight forwarding and customs clearance;
- Handling of duty-free goods;
- Banking, stock exchange and other financial services, insurance and reinsurance;
- Import of goods for special services, exhibitions and publicity;
- International commercial arbitration services;
- Activities relating to integrated zones; and
- Other activities deemed appropriate by NEPZA.

Applications for permission to invest in the zones are received directly by NEPZA, which can grant a license whether or not the business is incorporated in the customs territory. The NEPZA Act also indicates that the grant of a licence shall constitute automatic registration within the zone. Up to 100 per cent foreign ownership of business is allowed. However, under the 2004 Investment Procedures, Regulations and Operational Guidelines by NEPZA, approved enterprises can engage in authorized activities provided an investment of at least $500,000, with no distinction between foreign and domestic investors.

Apart from the specific incentives that will be discussed later in this chapter, investors in the zones are offered such guarantees as repatriation of foreign capital investment at any time, including the capital appreciation of the investment, remittance of profits and dividends and the possibility to employ foreign managers and qualified personnel. Immigration and employment permit applications are received directly by NEPZA together with the application for a licence to establish in the zone or at any time thereafter.

As mentioned above, dispute settlement falls under the competences of NEPZA, which is empowered to decide on disputes arising between licensees and to represent a licensee in all negotiations, arbitration and settlement of disputes with any other government agency or department in the zones. In the latter scenario, the 2004 Guidelines specify that the Arbitration and Conciliation Act Cap 19 Laws of the Federation of Nigeria shall apply. NEPZA also receives disputes between licensees and their employees and, according to the guidelines, it shall take all necessary steps to reach settlement between the parties. In all the above cases, NEPZA maintains "the right to intervene at any stage of any dispute in order to maintain industrial peace in the zone".

Source: UNCTAD

Box II.2. Nigeria's One-Stop-Shop Investment Centre is created

A One-Stop-Shop Investment Centre (OSIC) has been operational in Nigeria since March 2006. It is housed within the premises of NIPC in Abuja and a site for the forthcoming Lagos branch has been acquired. OSIC was opened with the stated objective of addressing "problems related to the multiplicity of agencies involved in various aspects of investment facilitation in Nigeria and the resultant inter-agency rivalry, complicated by conflicting statutory laws/legal frameworks; arbitrary use of discretion in granting approvals; limited transparency; bureaucratization in procedures; and poor service orientation" (NIPC, 2006). Since inception, OSIC has registered more than 2,500 companies.

While the ultimate goal is to get the agencies involved in the OSIC to work in harmony to reengineer and streamline their processes, procedures and requirements for granting business entry permits, licences and approvals, it was decided to adopt a "Coordinated One-Stop Approval Framework for the One-Stop-Shop (OSS) of Nigeria. This model implies that the various agencies/authorities maintain their existing mandates and responsibilities within the structure of the OSIC. In this regard, the following agencies have opened desks in the Centre:

* The Nigerian Investment Promotion Commission (NIPC);
* The Corporate Affairs Commission (CAC);
* The Central Bank of Nigeria (CBN);
* The Ministry of Federal Capital Territory;
* The Ministry of Solid Minerals Development;
* The Federal Ministry of Finance;
* The National Bureau of Statistics;
* The Nigeria Immigration Service (NIS);
* The Nigeria Customs Service (NCS);
* The Federal Inland Revenue Service (FIRS);
* The National Office for Technology Acquisition and Promotion (NOTAP);
* The Standards Organization of Nigeria (SON);
* The National Agency for Food and Drug Administration and Control (NAFDAC);
* The Nigeria Maritime Administration and Safety Agency;
* The Northern Nigeria Development Corporation; and
* The O'dua Investment Corporation Limited.

OSIC is currently envisaging an e-payment solution to facilitate payment of fees charged by the various agencies. To this end, all agencies involved need to conform to the agreed service standards as shall be enunciated in the forthcoming Client Charter.

UNCTAD, invited to comment on the OSIC initiative on the occasion of the Presidential Retreat of 20 March 2006, recommended that the creation of the OSIC did not obviate the need to streamline business regulation, nor bring a better service culture within key regulatory agencies. UNCTAD's recommendations, geared towards achieving a "Team Nigeria" approach, include:

(a) The NIPC should negotiate protocols of cooperation with the agencies participating in OSIC. These should spell out the extent of empowerment of OSIC-located officers, NIPC oversight arrangements, the quality and number of staff assigned and service delivery expectations;

(b) OSIC should function in large part as a "virtual" OSIC, taking advantage of the opportunities opened by Internet technology. Online applications and inter-agency exchange would not only lead to faster information flow, better monitoring and accurate and timely reporting, but also extend the OSIC services to all areas of the country with Internet access. This has now been adopted as an official objective with proposed full implementation in three years.

(c) Use of OSIC services should not be mandatory. Investors should be able to apply directly to the regulatory agency if they choose. It is up to OSIC to perform. This is now official policy and the authorities are now determined to make OSIC an irresistible choice for investors.

Wherever feasible, regulatory officers sitting in OSIC should be "empowered" to approvals as distinct from channelling applications back to their headquarters.

Source: UNCTAD, based on information from the NIPC.

The objective of NEEDS mentioned above can be readily accomplished by restricting NIPC's role in the approval process to the registration of foreign investors only. Expatriate entry rights should be obtained directly by application to the Immigration authorities. NIPC can facilitate this by housing the Immigration representatives in its OSIC. In this regard, the NIPC should no longer purport to have a regulatory role, but one of supervision of the quality and efficiency in the procedure.[25]

An important outcome of this de-merger will be the right of all foreign investors to obtain guarantees of treatment and protection through registration with the NIPC. Another practical implication is that the registration requirements would be greatly simplified, bearing in mind that it is a *registration,* not a *licence.*[26]

The launch of the OSIC in March 2006 to facilitate business establishment is an important initiative. To fully meet its objectives, the OSIC will require strong support and mentoring from parent agencies and from NIPC's management if it is to be useful and credible to investors. The quality of seconded staff is equally vital. They should be trained and motivated – financially and in seeing career enhancement perspectives (box II.2). This applies to both the NIPC and the regulatory agencies represented in the OSIC.

2.   Treatment and protection of FDI

Most of the standard provisions relating to the treatment and protection of foreign investment are contained in the NIPC Act. The fund transfer undertakings are also given in the Foreign Exchange Act of 1995 and the Nigerian Export Processing Zones Act of 1992. There are, nonetheless, gaps in the treatment provisions of the NIPC Act. Furthermore, Nigeria has also signed a number of bilateral investment treaties (BITs) containing all the usual provisions on treatment and protection.

a. The BITs framework

BITs' negotiations in Nigeria are conducted by the Inter-Ministerial Committee on Investment Promotion and Protection Agreements, which comprises representatives of the Ministries of Finance, Commerce, Justice, Industry, Foreign Affairs; the National Planning Commission; the Central Bank; and the NIPC. Official sources have indicated that, since 1990, the country has signed 22 BITs. However, only those with France, the Republic of Korea, the Netherlands and the United Kingdom have entered into force (table II.1).[27]

The official explanation for the low rate of treaty ratification is the lack of action by treaty partners. However, the process of seeking ratification within Nigeria is not proactive and not well organized. In this respect, a more coordinated and energetic approach on the side of the Nigerian BITs negotiators should be considered, both to (a) obtain ratification of negotiated BITs with strategic partners such as South Africa or China; and (b) conclude new BITs with countries that are emerging as potentially large investors in Nigeria in the short to medium run, such as India. Furthermore, those BITs should represent the building block of broader instruments of economic diplomacy to be negotiated between Nigeria and its strategic partners.

---

[25] Following a recent change, this is now being accomplished indirectly. While NIPC appears still to be approving business permits, it may no longer apply the statutory minimum capital requirement and is thus able to issue the permit quickly and routinely. While this has the effect of speeding up the expatriate hiring procedure and removing an administrative limit to registration of FDI, it is not the role of a typical IPA. The business permit is a form of substance test on employers seeking to hire abroad and should be retained and improved (see subsection 4 below), not disregarded. It should, however, be administered by immigration representatives. NIPC need not have this regulatory role and should not apply an important policy instrument in a cavalier fashion, albeit in good faith.

[26] The present merged documentation (the NIPC Form 1) is quite intrusive. Apart from general information on the investing company and its intended operation in Nigeria, a feasibility study is required, as well as information on the number of Nigerians and expatriates to be employed, the training programme to be offered to the local workforce and the time-frame for replacement of expatriate labour with Nigerian workers (understudy programme). In addition, Form 1 is to be accompanied by a certificate of capital importation and evidence of the acquisition of business premises (tenancy or lease agreement). The NIPC reports that it has recently overhauled the process and drastically reduced the steps involved.

[27] It should be noted that there are other sources of information that suggest a different number of BITs have entered into force – see the website of the Ministry of Industry, Planning, Research and Statistics Department. However, such information appears less reliable.

Table II.1. Bilateral investment treaties of Nigeria

Partner	Signed on:	Entry into force:
Algeria	14 January 2002	Partner yet to ratify
Bulgaria	21 December 1990	Partner yet to ratify
China	27 August 2001	Partner yet to ratify
Egypt	20 June 2000	Partner yet to ratify
France	**27 February 1990**	*19 August 1991*
Finland	22 June 2005	Nigeria yet to ratify
Germany	28 March 2000	Partner yet to ratify
Jamaica	5 August 2002	Partner yet to ratify
Korea, Rep. of	**27 March 1998**	*01 February 1999*
Korea, Dem. Peoples' Republic of	11 November 1996	Partner yet to ratify
Italy	27 September 2000	Partner yet to ratify
Netherlands	**02 November 1992**	*01 February 1994*
Romania	18 December 1998	Partner yet to ratify
Serbia and Montenegro	01 June 2002	Partner yet to ratify
Spain	09 July 2002	Partner yet to ratify
South Africa	29 April 2000	Partner yet to ratify
Sweden	18 April 2002	Partner yet to ratify
Switzerland	30 November 2000	Partner yet to ratify
Taiwan Province of China	07 April 1994	?
Turkey	08 October 1996	Partner yet to ratify
Uganda	15 January 2003	Partner yet to ratify
United Kingdom	**11 December 1990**	*11 December 1990*

Sources: Government sources and UNCTAD BITs database.

In this respect, effective mechanisms should be put in place to ensure coordination and consultation among the different government agencies involved in the negotiation, ratification and implementation of BITs. The NIPC should take a leading role in this process, and act as the secretariat for processing BITs through the government machinery. This new function would also entail ensuring consistency between the provisions of the ratified BITs and the national legislation, thereby strengthening the supporting role of NIPC in investment policy advocacy, as proposed in chapter III of this report.

Box II.3 summarizes the key treatment and protection provisions contained in the BITs that have been ratified.

The BITs in force thus provide sound standards of treatment and protection for investments originated from signatory countries. The relevant provisions in national law and practice are considered below.

b. Treatment

There is no explicit legal provision granting national treatment to foreign investors in Nigeria apart from those appearing in the signed BITs. All existing BITs provide such guarantees as national treatment, fair and equitable treatment and MFN provisions (box II.3).

Box II.3. Key provisions of Nigeria's bilateral investment treaties

Since as early as 1990, Nigeria has signed 22 Bilateral Investment Promotion and Protection Agreements (table II.1). However, only four of them have entered into force: the United Kingdom (1990); France (1991); the Netherlands (1994) and the last one with the Republic of Korea (1999). Most others are awaiting ratification of the partner countries. Negotiations for further treaties are also in progress with Belgium, the Russian Federation and the United States.

All four ratified treaties contain guarantees of national treatment (NT) of foreign investors, most favoured nation (MFN) provisions, fair and equitable treatment and standard guarantees for unrestricted repatriation of investment and returns. Expropriation is only allowed for public purposes and is subject to prompt, adequate and effective compensations, based on market value. The coverage of the BITs provisions extends to all investment originating from the signatory countries, irrespective of whether they are registered with the NIPC.

Exceptions to NT and MFN feature in all four BITs in respect to any existing or future free trade zone, customs union, regional economic organization or other similar international agreements to which one of the parties might adhere (regional exception). The BITs with the United Kingdom and the Republic of Korea also allow for exception to NT in relation to any international agreement or domestic legislation relating wholly or mainly to taxation, while the BIT with the Netherlands limits such exclusion to fiscal advantages accorded under double tax treaties (DTTs). The BIT with the United Kingdom further provides for exclusion to NT and MFN for special incentives to stimulate the creation of local industries. Such exclusions are not unusual.

In case of disputes between a foreign investor and the State, all BITs in force provide for reference to the International Centre for Settlement of Investment Disputes (ICSID).

Sources: UNCTAD and the World Trade Organization (WTO).

Nigeria thus relies strongly on its track record of dealings with foreign investors and only two exceptions could be identified to the otherwise non-discriminatory treatment of national and foreign investors. The first is with respect to the minimum share requirement of ₦10 million to hire foreign labour and the obligation to obtain a business permit for such purpose, which is not required for national investors.[28] The second is the different minimum investment threshold to obtain the main form of tax incentive, the "Pioneer Status", which is higher, but by no means prohibitive, for foreign investors.

c. Funds transfer

As per the Foreign Exchange (Monitoring and Miscellaneous Provisions) Act of 1995, any investor is guaranteed the free importation and convertibility of foreign exchange and the unconditional transferability of funds, through an authorized dealer, in freely convertible currency of:

- Dividends or profits (net of all taxes) attributed to the investment;
- Payments in respect of loan servicing where a foreign loan has been obtained; and
- The remittance of proceeds (net of all taxes) and other obligations in the event of sale or liquidation of the enterprise or any interest attributable to the investment.

---

[28] The NIPC advises that the overall requirement for a business permit is under review. Meanwhile, it has a working arrangement with the immigration authorities that the minimum capital requirement will be waived for applications processed through the OSIC and says that applications are processed in a matter of minutes.

The act constitutes an important liberalization effort with respect to the repealed Exchange Control Decree of 1984 (section B.2 on general foreign exchange arrangements). The Central Bank guarantees unconditional transferability and repatriation of funds for holders of the Certificates of Capital Importation. These are issued by the Authorized Dealer (i.e. the commercial banks) within 24 hours of the importation (according to the act) and confer a right to repatriate dividend earnings and capital, subject of course to compliance with the tax regulation.

The NIPC Act reaffirms that the above provisions shall be guaranteed to all foreign investors to whom the act applies, but for the reasons mentioned above, the coverage of the NIPC's guarantee is limited to investments above ₦10 million.

d. Expropriation

The Constitution provides that expropriation can only occur if an enabling law is enacted to provide for prompt payment of compensation and for access to a court of law for the determination of interest and compensation amount (section 44). It further grants right of judicial appeal.

The NIPC Act is more specific, providing that no enterprise shall be nationalized by any Government of the Federation and that no law can force an investor to surrender his interest, unless the acquisition is in the national interest or for a public purpose. In those cases, investors are entitled to fair, adequate and prompt compensation (including authorization for its repatriation) and the right to access the courts to determine the investors' interest or right, and the appropriate compensation.

e. Dispute settlement

Nigeria's dispute settlement regime is in line with international best practice. Among the very first countries in the world to ratify the ICSID Convention, Nigeria was also the first country in Africa to adopt the Model Arbitration Law and Conciliation Rules elaborated by the United Nations Commission on International Trade (Asouzu, 2001).[29]

Part V of the NIPC Act establishes that in case a dispute between the State and a foreign investor is not settled amicably, recourse to arbitration can take place either via the settlement mechanisms of the bilateral or multilateral investment protection agreement of which they are parties, or via other national or international dispute settlement mechanisms, as mutually agreed. In case of disagreement on the arbitral tribunal, the ICSID applies.

Only one case of investor–State dispute, the Guadalupe Gas Products Corporation vs. Nigeria (Case No. ARB/78/1) in 1980, resulted in arbitration before ICSID so far. The case was settled by the parties and made an ICSID reward at their request.

---

[29] Arbitration and Conciliation Act, No. 11 of 1988, Chapter A18.

B. General measures

This section reviews those areas of the policy and operational framework that affect all investors and form part of the investment climate that has an impact on FDI.

1. Taxation

The allocation of taxation powers within Nigeria's federal system is relatively simple. The federal Government imposes corporate income and withholding taxes, oil and gas production taxes and charges, value added tax (VAT) and import duties. The State Governments collect personal income tax, individual capital gains tax, stamp duties, urban land rentals, business registration and road and gaming taxes. Local Governments collect personal, social and commercial permit fees. The federal Government collects about 95 per cent of all taxes. Substantial amounts are shared with local and State administrations, which account for around 45 per cent of national public expenditure.

Corporate income is taxed at a rate of 32 per cent[30] with a small minimum tax applicable four years after business start-up (and from which all companies in agriculture or with at least 25 per cent foreign ownership are exempt). An unusual "excess profits" tax also applies. Excess profits tax is payable either as 15 per cent of the shortfall between actual taxable income and a flat amount (the equivalent of about) of $40,000 or at 15 per cent of a weighted average concept of capital employed.[31] The "excess profits" tax is effectively a second-tier minimum tax (when applied to the flat amount) but without the grace period and exemptions available on the minimum tax. The Government advises that this onerous tax is not applied in practice. It should therefore be repealed.

The corporate tax base allows comprehensive deductions including:

- Attractive annual capital allowances (including 10 per cent on buildings, 25 per cent on plant, 20 per cent on furniture and fittings) supplemented in many cases by substantial initial year allowances (including 50 per cent on plant, 15 per cent on buildings and motor vehicles). Agricultural, mining and public transportation assets have especially favourable initial year allowances. Replacement plant and machinery have an initial allowance of 95 per cent. However, the deduction of capital allowances is capped at two thirds of annual assessable profits, except in agriculture and agro-processing, and the total allowance is limited to 95 per cent of asset cost;
- Additional investment allowances of 10 per cent are allowable on all plant and equipment ("reconstruction" investment allowance). Businesses located at least 20 km away from reticulated electricity and water and a sealed road are entitled to allowances for self-provision of such facilities ("rural investment allowance");
- These allowances may only reduce taxable income by two thirds in any year except in agriculture and manufacturing.

Losses may be carried forward for four years (indefinitely in agriculture). The short carry-forward provision and the cap on use of allowances attenuate the incentive value of the capital and investment allowances. The current tax reform measures would allow indefinite loss carry-forward in all sectors.

---

[30] 30 per cent general tax rate plus a 2 per cent "education tax". A 20 per cent general tax rate applies to microenterprises – those with turnover less than about $8,000.

[31] The capital employed formula is paid-up capital (40 per cent) plus capital or statutory reserves (20 per cent) plus general reserve (20 per cent) plus long-term loans (20 per cent).

Box II.4. Fiscal incentives in Nigeria

Pioneer industry incentive

Designated "pioneer" industries may qualify for a five-year profits and dividends tax holiday. There are currently 69 designated types of pioneer industries in agriculture, agro-processing, mining, quarrying, manufacturing, tourism, property development and utilities. Minimum capital invested to qualify is about $2,500 for nationally-owned companies and about $40,000 for foreign-owned companies. Capital allowances only commence at the end of the tax holiday period and any tax losses can also be carried forward. These have the effect of extending the period of tax relief available to pioneer industries. Despite the generosity of this scheme, there appears to have modest take-up.

Sectoral incentives

Agriculture attracts accelerated depreciation of capital allowances (up to 95 per cent on some assets in the first year) and the deductibility of such allowances is not capped at two thirds of a year's profits. Losses can be carried forward indefinitely. Many kinds of agriculture are also eligible for pioneer status.

Agro-processing industries can qualify as pioneer industries (see above). In addition, the cap on use of capital allowances does not apply.

Mining qualifies for three-year tax holiday.

Manufacturing, not otherwise a pioneer industry, is entitled to rapid depreciation allowances, although these are somewhat vitiated by the cap on aggregate capital allowances and the four-year limit on loss carry forward. Also, manufacturing plant and machinery receives a 10 per cent investment allowance.

Services have few specific incentives. However, investments in several important services industries may qualify for pioneer status (see above). Also, earnings from services exports are tax-free if repatriated to official "domiciliary accounts".

Outcomes' incentives

Exports: Designated "export processing factories" and firms located in EPZs are "extra-territorial" and not subject to any taxes, including income tax, VAT and import duties. Approved activities include manufacturing, warehousing, logistics and financial services. The amount invested must be at least $500,000. Draft legislation prepared in 2005 proposes an important amendment to zone corporate taxation. The income tax relief would be made proportionate to the amount of exports in relation to total turnover. (Previously, 75 per cent of output had to be exported in order for total income to be tax exempt.) he effect of this change is to enable companies to establish in zones, and take advantage of their superior facilities and services, even if they are not primarily exporters.

A separate scheme permits manufacturers that export at least 50 per cent of output to qualify for pioneer status. It is also possible for exporters to qualify for financial assistance for export marketing expenses (the Export Development Fund), for expansion and export diversification (the Export Expansion Grant Fund) and to compensate for higher production costs arising from poor infrastructure or factors beyond the exporters control (the Export Adjustment Scheme Fund).[32]

Tax law provides that profits earned from goods exports may, if reinvested, be exempt indefinitely from income tax.[33] However, it seems that this scheme does not operate in practice due to the difficulties of monitoring the reinvestment conditions.

[32] Export (Incentives and Miscellaneous Provisions) Act, 1986.
[33] Companies Income Tax Act, section 23(9).

Dividends received from wholly export-oriented businesses are also exempt from tax.

R&D: Nigeria has several fiscal incentives to encourage R&D by firms. Some are duplicative in that they cannot all be applied in a given situation.

The general provisions are that, for any business, up to 10 per cent of profits set aside as a reserve for R&D qualify as allowable expense. In addition, expenditure on commercializing R&D qualifies for a 20 per cent investment tax credit. Other, not necessarily consistent provisions, allow (a) 100 per cent expensing of R&D, deemed to include a levy payable to a qualifying R&D institution; and (b) corporate contributions to R&D carried out by universities and research institutes to be tax deductible up to a maximum of 10 per cent of profits (draft legislation prepared in 2005 proposes to raise this cap to the higher of 15 per cent of profits or 25 per cent of the tax bill). Overall, this regime provides substantial incentives for local R&D and has been in place for at least 10 years.

Local sourcing: local manufacturers of spare parts, tools, equipment supplied to other local businesses or exported can obtain a 25 per cent investment tax credit on their capital expenditure. A company buying locally manufactured plant, machinery and equipment is entitled to a 15 per cent investment tax credit. (Draft legislation prepared in 2005 proposes to eliminate these incentives.)

There is also a deemed export scheme in which suppliers of inputs to exporters can obtain total exemption from profits taxation.

SMEs: such businesses are exempt from minimum tax, pay a lower profits tax rate of 20 per cent in the first five years in several sectors, and dividends are exempt from tax. Under the Small and Medium-Sized Enterprise (SME) Investment Equity Scheme, banks are required to set aside 10 per cent of profits to provide funding for new ventures. NEEDS proposed to legislate a 100 per cent investment allowance to banks and to give beneficiary SMEs a 10 per cent corporate tax rate plus a five-year tax holiday at inception. As of 31 March 2006, 212 projects had been funded with investment totaling about $8.6 million.

Outward investment: Dividends from Nigerian affiliates abroad are exempt from tax in Nigeria, if repatriated to official "domiciliary accounts".

Sources: UNCTAD and Federal Revenue Service.

Withholdings on payments to non-residents are set at 10 per cent of dividends, interest and rent, and at 15 per cent on royalties. These statutory rates are mostly below the maximum rates set in Nigeria's DTTs. Further, a unilateral reduction to 7.5 per cent in these rates was made for Nigeria's tax treaty partners in 1999.[34] There appears to be no withholding system for services' payments to non-residents in either Nigeria's law or tax treaties. But such payments would be caught in the general measure of withholding 10 per cent of contractor payments.

Significant corporate tax incentives are available, including tax holidays and favourable treatment of capital expenditure (box II.4). In addition to documented incentives, the President may exempt any project from income tax or vary allowances.

[34] Nigeria has DTTs in force with Belgium, Canada, France, Pakistan and the United Kingdom. Agreements with China, South Africa and Sweden are awaiting ratification.

How competitive is Nigeria's taxation of business? Figure II.1 provides a comparison of the burden of taxation in Nigeria on various business activities with that in a selection of other developing countries. It is based on UNCTAD's comparative tax methodology (annex III). The (discounted) present value of tax is measured as a percentage of investor cash flow (PV tax per cent). The higher the PV tax per cent, the larger is the tax on an investment.

Figure II.1 suggests that Nigeria has a relatively high standard regime of corporate taxation in keeping with other known higher tax jurisdictions such as Brazil, India and South Africa. The pioneer scheme significantly reduces the tax burden but it is mostly confined to manufacturing and specialized services. It provides a similar outcome to the pioneer schemes of Malaysia but not always as favourable as China's incentive schemes (which, however, tend to discriminate in favour of foreign investors). Obviously, the tax holidays offered by export processing zones in Nigeria and elsewhere mean that insignificant tax is paid – but only by those able to export at least 75–80 per cent of output.

Figure II.1. Comparative taxation of investment, 2006

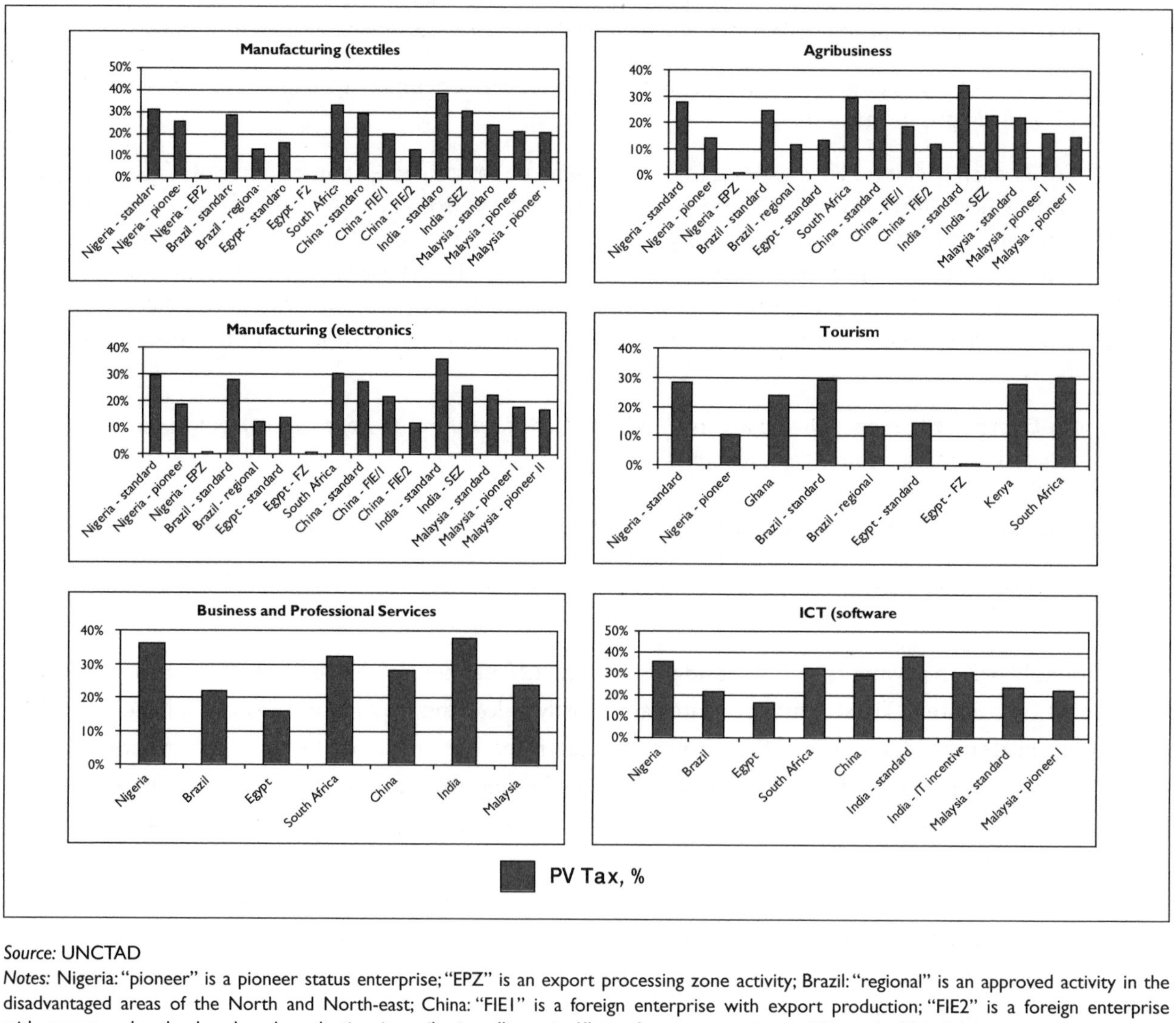

Source: UNCTAD

Notes: Nigeria: "pioneer" is a pioneer status enterprise; "EPZ" is an export processing zone activity; Brazil: "regional" is an approved activity in the disadvantaged areas of the North and North-east; China: "FIE1" is a foreign enterprise with export production; "FIE2" is a foreign enterprise with export and technology-based production; in agribusiness,"incentive1" is a foreign enterprise and "incentive2" is foreign enterprise in export production; Egypt:"FZ" is an export activity from a free zone; India:"SEZ" is an export activity from a special economic zone; Malaysia:"pioneer1" is a pioneer status activity;"pioneer2" is a pioneer status activity in a promoted area.

Nigeria's tax regime has much in common with an Asian dual approach of combining high general taxation with generous incentives for selected activities. When the gap between the dual regimes becomes wide and incentive schemes proliferate, it can easily lead to undue discrimination among industries and between large and small investors. It also creates compliance issues. Egypt has recently adopted a "flat" 20 per cent tax with standard capital allowances for virtually all activities. Figure II.1 shows that this regime is highly competitive whilst being simple to administer and available to investors of all types in all industries. This approach is worth considering for Nigeria rather than going further down the path of selective incentives.

The same conclusions are shared by the Presidential Committee on the Review of Incentives, Waivers and Concessions, created by the new Government in September 2007. The role of this committee is to analyse the existing tax and incentives policy, and recommend any improvements required to better achieve the fiscal objectives. In its report of February 2008, the committee found that at least 20 incentive schemes had been introduced over time in an ad hoc manner. These were administered by different agencies and their impact was not monitored. The report further indicated that it was not possible to identify all other incentives that may have been available and which ones were in operation. Finally, it recommended reducing reliance on incentives and instead adopting a generally applicable corporate tax rate of 20 per cent or less.[35]

VAT was introduced in 1994 at a rate of 5 per cent, among the lowest in Africa. The VAT has, however, unusual features. First, capital purchases and indirect costs (such as overheads) attract input VAT but cannot be credited against output VAT. Second, export income is exempt rather than zero-rated. In this respect, the VAT is partly a sales tax rather than a true tax on value added. While this accounts for the comparatively low rate adopted, its features also simplify administration of refunds. However, it disadvantages exporters because they cannot obtain relief on their input taxes.[36] It also adds non-relieved elements to the cost base of import competing producers.

Recommendations:

(i) Nigeria should consider introducing a flat 15 or 20 per cent tax rate on corporate income for all non-extractive businesses whilst maintaining and rationalizing the current attractive capital allowances. This approach, in line with the conclusions of the Presidential Committee on the Review of Incentives, Waivers and Concessions, would provide internationally competitive taxes for all investors (not just SMEs or those eligible for the pioneer scheme) and would be a simple and powerful investment promotion message.[37] Any revenue loss is likely to be inconsequential, as corporate tax receipts account for less than 3 per cent of all total fiscal revenues. The recent proposal to reduce the corporate income tax rate to 25 per cent is a step in the right direction. But it possibly does not constitute the highly visible "low, flat" tax regime that would obviate recourse to large-scale incentives;

(ii) The pioneer industry scheme should be removed as a consequence of the above recommendation. It is overly generous (especially in relation to providing for full capital allowances at the end of the tax holiday period) and limits competitive tax arrangements to the few eligible businesses rather than all;

(iii) The current caps on utilization of capital allowances and the limitation of loss carry-forward to four years should be eliminated. The current restrictions are technically muddled and in any event need not apply as a corollary to introducing a low flat tax and rationalizing capital allowances.

---

[35] Federal Ministry of Finance (February 2008). Report of the Presidential Committee on the Review of Incentives, Waivers and Concessions, Abuja, Nigeria.

[36] The impact of restricted input VAT creditability was modeled in the case of textiles and garment manufacturing for export using the UNCTAD tax methodology. It was found to be the equivalent to raising the corporate tax burden from 31 per cent to 36 per cent (PV tax per cent), a significant jump.

[37] Egypt has recently undertaken a similar reform.

(iv) The removal of domestic sales restrictions on zone companies is sensible and the proposed dual basis of taxation by income source is a natural consequence. Income from domestic sales would attract the lower flat tax rate and there seems no need to impose a minimum investment size of $500,000;

(v) VAT should be restructured into a genuine VAT system to remove the bias against exports, among other benefits;

(vi) The excess profits tax (which could operate as a burdensome second-tier minimum tax when applicable to turnover) should be formally abolished, to accord with de facto situation;

(vii) The tax treatment of services payments to non-residents should be clarified and brought into line with standard practice;

(viii) The conclusion and ratification of DTTs should be pursued more energetically with key investment partners and to aid Nigerian business within ECOWAS.

2. Foreign exchange arrangements

The history of Nigeria's foreign exchange market since independence is characterized by alternate phases of comprehensive and more relaxed controls, interventions by the Central Bank which led to a misalignment between the exchange rate and the underlying market conditions, and to the abandonment of convertibility. A significant liberalization effort took place in 1995, when the new Foreign Exchange Act (Monitoring and Miscellaneous Provisions) came into force. This act was introduced in parallel to the NIPC Act, with the explicit purpose to "ensure free flow of investments and investible funds into Nigeria and improve the investment climate in the country" (Sofowora, 2003). From a business perspective, the reforms have generally liberalized access to foreign exchange, and further improvements are underway, albeit under a foreign exchange control regime. The key liberalization since 1995 has been:

- Foreign exchange proceeds must be brought back in Nigeria (surrender requirement), but can be maintained in local foreign currency accounts ("domiciliary accounts") and used for any valid purpose from such accounts; and

- No prior approval is needed to initiate capital account transactions – FDI, borrowings – and holding a Capital Importation certificate against such inflows provides a guarantee of repatriation of associated outflows of profits, capital or debt service.

However, the system did not provide certainty of convertibility for non-exporters (i.e. the great majority of businesses that sell to the domestic market). Furthermore, Nigeria has not accepted the obligations of article VIII of the Articles of Agreement of the IMF that ensures currency convertibility for current account transactions and bans multiple currency practice.

Controls placed on the foreign exchange market are a problem. Until recently, there were two main markets in place: (a) the retail Dutch Auction System (DAS), where authorized banks can bid on behalf of their customers, who then can use foreign currency for eligible transactions only[38] (this excludes import of banned items); and (b) the inter-bank market, where foreign exchange can be obtained from other sources than the Central Bank, including local currency purchases from domiciliary accounts. In this case, the exchange rate was freely negotiated among authorized dealers. A parallel market, illegal but tolerated, continues to exist and is primarily used by smugglers to finance the import of banned items or to evade duties and border clearance administrative difficulties.

---

[38] These are listed in CBN's published foreign-exchange instruction manual and include visible imports, excluding banned items, contract service fees and other invisible trade items such as educational expenses and travel allowances.

This system posed two key problems: (a) with the inter-bank market playing only a minor role (representing about 20 to 30 per cent of the DAS sales)[39], companies seeking to remit profits and service debt needed to resort to the DAS, with uncertainty regarding the outcome of their bidding; and (b) a cumbersome administrative procedure, which prompted many to resort to the illegal market.[40]

The practical implications were as follows:

- Exporters had ready access to foreign exchange; and

- Non-exporters were often faced with the uncertain outcome of bidding in the DAS and the bureaucratic requirements involved.

In February 2006, the Central Bank replaced the DAS with a Wholesale Dutch Auction System (WDAS) in the effort to decentralize foreign exchange management and make it more efficient. The WDAS is an inter-bank foreign exchange market for foreign currency released by the Central Bank. It is organized around authorized dealers, where participants are free to establish buying and selling rates for transactions among themselves and with the customers. The benefit for business is that those who used to bid transaction-by-transaction in the DAS system, run by the Central Bank for some of their foreign exchange needs, can now be accommodated by their own commercial bank. The commercial banks handle the documentation, including responsibility for ensuring that their customers' needs are legitimate.

There is still a parallel market rate however. The Central Bank attributes its existence to two main reasons: (a) the long list of banned items for imports; and (b) the continued existence of a heavy documentation burden on those intending to use the formal market. It intends, therefore, to further liberalize the market by reviewing or eliminating many of the restrictions imposed on users of the official market and simplifying the administrative requirements for access to foreign exchange.[41]

Nigeria has clearly made serious efforts at foreign exchange liberalization and is moving gradually towards accepting the obligations of the IMF article VIII. As things stand, including the new WDAS, the arrangements are workable for business, especially for those eligible for domiciliary accounts. But foreign exchange arrangements will not become best practice as long as they continue to be used as an instrument to support import bans.

3.   Labour

Nigeria has a rather liberal labour regime, based on English common law, and set out in few pieces of legislation, mostly from the 1970s.[42] However, most labour norms, including strikes and lock-outs, are regulated via collective bargaining agreements between the unions and management.[43] The majority of Nigerian workers are unionized and Nigeria has ratified all eight core ILO labour conventions. Yet, according to the International Confederation of Free Trade Unions (IFCTU), serious restrictions exist with regard to the freedom of association, collective bargaining and the right to strike (IFCTU, 2005). Cited examples include a new law, signed on March 2005 (Trade Union Amendment Act), which made union membership voluntary and introduced a strike ban on essential services other than those so defined by the ILO (including among others telecommunications, public transport and education).

---

[39] Estimate from the IMF, Country Report No. 04/242, August 2004.

[40] Authorized dealers were in fact required to submit documentation establishing their clients' eligibility, including the official foreign exchange form of authorized imports (Form M), which must be registered with an authorized dealer and certified by the negotiating bank and, in the case of exporters, submission of original copies of the bill of lading, with evidence of payment of the relevant administrative charges, to the collecting bank.

[41] For details, see: Press Briefing by the Governor of the Central Bank, Prof. C. Soludo, on *Programme for Further Liberalization of the Foreign Exchange Market in Nigeria*, 27 March 2006.

[42] The former include, among others, the Labour Act of 1974, the Trade Disputes Act of 1976 and the National Minimum Wages Act of 1981.

[43] For professional and managerial staff, all conditions are set in individual contracts.

Encouragingly, the entire labour regime is currently being revised with the support of ILO, in full consultation with employers' and employees' representatives. The new set of laws is meant to codify fundamental principles and minimum standards of treatment which comply with internationally agreed labour standards.[44] If implemented, Nigeria will have one of the most modern and balanced labour regimes in Africa, at least on paper.

A single national minimum wage, reviewed infrequently in tripartite consultation, is set under the National Minimum Wages Act.[45] In mid-2007, the level of the minimum wage was set at ₦8,625 (about $68 per month). The minimum wage applies to all firms with more than 50 employees, with the exception of employment paid at piece-rate, on commission basis, part-time or seasonal and in merchant shipping or civil aviation. The set minimum wage does not appear to impose economic distortions to the labour market, as it is lower than average monthly wages for all levels of skills. The Minister of Labour could also set sectoral minimum wages, but none is in place. No relevant changes are introduced by the new set of labour laws on this matter.[46]

No major rigidities in hiring and firing exist and provisions related to the termination of contracts are fairly straightforward, as confirmed by Nigeria's high rank in the *employing workers* index of the World Bank (table II.2). Government approval is not required, as is sometimes the case in other countries, and termination results from expiration of the contractual period or notice, both in the current and proposed regimes. While in the current Labour Act, notice time depends on the effective duration of the employment and ranges from one day to one month, the draft Labour Standards Bill proposes notice periods of not less than one month (or as agreed by the parties for contracts of limited duration). Under both regimes, the parties can also agree on payment in lieu of notice.[47]

Table II.2. Employing workers in Nigeria and selected economies
(Country rankings, 1 = less difficult to 178 = most difficult)

	Employing workers rank
Nigeria	30
Kenya	66
South Africa	91
Egypt	108
Algeria	118
Ghana	138
Morocco	165

Source: World Bank, *Doing Business Database*, 2008.

The Labour Standards Bill follows the formulation of the Labour Act of 1972 in respect of redundancy provisions: the employer needs to notify the trade union concerned of the reasons and extent of the redundancy. The principle of last in, first out applies, although this principle is subject to a qualification

---

[44] Including a new "Labour Standards Bill", a "Collective Labour Relations Bill", a "Labour Institutions Bill", and an "Occupational Safety and Health Bill".

[45] The federal Government sets the minimum wage upon recommendation from the "National Salaries, Incomes and Wages Commission", which includes Government representatives, one representative of the Nigerian Employer's Consultative Association and one of the Nigeria Labour Congress, the federation of trade unions.

[46] Although the prohibition for the employers to grant general or percentage wage increases to any group of employees without the approval of the Minister of Labour currently set in the law (Trade Disputes Act, section 19) would be cancelled.

[47] Although the draft Labour Standards Bill is also new in that in the calculation of pay in lieu of notice, leave pay and sickness, only the part of the remuneration which the worker receives in money is taken into account.

that an employee's merits can be considered. Both existing and proposed legislation empower the minister responsible for labour to make regulations providing for compulsory payment of redundancy allowances. But the current power of the minister to regulate redundancy payment would be changed somewhat. The minister could continue to make general regulations but, in the future, he would only step in to regulate if the parties were unable to agree. It would be advisable for the minister to remove opportunities for dispute by setting an international standard regulation, which would then guide all collective bargaining agreements. This regulation should be drafted so as to come into effect with the passage of the bill. Otherwise, it will be an area of uncertainty for business.

Neither the current nor the proposed labour laws contain any statutory protection against unfair dismissal or statutory severance pay. However, unfair dismissal may constitute a "trade dispute" under the Trade Disputes Act and the ILO reports. Therefore, the National Industrial Court has, on occasion, awarded severance pay as additional compensation to unfairly dismissed workers (ILO, 2000).

Figure II.2. Nigeria: trade disputes 1990–2004
(Number)

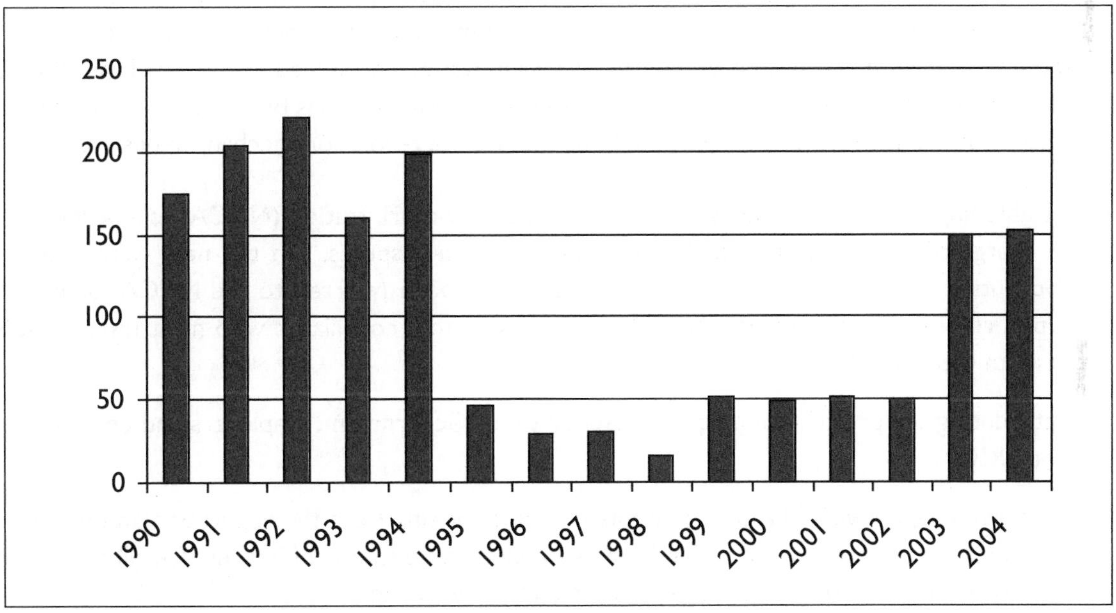

Source: Federal Ministry of Employment, Labour and Productivity.

Industrial relations are quite litigious and have worsened since 2003 (figure II.2), when the controversial draft Trade Union Amendment Act mentioned above was proposed to the National Assembly and a series of strikes took place in response to the plans announced by the Government to increase petrol prices by 50 per cent. The following year, the total number of days lost due to strikes and lockouts was higher in Nigeria than in any other large comparator country in Africa, with the exception of South Africa (table II.3).[48]

---

[48] An appropriate comparative analysis would take into consideration the relative weight of the workforce in each country; this was not possible due to data availability issues.

Table II.3. Strikes and lockouts, most recent available data

	Number of days not worked
Algeria	628,838 (in 2004)
Egypt	19,969 (in 2003)
Ghana	n.a.
Kenya	217,012 (in 1997)
Morocco	141,083 (in 2002)
Nigeria	**2,737,399 (in 2004)**
South Africa	4,152,565 (in 2006)

Source: ILO, LABORSTA Database 2006.

Note: The number of days not worked as a result of <u>strikes and lockouts</u> is usually measured in terms of the sum of the actual working days during which work would normally have been carried out by each worker involved had there been no stoppage.

Under the Trade Disputes Act of 1976, after the initial attempts to explore an amicable settlement,[49] each trade dispute is referred to the Minister of Labour, who sets up an Industrial Arbitration Panel.[50] The panel's decision is binding, but can be reviewed by the National Industrial Court. In this context, the reform of the dispute settlement mechanism is one of the major innovations proposed by the new legislation. On the basis of the South Africa and Lesotho examples, the draft "Labour Institutions Bill" and the "Collective Labour Relations Bill" would bring to best practice standards the dispute resolution mechanism described above by:

(a) Establishing a National Commission for Conciliation and Arbitration (NCCA) as a permanent body in charge of the conciliation and arbitration of labour disputes.[51] In the new system, strikes and lockouts would not be lawful unless the dispute has been referred to the NCCA for conciliation. Upon receipt of a referral, the NCCA would designate a conciliator who must try to resolve the dispute within 30 days;

(b) Introducing the principle of equal representation of Government, employers and employees within the NCCA;

(c) Distinguishing between disputes of rights (i.e. those arising from the application and interpretation of labour laws, contracts and collective agreements) and disputes of interest (i.e. all other disputes) with respect to the resolutions mechanisms that apply to each.

In a dispute of right, striking is not allowed, but the parties can refer the dispute directly to the National Industrial Court for final decision. On the other hand, in a dispute of interest, the right to strike is preserved. The parties can then refer the dispute to the NCCA, which designates an arbitrator, whose award can only be reviewed by the National Industrial Court in case of misconduct, gross irregularities or excess of power. An alternative "voluntary arbitration" applies where the parties to a collective agreement have provided for labour disputes to be referred to private arbitration. In this case, they can appoint an arbitrator by common agreement (or the NCCA may do it on their behalf).

---

[49] In the current system, the parties shall first attempt to settle disputes via the existing agreements between employers and workers organizations. If the dispute remains unsettled or no agreement exists, the parties must meet within seven days, under the presidency of a mediator mutually agreed upon.

[50] The panel is composed of not less than 10 members, two of them "appearing to the Minister as representing the interest of employers and two (...) the interest of workers".

[51] The proposed structure could be: one chairperson, three representatives of Government, three representatives of employers, three representatives of organized labour, three full-time Commissioners representing the social partners, two persons representing the public interest and the Director General of the Commission.

4.   Entry of foreign workers and business visitors

One recurring bottleneck to investment, reported by the international private sector in Nigeria during interviews conducted by UNCTAD, is the scarcity of well-trained executive staff and specialized technical staff in the Nigerian workforce (see more in chapter III). On the other hand, there is some feeling within the Government that foreign investors are too keen to quickly hire overpaid and inexperienced foreign workers. Obtaining a balance between the legitimate interests of investors to obtain appropriate staff and the national interest of citizen job protection, training and advancement is not easy. In Nigeria's case, the procedures are not yet in place to obtain such a balance efficiently. The current approach to the entry of foreign workers is not only cumbersome and anachronistic, but also highly discretionary, unpredictable and open to rent-seeking. Procedures for temporary entry of business visitors and service providers are also problematic. Both need urgent revision.

Immigration is an area of sole federal jurisdiction and statutory responsibility for work and residence permitting rests on the Nigerian Immigration Service in the Ministry of Internal Affairs.[52] The statistics from the Ministry of Internal Affairs indicate that the number of work permits issued in Nigeria to non-citizens is comparable to that of other large developing countries, although much smaller than that of large developed ones (table II.4).[53]

Table II.4. Non-citizen work and residence visas issued

	Temporary work and residence permits issued
Nigeria (2005) – total	26,492
Nigeria (2005) – via NIPC	140
Brazil (2004)	20,162
Mexico (2002)	24,649
Australia (2002/03)	37,859
Canada (2001)	58,860
United Kingdom* (2003)	113,960

Source: National authorities.
*Top 10 countries of origin of immigration only.

a. Business visas

Investors going to Nigeria on a business trip must apply for a business visa for up to 90 days (not valid for employment or remuneration).[54] They need to provide the Nigerian missions abroad with evidence of sufficient funds to sustain themselves in the country, a valid return ticket and a letter of invitation from companies or business organizations stating the reason for the travel, and accepting "immigration responsibilities". This involves responsibility for accommodation/feeding, transportation and, if needed, the cost of repatriation or deportation. UNCTAD interviews with foreign investors in Nigeria indicate that such visas can be difficult to obtain and that the immigration officials often question the necessary duration of the trip upon entry. This can be a severe problem for prospective investors, who may not have a suitable Nigerian counterparty to accept "immigration responsibilities".

---

[52] An immigration desk was, however, opened within the NIPC premises in Abuja to facilitate foreign investors' applications for expatriate labour.
[53] The statistics also point at a large gap between the permits issued through the NIPC channel and those issued directly by the Ministry of Internal Affairs
[54] As of December 2006, all visa application forms are available online at the NIS website: www.immigration.gov.ng.

The procedures should be made more flexible and hospitable for business visitors to support the attraction of FDI. The following changes are recommended:

- Business visa applicants only need to provide evidence of a return ticket and availability of funds to support their visit. The "immigration responsibility" requirement should be removed altogether.[55]

- Introduce a "Green Channel Business Visa" to fast track applicants who meet the ticket and funds criteria and whose application is supported by the NIPC, which endorses the "bona fides" of the applicant. Nigerian missions abroad should approve these applications within 24 hours.

b. Temporary work permits (less than three-month stay)

Foreigners providing specialized services (such as maintenance and after-sales installation) for less than three months must obtain a temporary work permit. The application is accompanied by the same documents needed to obtain a business visa, with the exception of the evidence of funds. The permits are obtainable only from the office of the Comptroller General of the Nigeria Immigration Service Headquarters in Abuja, who retains power to determine on the request.

c. Work and residence permits

Obtaining visas to work in Nigeria for up to three years is far more complicated and involves various steps, as summarized in box II.5.

According to the wording (and interpretation) of the Immigration Act of 1963, business permits (box II.5) are a precondition to obtaining EQ positions and are only necessary for companies with some degree of foreign investment. In addition, the immigration authorities only receive applications for BP/EQs from companies whose share capital is at least ₦10 million ($80,000)[56] This represents a clear bias against foreign investment, especially against small foreign investors and start-ups. Also, the determination of the number and qualifications of foreign workers allowed to enter the country appears entirely discretionary and favours rent-seeking behaviour.

NEEDS recognizes that the current approach to the entry of foreign workers in Nigeria requires revision and proposes to "consolidate immigration matters, including visas, EPs, work permits, and "Permanent until Reviewed" (PUR) status".[57]

It is recommended that reforms are carried out in two phases. The first and immediate need is to streamline the entry procedures for key expatriate personnel required by new investors. For this purpose, Nigeria should adopt an *Automatic EQ Scheme*, which would allow investors to recruit for a select number of positions without the requirement to justify the need to hire abroad or to engage understudies. Of course, the applicants hired for those positions must undergo the normal credentials, character and health checks.

---

[55] Or applied only to citizens of high-risk countries, i.e. where there is a history of unacceptable rates of overstaying.
[56] Federal Ministry of Internal Affairs (2004).
[57] National Planning Commission (2004), p. 56.

Box II.5. Procedure to obtain work and residence permits in Nigeria
The BP/EQ Scheme

1. The foreign investor requests a Business Permit (BP) and applies for the right to hire expatriates for designated positions, the Expatriate Quota (EQ). This is done either through the NIPC, by means of Form 1 mentioned earlier, or directly at the Ministry of Internal Affairs, through the corresponding Form T1.[58] Most applications are made directly. Each expatriate position requires the employment of two Nigerian understudies who must be trained to take over within three years.

2. It appears that, where the investor was already granted an EQ, the consulates can grant the entry visa before the employment permit requests are completely processed, Thus character, credentials and health checks are administered by the missions abroad (mission interviews and Investor's Roadmap). Hiring against an EQ requires an application to the Comptroller General of Immigration for a Subject to Regularization Visa (STR). STRs are collected at the consulate nearest the entering expatriate's place of residence.[59] Among other forms, the application must be accompanied by the letter of invitation accepting "immigration responsibility".

3. Statutory responsibility for issuing EQs rests with the Ministry of Internal Affairs (the parent ministry of the Nigerian Immigration Service), which decides on a discretionary number of expatriates (EQ positions) per company that can enter Nigeria.

4. Once in Nigeria, expatriates apply for regularization of their STR visas to obtain a "Combined Expatriate Residence Permit and Alien Card" (CERPAC), i.e. a one-year residence and work permit (the validity is two years according to the guidelines issued by the Nigerian Immigration Service, but it appears that, in practice, most CERPAC are issued for a one-year period).

5. An alternative to CERPAC is the "Permanent Until Reviewed" (PUR) Status. PURs are available only for sole owners/CEOs of a foreign invested enterprise and are subject to the employment of Nigerian Deputy CEO and payment of a $10,000 fee. The company needs also to show proof of an appreciable net profit of which not less than N2 million ($15,500) has been paid as corporate tax. Other factors considered are the "political/policy direction of Government; the company's area of business; evidence that the PUR would guarantee technology transfer and that the company has a large quota portfolio and corresponding share holdings as an added qualification".

Exceptions to the above EQ approval procedure apply to ECOWAS nationals, who do not need an EQ or residence permit and are required only to register with the authorities for record-keeping purposes. Also, Free Zones are not subject to the EQ process because they are deemed to be extraterritorial. However, the STR, then residence permit is, strictly speaking, only for sojourn in a zone. Foreigners with this status need a pass to travel to the "hinterland", but according to the Nigeria Immigration Service, these are readily issued by its officers stationed in the zones.

Sources: UNCTAD and Nigeria Immigration Service.

---

[58] Form 1 asks the investor to list the posts for which the expatriates are required, their qualifications and the particulars of the training scheme for Nigerians understudies to fill the posts, as well as the time when they will take over from the expatriates. Other documents required are, among others, the receipt of payment for the form's fees, the Certificate of Incorporation, the feasibility report, the joint venture agreement (where applicable), the tax clearance certificate, the lease agreement for operating premises, evidence of imported machinery (form M, pro forma invoice, shipping documents and pre-shipment inspection certificates) and the proposed annual salaries to be paid to the expatriates.

[59] It appears that, where the investor was already granted an EQ, the consulates can grant the entry visa before the employment permit requests are completely processed, Thus character, credentials and health checks are administered by the missions abroad (mission interviews and Investor's Roadmap).

Many countries employ this kind of scheme. The number of key positions allowed usually depends on the capital invested and, in some cases, the priority attached to attracting investment in the sector. For example:

- Ghana offers key positions based on paid-up capital – one position for $10,000<100,000 invested, two positions for $100,000<500,000 invested and four positions for $500,000 or more invested;

- In Malaysia, a manufacturing investor may be entitled to one key position if a minimum of RM 500,000 (about $130,000) is invested and up to five positions for investment of RM 5 million (about $1.3 million). A key position scheme also operates for investment in the Multimedia Super Corridor, which is accorded high priority as a strategic initiative.

- The United Republic of Tanzania provides an "automatic immigrant quota" of up to five positions, which is available during a start-up period for qualified investors who invest at least $300,000.

Nigeria's *Automatic EQ Scheme* should be similar to that of Ghana, but perhaps with a higher minimum investment threshold of $50,000 (to match the new BP threshold proposed below) and up to 10 key positions for large-scale investments. The automatic EQ positions would be converted into work and residence permits valid for up to five years, depending on the duration of the employment contract. Moreover, a higher number of EQ positions could be granted if the investment takes place in priority sectors, including IT and other key services (Priority Sectors Scheme). Finally, in this first phase, any additional EQ position would be allocated on the basis of the current BP/EQ system. However, the current BP threshold would be lowered to $50,000 and apply to both foreign and national investors, so as to remove the bias of the current regime against small foreign investors and start-ups.

A second stage of reforms should entail moving towards international best practice in a full-scale revamp of the present system for approving employers, assessing needs for foreign skills, allowing employers reasonable predictability in visa applications and renewals and catering for local skills development.

Table II.5. Entry of foreign labour, recommended regime

Phase I	*Phase II*
Automatic EQ Scheme	**Extended EQ Scheme**
Automatic EQs assigned according to size of investment Validity of permit – up to 5 years (according to duration of contract) No understudy programme	- Scarce skills list based on objective research for fast-tracked EQs
Priority sector scheme	
Increase the automatic EQ quota in priority sectors Validity of permit – up to 5 years (according to duration of contract) No understudy programme	- No understudy programme, but introduction of a company-wide training performance assessment to inform the allocation of EQ positions
Additional EQ	
Current BP requirement, but Investment threshold lowered to $50,000 and applied to both domestic and foreign investors Determination of EQ quota by Internal Affairs/Immigration Understudy programme	- Validity of permit – up to 5 years, renewable (according to duration of contract)

Source: UNCTAD.

Based on an UNCTAD study of international best practice (UNCTAD, 2005a), it is recommended that Nigeria move away from the understudy approach to adopt a system based on the assessment of company-wide training performance to ensure that expatriate hire goes hand in hand with local skills development (table II.5). In this new system, which could be called *Extended EQ Scheme*, Nigeria would introduce a "scarce skills" list to be based on objective research, carried out in collaboration with the private sector. The list would signal to employers where expatriate hire can be fast-tracked. At the same time, an investment threshold to qualify for expatriate hire would be retained to ensure that the employer has sufficient substance to cover the upkeep, health costs and departure costs of expatriate employees.

The proposed changes would make the expatriate labour regime more predictable and, at the same time, provide an appropriate regime to foster the training and advancement of the local workforce.

5. Land

The land system is a serious constraint in the investment framework of Nigeria due to misdirected land policy and decades of underinvestment in land administration. It is one of the most important impediments to NEEDS' goal of creating a competitive private sector.

As result of a major reform of the land regime in the 1970s, which sought to consolidate and simplify the previous mixture of customary and statute law (Hodgson et al., 1999), the Land Use Act of 1978 vested all proprietary rights on land in the State. The reform also introduced a distinction between urban and non-urban land: State Governors can grant *statutory* rights of occupancy and determine the lease conditions in respect to both, while local Governments can grant *customary* rights of occupancy only in respect to non-urban land. Lease period is 99 years for residential plots and 40 for industrial plots.

The act empowers the State Governors to revoke rights of occupancy for reasons of overriding public interest. However, compensation may be paid only on the value of the "improvements" to the land (such as buildings, roads, plantations, etc.), and not on the value of the land itself. This compensation regime only covers part of the market value of the expropriated land and is therefore hardly protective of the legitimate interests of the land "occupant" to receive fair compensation. Furthermore, it provides undue incentives to State and local Governments for land expropriation.

Apart from frustrating the proprietary rights and interests in land, the reform inhibited the development of a land market in a second major way. An administrative system overlays market forces in the disposition of land, as the Land Use Act prohibits the alienation of the rights of occupancy by either "assignment, mortgage, transfer of possession, sublease or otherwise howsoever without the consent of the Governor" (section 22). All transfer procedures must hence be submitted to the State Governors' approval of otherwise straightforward commercial transactions. This is an obvious source of non-transparency given the potential for delay and undue discretionary treatment in this process. Attempts to avoid this procedure could lead to the formation of corporate entities to hold and transact land or to use powers of attorney. Interviews reported that fraud is a serious problem in leasing transactions, including fraudulent subleasing. For instance, in response to the fraud problem, all titles in the Federal Capital Territory are being recertified and new lease allocations suspended for 12 months.

Identification of available land is also difficult, because of poor record-keeping and lack of computerized land registries in many States, which contribute to a backlog of unresolved title disputes. In this respect, however, the States of Lagos, Niger and The Federal Capital Territory appear to constitute positive exceptions, having digitalized their land records. The last, in particular, is now digitizing cadastral maps with the support of GPS technology.[60] Other States, such as Cross River and Enugu, are also making efforts to

---

[60] *Abuja Geographic Information System* on http://www.abujagis.com/.

modernize their registries. For instance, the Department for International Development (DFID) of the British Government is supporting a pilot Land Registry Improvement Programme in five States. The issue of land registry is also being considered by the Presidential Committee on Doing Business, which is working with the Commissioners of Lands and Housing towards the establishment of an information technology-driven Land Registry.

Although the matter was not researched by UNCTAD during the mission, previous reports suggest that the cost and time required for the range of transactions involving land titling is problematic. There are, however, signs that significant progress was achieved in recent years. In this regard, the 2008 Doing Business survey of the World Bank points out that an entrepreneur seeking to buy property free of dispute and officially recorded must complete 14 procedures (as opposed to 21 in 2005), in a process that takes 82 days (274 in 2005) and requires official fees amounting to 22 per cent of the property value in Nigeria. This compares, for example, to one day and payment of a registration fee and 2.5 per cent of the property value in stamp duties in Norway (World Bank, 2008).

There is broad agreement in the literature that secure individual land rights increase incentives to undertake productivity enhancing land related investment.[61] However, the evolution of the land system in Nigeria has not permitted the development of a sensible land market in which investors and others requiring land are able to readily purchase and encumber titles from others and put the land to improved commercial use. In 2002, UNCTAD recommended the Nigerian Government to amend the Land Use Act so as to address the problems arising from its enactment, which has impeded secure access to land. This is central to farming and its absence has created additional barriers to access credit for example by investors in horticulture.[62]

NEEDS calls for streamlining the process for land access and transfer, but does not indicate how. In this regard, the National Assembly recently concluded a public hearing on land allocations/acquisitions, in which a number of the above issues were brought to light. As a result, the creation of a Land Allocation Committee was recommended and is currently in the works. These recent initiatives suggest that a fundamental policy change is required. The following are therefore recommended actions:

- Abandon the requirements of State Governors' approval for all land transactions. Governors should retain powers to allocate new lease titles, under transparent conditions, but title transfer and encumbrances would simply be registered in conventional fashion by the deeds' registry. Apart from streamlining a very cumbersome process, this would promote a freer market in land with more private sector involvement (domestic and foreign). The public interest lies in appropriate land *use* (such as through zoning laws) rather than in land *occupancy* (which should be left to market forces);

- Institute full compensation at market value for land resumed by Government;

- Outsource land surveying and the administrative support to land registries to specialized commercial enterprises to reduce delays;

- Encourage the transformation of free zones into multi-facility zones so as to provide ready to use plots of land for investment, but recognize that this is a palliative measure and does not obviate the need for thorough policy and administrative reform.

---

[61] 1999 literature review by Deininger K and Binswanger H. The Evolution of the World Bank's Land Policy: Principles, Experience and Future Challenges. *The World Bank Research Observer* , Vol. 14, #2, pp. 247–76.

[62] Recommendations stemming from the National Workshop on "Horticulture for National Development", held at Women Development Centre, Abuja 23–25 April 2002.

6. Environment

Environmental damage in Nigeria, also by foreign investors, is subject to much debate. Oil exploration and development, in particular, have had a severe environmental impact. In this regard, Nigeria continues to suffer the detrimental effects on marine life and human health from oil spills as well as from air pollution that results from the flaring of associated gas that occurs during the production of oil (Energy Information Administration, 2003).

Modern and comprehensive environmental management legislation was introduced in 1992, with the Environmental Impact Assessment Decree. According to the decree, proposed projects, both from the public and private sector, must identify the expected environmental impact. If that impact is likely to be significant, an environmental impact assessment (EIA), including a description of planned efforts to mitigate any damage deriving from it, must be prepared. EIAs were to be submitted to the Federal Environmental Protection Agency (FEPA),[63] which was responsible for the protection and sustainable development of the environment. The FEPA was integrated into the new Ministry of Environment created in June 1999. With respect to the oil sector, the Department of Petroleum Resources, within the Ministry of Petroleum Resources, is charged with the responsibility of ensuring a clean environment where the oil industry is operating. For this purpose, the department has produced specific "Environmental Guidelines and Standards" for oil-related projects since 1991 and is in charge of their enforcement.

The decree distinguishes between three types of projects:

(a) *The Mandatory Study Activities:* These are projects that are specified by the decree as requiring the production of a Mandatory Study Report. This list includes projects relating to agriculture, airports, land reclamation, logging and conversion of forestry to other uses, housing schemes covering more than 50 hectares, large industrial developments, infrastructural developments, mining, petroleum developments, power generation and transmission projects;

(b) *Projects excluded form EIA requirements:* These are projects that have been deemed to have minimal effects on the environment by the President, or are projects which are undertaken during national emergency;

(c) *Projects for which EIA is not mandatory but which require a screening report:* This report indicates potential adverse effects. The project proposal has to go through the process(es) of mediation and review.

The decree also contains a comprehensive process for reviewing EIAs and determining appropriate action to safeguard the environment.

Despite the quality of the environmental legislation, its enforcement has so far been weak. The environmental protection agency is underfunded and viewed as not capable of adequately protecting the environment (Dung-Gwom, 2004). Another issue raised relates also to poor linkages and coordination among the different tiers of Government. Under the Nigerian Constitution, environmental protection is the responsibility of the federal Government. Yet the FEPA Decree encouraged States and Local Government Councils to set up their own environmental protection agencies. Many of them were unnecessarily charged with identical responsibilities to those of FEPA, effectively undermining the latter's role (Echefu and Akpofure, 2002).

The creation of the Ministry of Environment in 1999 was the first response to the above problems by the current administration. Although FEPA was absorbed and its functions taken over by the new ministry, enforcement and funding problems remained. For that reason, NEEDS formulates a proposal for the establishment of a "central self-sustaining regulatory agency responsible for environmental enforcement,

---

[63] Established via the *Federal Environmental Protection Agency Decree,* No. 58 of 1988 (revised in 1992 and 1999).

compliance, monitoring, environmental auditing, impact assessment and standards setting" (National Planning Commission, 2004, p. 66). This is in fact a proposal to revive the former FEPA. This initiative is welcome assuming that the new FEPA would be adequately funded and professionally staffed.

The Government is looking into new solutions to the environmental damage caused by oil spills and gas flaring. In 2002, the Nigerian Government ordered oil companies operating in the country to comply with the "Environmental Guidelines and Standards for the Oil Industry" or risk paying a fine (Energy Information Administration, 2003). A sign of the seriousness of the obligation came in 2003, when Shell Nigeria was ordered to pay $1.5 billion to the Ijaw tribe in compensation for the environmental damage caused to the ethnic group region since 1956. Moreover, the Government set the objective of zero gas flare by 2008 and created a National Forum on the Monitoring of Natural Gas Utilization and Implementation of Related Projects to ensure its achievement.

In addition to these measures, a National Oil Spill Detection and Response Agency (NOSDRA), the first such agency in a developing country, was established in 2003 and a National Oil Spill Contingency Plan (NOSCP), for the agency to manage, was also prepared. Accordingly, a three-tier response system was devised, to regulate the agency's response and involvement in case of spillage.[64]

In this context, tighter regulation – and better monitoring and enforcement of existing environmental laws – should indeed stop the degradation of the environment and prevent the most serious environmental problems in the future.

7. Rule of law and administrative issues

Nigeria is perceived as being among the most corrupt countries, not only in Africa but worldwide. Corruption in the public and private arenas hampers development and affects both the cost of doing business in the country and its international image. It therefore constitutes a serious impeding factor in the country's capacity to diversify foreign investment inflows away from oil.

Box II.6. Governance in resource-rich countries: the Extractive Industries Transparency Initiative

The EITI supports improved governance in resource-rich countries through the verification and publication of company payments and Government revenues from oil, gas and mining. The sponsors of the initiative intend to improve governance – through greater transparency and accountability – so that oil revenues stimulate economic growth, reduce poverty and foster sustainable development.

Some 20 countries have either endorsed or are now actively implementing EITI across the world. The countries involved include Azerbaijan, East Timor, Nigeria (where the EITI initiative is implemented at all three tiers of Government – federal, State and local), Peru, and Trinidad and Tobago.

EITI is supported by an international secretariat presently based in the United Kingdom's Department for International Development. The secretariat works closely with the World Bank and the IMF. In addition to the implementing Governments, EITI is supported by donors, many of the largest oil and mining companies in the world, investors in large oil and mining TNCs, and different civil society groups.

Source: EITI Secretariat website: http://www.eitransparency.org.

---

[64] Up to oil spills of 50 barrels, NOSDRA is only to be notified. For oil spills up to 5,000 barrels, a formal process of cooperation with the agency is initiated and for larger spills, NOSDRA takes over response management and coordination.

Box II.7. The Economic and Financial Crimes Commission

The "419" advance fee fraud is one of the best known international financial scam which bilks hundreds of millions of dollars annually and contributes to worsening Nigeria's image internationally. Its pervasiveness had severe negative consequences on Nigeria. These include reduced FDI flows to the country and difficulties in business prospecting for genuine Nigerian businesspeople, spurned by the international business community because of distrust.

To tackle financial and related crimes, including the "419" fraud, the Government of Nigeria set up the EFCC in 2002. It became operational in April 2003. The EFCC Establishment Act of 2002 was a major departure from the past laws for fighting economic and financial crimes in terms of powers and functions attributed to the commission, which holds responsibility for the enforcement of all laws and regulations relating to economic and financial crimes.

The two main functions of EFCC are prevention and investigation. The commission identifies trends and all issues associated with economic and financial crimes, takes measures to prevent unlawful activities and investigates all financial crimes. It enjoys cooperation and support from (a) national and international agencies such as INTERPOL, EUROP, and customs and immigration services; (b) Governments of partner countries such as the European Union, the United States and South Africa; and (c) the private sector for banking, financing, etc.

Early in 2006, after only three years since its creation, the EFCC had some concrete achievements to showcase:

* Recovered money and assets derived from crime, worth over $700 million;

* Recovered £3 million in looted assets from the British Government;

* Had over 500 suspects in custody, most of them standing trial in the various courts in the country;

* Was prosecuting over 100 cases in court and investigating over 500 cases at various stages;

* Recovered billions for the Government in respect of failed Government contracts; and

* Established a sub-unit called The Nigerian Financial Intelligence Unit in 2004, which is saddled with the responsibility of checking transactions in banks in order to detect any fraudulent activity.

However, the greatest success of the EFFC was its capacity to start the process of sanitizing the business environment, fighting corruption, ensuring accountability in Government, reforming and stabilizing the banking sector through loan recoveries.

Sources: UNCTAD and EFCC (website: www.efccnigeria.org).

Since 1999, however, the Nigerian Government has taken determined action against corruption. A series of anti-corruption agencies and practices have been introduced. The main ones of a long list include:

* The Independent Corrupt Practices and Other Related Offences Commission (ICPC), established by the Corrupt Practices and Other Related Offences Act of 2000. Its functions are not only to investigate and prosecute corruption cases, but also to correct corruption-prone systems and procedures of public bodies and to educate the public against corruption and enlist its support;

* The Economic and Financial Crimes Commission (EFCC). It began operating in 2003 and has already developed a highly impressive track record (box II.7);

- The Due Process Office, which oversees procedures to be followed in the execution of Government activities and projects;

- EITI, under which oil companies agree to publish what they pay to Governments (box II.6);

- Publication of monthly revenue allocations to all three tiers of Government (federal, State and local) as of January 2004.

As a result of the above initiatives, the former inspector general of the police was tried and sentenced to jail, two judges have been suspended and two lost their jobs outright, five former State governors were arrested, and three ministers and top customs officials were dismissed.[65]

NEEDS is clear about the extent of the problem and the systemic changes that are needed to complement its direct compliance measures. According to NEEDS, the Government must become "smaller, stronger, better skilled and more efficient at delivering essential services", in order to "transform it from a haven of corruption to an institution that spurs development and serves the people". In that respect, the Government is committed to fast-track public sector reforms which reduce the scope for corrupt practices.

Although some progress is recognized, the international perception is that Nigeria is irretrievably mired in corruption.[66] Important changes are taking place and (chapter 3) the time is coming when a more positive message can be, credibly, communicated to international business.

Another key issue for investors – both domestic and foreign – is the ability of courts to deliver commercial justice impartially, promptly and consistently. On these matters, Nigeria's record remains poor. A recent comparative survey – the World Bank's World Business Environment Survey (WBES, 2000) – found that over 60 per cent of investors were dissatisfied with respect to the fairness and impartiality, honesty/absence of corruption, and consistency of judgements. Ninety per cent had negative opinions regarding the speed of the judicial system. Among Nigeria's main competitors for FDI attraction in the continent, only Kenya scored worse on all counts (table II.6).

Table II.6. Investors' perception of court system, 2000
(Percentage assessing poorly)

	Fairness	Honesty	Speed	Consistency	Enforcement
Nigeria	61.4	69.8	90.6	68.6	52.3
Egypt	8.1	6.1	30.3	13.1	14.1
Ghana	46.2	54.0	83.2	59.0	46.5
Kenya	70.6	82.8	94.9	83.0	70.0
South Africa	5.1	7.6	84.7	23.9	28.2

Source: World Bank (2000), *World Business Environment Survey.*
Note: Values refer to percentage of investors assessing performance as "slightly bad", "bad", or "very bad" as opposed to "slightly good", "good" or "very good".

---

[65] Interview with Mrs.Ngozi Okonjo-Iweala, Nigerian Finance Minister, by Paul Vallely, "The Independent", 16 May 2006.

[66] In 2002, Nigeria topped the Transparency International poll as the most corrupt nation on Earth. In 2007, its position in the rankings, while still low, had improved markedly to 147 out of 179. As a result, Nigeria was identified as one country that had witnessed very significant improvements.

The Nigerian authorities are well aware of the difficulties of obtaining remedy from the commercial justice system and that many firms are given little option but to seek unsatisfactory extra-judicial solutions. In the interviews conducted by UNCTAD to prepare this report, they acknowledged the main problems as being:

- Lack of funding and human capacity issues (lack of specialization). Judges are not specialized and are expected to hear a wide range of civil, administrative, commercial and family matters. They have inadequate staff and courts are not computerized. Therefore, judges themselves have to record the presented evidence by hand and there are long delays in getting opinions typed and published;
- Slow and archaic procedures, which make it easy for defendants to prolong matters;
- The maximum cost (set by the judiciary) for awarding against unsuccessful plaintiffs that amounts to a derisory N10,000 (about $80); and
- Corruption.

Solutions are, however, being considered and progress is being achieved in many areas. The Government's tough stand on corruption is beginning to pay off. Some judges have been removed from office and a new appointment system is being introduced. The new system will involve the Bar Association in a peer review of the candidacies. A useful development in this regard is the World Bank-supported project to improve commercial dispute settlement in two States, including the commercial capital Lagos. Moreover, with the support of the United Kingdom Department of International Development (DFID), the Attorney General's office, in consultation with the judiciary, is introducing the following reforms:

- Promotion of alternative dispute resolution mechanisms to be a part of the court system and not seen as a competing system by the judiciary;
- Streamlining of the court civil procedures system to avoid overlapping jurisdictions as between the federal, State and local levels;
- Introduction of a fast-track channel to treat commercial matters more urgently and minimize adjournment;
- Review of costs to reduce frivolous suits; and
- Review of commercial laws by the "National Committee on the Review of Investment Laws in Nigeria", inaugurated in May 2005.

A positive feature of the Nigerian system is the courts' independence from government pressure in disputes involving private investors, including the foreign ones, which is not always the case in many countries.

Another area where administrative backlogs and rent-seeking constitute a major obstacle to business development is customs administration. Import clearances are lengthy and irregular payments are rife.[67] Documentation requirements and processes are especially burdensome, exacerbated on the import side by Nigeria's long list of banned imports.[68]

---

[67] World Economic Forum, Global Competitiveness Report 2005–2006. According to the irregular payments in exports and imports ranking, firms estimate that undocumented extra payments or bribes connected to export and import permits are commonly made. Nigeria ranks 102 of 117 countries in this regard.

[68] For example, this necessitates the completion and filing with various agencies of six copies of a special form, Form M, in addition to normal documentary requirements.

The Government is, however, undertaking reforms to bring efficiency to the customs services. One of the main projects is the implementation of the Automated System for Customs Data Entry (ASYCUDA) with the support of UNCTAD. ASYCUDA++ is the third generation of an automatic data processing system developed by UNCTAD. This software automates data for customs control, duty tax collection and statistical economic analysis. It also provides for Electronic Data Interchange between users and the customs administration.

As of June 2008, the ASYCUDA++ programme had been installed in the two main ports of Lagos and in Port Harcourt, with plans to expand it to the remaining ports in the near future. ASYCUDA has already helped to reduce clearance time from two to three weeks to two to three days.

Also, in a bid to achieve 48 hours clearance at ports, the Government has constituted a "Special Presidential Committee on 48 Hours Clearance of Cargo at the Nation's Ports". Its mandate includes capacity-building for ports' officers, process and procedures' streamlining and tackling of infrastructure and cost issues.

Although it is too early to comment on the success of such an initiative, it is encouraging that these matters are receiving attention at the highest level. The implementation of first-class systems and procedures in the commercial justice system, however, should get higher priority. They are an essential complement to the fight against corruption and are key to restoring confidence of investors in the rule of law.

8. Protection of intellectual property

Nigeria is a member of the World Intellectual Property Organization (WIPO) and a signatory to, or a member of, the Universal Copyright Convention, the Bern Convention, the Paris Convention and the Rome Convention. Intellectual property infringement remains, however, a serious problem. It is estimated that Nigeria is the largest market for counterfeit products in Africa.[69]

The national framework for intellectual property protection is characterized by a multiplicity of legal instruments, including the Patent and Design Act of 1970, the Trademarks Act of 1967 and the Copyright Act of 1988 (revised in 1999), matched by a number of implementing agencies. The Ministry of Commerce is in charge of the industrial property protection, through the Registry of Trade Marks, Patents and Designs, while copyright is administered by the Ministry of Justice,[70] via the Nigerian Copyright Commission (NCC). The National Agency for Food and Drug Administration and Control (NAFDAC), under the Ministry of Health, is responsible, among others, for the registration of food and drugs and for combating counterfeit drugs in Nigeria. The Registry of Trade Marks, Patents and Designs appears to have orphan status within its parent ministry. It is poorly supplied with funds, staff and equipment. Applications may not be properly assessed (for example, patent applications appear to receive only cursory examination). While this may reduce delays in approvals, the public interest is not necessarily served.

Although much progress is being achieved, notably by the Copyright Commission (Box II.8.), law enforcement is considered weak, particularly for patents and trademarks. Companies rarely seek official help in trademark or patent protection as the judicial process is slow and far from transparent. Shortage of funds, IT facilities, staffing and awareness of intellectual property issues further contribute to a weak intellectual property climate (WTO, 2005; and the United States Commercial Service, 2005).

---

[69] From the address by Ms. Karen Burress, United States Department of Commerce, at the "CTO business and technology summit", Lagos, 16 May 2005, available at: http://www.microsoft.com/africa/press/ng_nigeria_ip.mspx.

[70] The Nigerian Copyright Commission was an agency under the Federal Ministry of Culture until February 2006 when it was relocated to the Federal Ministry of Justice in order "to strengthen the Commission to achieve its mandate". See Nigerian Copyright Commission (2006). *Update on the Strategic Action against Piracy (STRAP)*.

Box II.8. The Nigerian Copyright Commission and the STRAP Initiative

In 1999, in response to widespread copyright infringement in Nigeria, affecting both local and foreign products, a series of amendments to the Copyright Act of 1988 gave the Nigerian Copyright Commission (NCC) new powers, shifting its focus from administration to enforcement. Among the new powers are the following:

* Powers to impose the use of anti-piracy devices (such as holograms, labels, marks, etc.) in connection with any copyrighted work;

* Powers to regulate businesses that make use of copyrighted material, including factories and rental outlets;

* Copyright inspectors have all the powers, rights and privileges of a police officer pertaining to the investigation, prosecution or defence of a civil or criminal matter under the act; and

* New fines and punishments for copyright infringement (up to five years imprisonment).

On the institutional side, the NCC was strengthened by the introduction of a governing board which includes, aside from a chair appointed by the President and the Director-General of the Commission, representatives of the Ministries of Justice and Education, of the Nigeria Police Force, the Nigeria Customs Service and of the authors' community, to reflect the role that each agency needs to play in the fight against copyright infringement in a country where more than 80 per cent of software in use is pirated.

The new NCC, run by a dynamic and competent team, reports satisfaction with the revised legal framework, although it stresses the importance of appropriate funding. Police awareness of intellectual property rights and their cooperation significantly improved over the last two years. Implementation at the border is more problematic, although the customs management is cooperative and it is hoped that the recently established Ports Monitoring Authority will help improve border control.

Finally, in 2005, NCC launched the STRAP (Strategic Action against Piracy) Campaign. By means of STRAP, NCC aims to create a copyright environment, which will not only benefit local investors in the copyright-based industries but also act as an incentive to foreign investors. STRAP, which is supported by Microsoft and other foreign and domestic businesses, has three components:

* An anti-piracy enforcement component with a zero tolerance approach;

* A public education programme (named "mass enlightenment"); and

* The introduction of a hologram scheme, a video rental scheme, optical discs manufacturing plants scheme and a database of copyright works.

The Standard Organization of Nigeria and the Nigeria Police are directly involved in the STRAP initiative. The latter has set up Special Copyright Enforcement Teams, to work in conjunction with NCC's copyright inspectors. A number of joint operations to confiscate pirated materials, arrest pirates and shut down illegal replication plants have already taken place. The NCC reports that, by May 2006, over N600 million ($4.7 million) worth of software, books and musical works had been seized in the anti-piracy operations.

Source: UNCTAD interviews.

A new legal framework is currently being discussed in the Ministry of Justice. The draft legislation proved however impossible to obtain. Nonetheless, it was reported that the reform aims at ensuring compliance with the Trade-Related Aspects of Intellectual Property Rights (TRIPs) agreement. In particular, the Patents and Design Act would be amended to make comprehensive provisions for the registration and proprietorship of patents and designs. The Trademarks Act would also be amended to improve existing legislation relating to the recording, publishing, and enforcement of trademarks and the protection for plant varieties (including biotechnology) and animal breeds.

On the institutional side, the reform would introduce a new Intellectual Property Commission, bringing together all Government agencies involved in the administration of intellectual property. This would be a welcome development.

9. Technology transfer requirements

Nigeria retains traditional thinking on the regulation of the entry and acquisition of foreign technology. Following the National Office of Industrial Property Act of 1979, all commercial contracts and agreements dealing with the transfer of foreign technology must be registered and approved by the National Office for Technology Acquisition and Promotion (NOTAP), an agency within the Ministry of Science and Technology.

For approval to be granted, such contracts must pass a number of criteria concerning, among others, their financial terms, the quality of the technology transferred, the existence of similar technologies in Nigeria, the training embodied and the avoidance of monopolistic practices.[71] The obligation to ensure proper registration falls both on the licensor and the licensee of the foreign technology. The 1979 Act further assigns NOTAP a monitoring role concerning the implementation of Technology Transfer Agreements. The objective is to ensure respect of the law, correspondence of the technology acquired with Nigeria's long term development objectives, to assess its diffusion and identify solutions to absorption constraints.

The stringent criteria for approval of technology transfer agreements were adopted over 25 years ago in response to a number of concerns by the Nigerian authorities. NOTAP reports that, before the introduction of the NOIP Act, "technology transfer contracts contained unfair conditions such as monopoly pricing, restrictive business practices, export restrictions, high royalty rates and tie-in clauses (with respect to equipment, raw materials, components etc.) but also little comprehensive training and management succession programmes and poor local R&D activities".[72]

Though the original functions are maintained, NOTAP recently shifted its focus from regulatory control and technology transfer to promotion and development of technology. In 1998, it was given an additional mandate to commercialize locally developed R&D findings, inventions and innovations from research institutes, universities, polytechnics, private laboratories and workshops. Since then, the office has undertaken some initiatives to assist SMEs in Nigeria to make effective use of Intellectual Property through the Patent Information and Documentation Centre (PIDC) established in NOTAP with the assistance of WIPO.[73]

---

[71] All relevant requirements are listed in the *Revised Guidelines on Acquisition of Foreign Technology under Noip Act Cap 268 LFN*, NOTAP, 2003.

[72] Okongwu DA (Director General of NOTAP) (2003). *IPRs and the Transfer of Technology – African Case Study*, presentation at the WIPO–WTO Joint Workshop on IPRs and Transfer of Technology, November, Geneva.

[73] WIPO. *Assisting SMEs to Make Effective Use of Patent Information: The NOTAP Case*. On the WIPO website at: http://www.wipo.int/sme/en/best_practices/notap.htm.

While a number of countries such as Brazil and Kenya still retain a screening – or regulatory – approach to transfer of technology, a more modern approach (the targeted approach), which does not rely on prior approval of technology transfer agreements, has emerged and is currently adopted by the majority of developing countries (box II.9.).

Box II.9. Evolution in the approach to technology transfer regulation

The discipline concerning technology transfer issues has evolved significantly over the last three decades. In this regard, the "regulatory" approach typical of the 1970s has been largely abandoned in favour of a more "targeted" approach. The characteristics of both are described below.

The **regulatory approach**. The underlying rationale is to control the potentially adverse economic consequences of technology transfers on the weaker party, which include both the licensee and the developing host country. Hence, the major features of such provisions include the prior screening of transfers of technology from abroad and the outright prohibition of certain terms in technology transfer transactions that are deemed to be detrimental to development goals. This approach was adopted in the national laws and policies of numerous countries during the 1970s, following a model well established in Japan and the Republic of Korea and later abandoned. It is most fully exemplified at the regional level by the Andean Community's policy on technology imports as contained in decision 24 of 31 December 1970, the "Common Regulations Governing Foreign Capital Movement, Trade Marks, Patents, Licences and Royalties", which has also since been superseded.

The **targeted approach**. With this approach, the technology transfer transaction is not necessarily seen as one between unequal parties. Rather, the private property character of the technology is stressed and a TNC that (in most of these cases) owns the technology is seen as being free to transfer it by the means it sees fit. However, given the potential inequality of market power between the owner and recipient of the technology, this freedom for a TNC is subject to certain obligations not to abuse its market power, whether in the case of an external transfer to a licensee or in the course of internal transfers within the TNC network. The willingness to prohibit specific terms in technology transfer transactions that is characteristic of the regulatory approach is abandoned. The targeted approach relies rather on adequate ex-post monitoring by those agencies that are most competent to address the various issues arising from technology transfer agreements. Hence, competition rules and agencies control market abuses, taxation authorities ensure correct reporting of taxable income, while training and transfer of technology is addressed by formulating general policies on these matters. These include incentive regimes by both the TNCs' home and host countries, so as to encourage technology transfer to developing countries.

Thus, over time, the emphasis has shifted away from the regulation of technology transfer transactions in the interests of the weaker party – normally the recipient in the developing country – towards a more market-based model in which increased technology transfer to developing countries is to be encouraged through the proper operation of the market, coupled with targeted regulation to counter potentially detrimental effects and an appropriate incentive structure to support diffusion.

Source: UNCTAD.

The current regulatory approach to technology transfer in Nigeria may have worthy objectives, but its criteria are far too sweeping and cumbersome to be effectively enforced. Moreover, the registration process and subsequent monitoring do not appear to have resulted in any assessment of the impact of foreign technology on Nigerian technological competence.[74] Monitoring the absorption of foreign technology and its diffusion within the national productive tissue is important and should be undertaken via competent analysis, but approval and registration of technology transfer agreements should cease as means of protecting or enhancing Nigeria's interests in technological advancement.

It is recommended that Nigeria embark on an overhaul of its public policy in the area of intellectual property rights and adopt a new generation of policies. Such policies should be consistent with the NEEDS' goal to make the Government "the enabler, the facilitator and the regulator", while leaving the private sector as the "executor, the direct investor and manager of businesses" (National Planning Commission, 2004: xi). Nigeria should therefore deploy market forces to provide competitive stimulus, which is in the interest of the private sector. It should at the same time support all firm behaviour, which has positive externalities to the country's development, by appropriate incentives (tax and/or subsidies).

In particular, NOTAP should complete the transition from a regulatory to a monitoring and promotion agency. NOTAP's key role should be to offer training to Nigerian businesses, especially at the SME level, in accessing foreign technology, including the negotiation of fair terms. Regulatory matters can be better handled by tax and competition law. Issues such as ensuring that payments under such agreements do not lead to underreporting of Nigerian taxable income could be dealt more effectively via anti-avoidance provisions in the tax legislation and enforcement monitoring by the tax authorities, while training and transfer of technology need to be addressed by formulating general policies on these matters, including via a regime of incentives and sanctions. In the same way, monopoly pricing and other anticompetitive practices should be contrasted by putting in place an appropriate competition regime.

10. Competition policy

On 24 August 2005, the Federal Executive Council approved Nigeria's first comprehensive Competition Bill, which foresees the setting up of Nigeria's first independent regulatory body, the Federal Competition Commission. Until adoption of the bill by the National Assembly, however, the main legislation on competition in Nigeria remains the Investments and Securities Act of 1999.

The bill covers the whole spectrum of anticompetitive agreements and conduct (abuse of dominant position, price maintenance, mergers and acquisition, monopoly, restrictive practices and intellectual property related issues) and gives the commission extensive powers to investigate (either on its own initiative, after receiving complaints or at the request of responsible minister) alleged anticompetitive conduct affecting business in the Nigerian market.

The initiative to introduce a full pro-competition regime is a welcome development and arguably overdue. The draft law is comprehensive, but often unclear in many of its provisions, which may create legislative uncertainty for business. For instance, the procedure for notification empowers the commission to review potential "dominance" arising from mergers and acquisitions (arts. 36 and 59). The bill could be shortened and simplified, and care should also be taken in formulating the application guidelines so as to ensure that the competition authority has the necessary flexibility in evaluating the potential anticompetitive effects of vertical constraints and other anticompetitive arrangements. In particular:

- At the moment, the Bill requires all mergers and acquisitions (M&As) to be notified by the parties to the commission, even if they result in a low combined market share. The commission will give clearance to all transactions not leading to dominance, defined as 40 per cent of market share or the ability of the merging parties to control prices, exclude competitors or behave independently

---

[74] No impact studies have been published, as required by the "Revised Guidelines for the Operation of NOTAP".

of competitors, customers or suppliers. Otherwise, the commission will proceed with a full investigation. It would be sensible to apply a minimum threshold to the notification requirement, as is the case in many countries. There is no substantive rationale to overwork the commission with minor mergers, which are unlikely to have an impact on competition, and such notification would impose unnecessary costs and delays to business;

- An M&A that might otherwise be prohibited could be allowed if the commission is satisfied that it creates a "public benefit". This concept is, however, not defined in the bill. In order to avoid abuse of discretionary power, "public benefit" should be made operational and spelled out (e.g. via an explicit employment target or an exports target). A second issue is that of which authority is best placed to ascertain public benefit.[75] If it is considered that the commission (and not the Parliament or the Government) should carry out that role, then it should be assigned an explicit mandate to address public interest and particular attention should be paid in ensuring transparency in its decision-making. Appeal should be possible if the parties are not satisfied with the decision taken;

- Monopolies are generally prohibited. A monopoly is defined by the bill as a single entity controlling sales or purchases of at least 51 per cent of a goods market, 25 per cent of services market and 25 per cent of the total national export of a good. However, a monopoly is normally understood to be a market situation with a single producer/supplier. Monopolies are not incompatible with competition law and policy if they emerge as a result of superiority in management, innovation or ownership of intellectual property rights, etc. Competition law and policy seek to prohibit monopolization, i.e. the conduct by enterprises which seeks to lessen or eliminate competition as a process. Moreover, the bill's definitions of monopolies are much too low and will make it impossible for firms to execute their business plans in a way that can allow them to prosper;

- Finally, the bill lists a number of exceptions to the abuse of dominant position (art. 37.3), including, for example, if the company's behaviour is the result of its superior competitive performance. A better approach would be to give a narrower definition of what constitutes anticompetitive behaviour, excluding de facto agreements and conducts which the exceptions seek to authorize, rather than take this broad and more intrusive approach, which puts the burden of proof on the enterprise to demonstrate both positive and negative conditions (art. 37.3).

During the Fifth United Nations Revision Conference on Competition Policy, the UNCTAD secretariat received a request from the Government of Nigeria for technical assistance with respect to the finalization of the Competition Bill.[76] This will be provided in the context of the follow-up implementation activities to this report.

11. Selected sectoral regulations

There has been a concerted effort to improve and modernize the regulation of the backbone services. The boundaries between public and private investment are being redrawn to an unprecedented extent (see the privatization section in chapter I). Major foreign investment cannot be expected in all areas, especially those involving heavy capital commitments and highly sensitive public services remunerated in local currency. Thus, privatization and concession are proceeding at different speeds in the various sectors. Major public funding will still be required, particularly in electricity and roads. But the conditions are being put in place to attract more foreign investment. Some questions are raised below about regulatory models and, although regulatory institutions have not all found their feet, there is a sense of progress.

---

[75] This is one of the competition policy issues which is still largely debated and was the object of the "Judicial Seminar on Competition Law", which took place in June 2006 under the auspices of UNCTAD in Bali.
[76] Belek (Antalya), Turkey, 14–18 November 2005.

a. Banking

Historically, the Nigerian commercial banking sector had not provided an adequate financial intermediation service in the economy. Private credit, as a proportion of GDP, stood at 24 per cent in Nigeria prior to recent reforms, in comparison to an African average of 57 per cent and over 100 per cent for South Africa (Soludo C, 2005). A long period of poor supervision led to a proliferation of banks and declining standards of compliance. Certain practices by less reputable banks also harmed Nigeria's international image. By 2004, there were 89 commercial banks, which had an average non-performing loan ratio of over 20 per cent (Central Bank of Nigeria, 2005).

A far-reaching programme of banking sector reform began in 2004 to address the above failings. Its central feature has been sector consolidation, pursued through the raising of the minimum base capital requirement to ₦25 billion ($200 million) from ₦2 billion ($16 million). Through mergers and acquisitions, capital injections and new capital raisings, 25 banks remained in operation while another 14 banks had their licences revoked after failing to meet the new requirements. Also, $3.2 billion of additional capital was raised through the exercise, including reported foreign investment of $650 million.

The speed and reach of the reforms undertaken since 2004 are impressive and the impact is tangible. According to a CBN interim progress report, bank liquidity has improved, interest rates have fallen and lending has increased. In January 2006, Nigeria received its first ever sovereign credit rating, BB-, and banking sector reform programme was an important factor in the agency's analysis.

On 23 June 2006, the Financial Action Task Force, recognizing the progress made, decided to remove Nigeria from its list of countries that are non-cooperative in the international community's efforts to fight money laundering. This is a signal of the improved quality of bank supervision.

Notwithstanding these reforms, Nigerian banks are still relatively small, reflecting the shallowness of financial intermediation in the country and the lack of international outreach of Nigeria's banking industry. Three Nigerian banks rank among the largest 20 banks in Africa, but they are minnows compared with the largest South African banks. The largest South African bank is 20 times bigger than the largest Nigerian bank.[77]

Foreign participation is also muted and has not, so far, changed as a result of the reforms. There are still only four foreign-owned banks operating in Nigeria at present: Stanbic; Standard Chartered; Ecobank (owned by ECOWAS member States); and the Nigerian International Bank, a Citigroup subsidiary. Barclays Bank, a stalwart African banking, was nationalized in the 1970s and has not returned.[78] Only 2 of the world's largest 10 financial institutions with a presence in Africa are active in Nigeria. The foreign banks represent a tiny 2.8 per cent of total banking assets. They have larger shares of total foreign assets (32 per cent) and the treasury bill market (29 per cent).[79] These statistics suggest that the foreign banks are little engaged with bread and butter corporate business. It seems likely that, as banking and wider economic conditions stabilize, there will be more interest in the Nigerian market by other foreign banks, probably through acquisitions.

---

[77] *Africa Business* October 2005. Size is measured by value of shareholders' equity.
[78] Thus, only two of the world's 10 largest financial institutions with a presence in Africa are in Nigeria.
[79] As at March 2006. Data supplied by the Central Bank of Nigeria.

b. Electricity

The Nigerian electric power system, which has been run since 1972 by the vertically integrated State-owned monopoly National Electric Power Authority (NEPA), is chronically dilapidated with respect to infrastructure, commercial standards and customer service.[80] As a result, over 90 per cent of industrial customers of NEPA have installed their own generators. High power costs represent the largest single source of non-competitiveness of Nigerian manufacturing (box III.1, chapter III). Yet Nigerian electricity costs could in fact be a source of competitive advantage, at least in thermal-based power, as Nigeria has the 10th-largest gas reserves in the world.

The electricity sector is to be liberalized, including the dismantling of NEPA, and private investment is sought. The new approach is set out in the Electricity and Power Sector Reform Act of 2005. The act provides a framework for private investment and for competition among private operators.

The Electricity and Power Sector Reform Act provides for the unbundling of NEPA into distinct business units, comprising generation, transmission, systems operation and distribution. The pro forma transfer took place in July 2005, when an initial holding company, the Power Holding Company of Nigeria, assumed the staff, liabilities and assets of NEPA. In turn, the Power Holding Company of Nigeria is composed of six generation entities, one transmission utility and 11 distribution companies created along previously existing regional arrangements. The Bureau of Public Enterprise (BPE) will attempt to privatize all of the operating companies, except for the transmission entity. The act establishes an independent regulator, the Nigerian Electricity Regulation Commission, which was formed in early 2006. The commission has appropriate independence and powers, including in relation to safety and consumer standards, operator licensing and tariff regulation (which must follow economic principles).

Independent power producers (IPPs) have been licensed to provide power to distributors and industrial users as a means of immediately reducing the shortage in supply, and to compete against the established generating units. There are already a number of IPPs operating or proposed (table 1.4). It is sensible to encourage IPPs and to permit them to contract directly with major industrial users.[81] They are a useful source of private investment in new capacity. The Government, with World Bank support, is enhancing grid capacity to cater for the increased supply.

The dismantling of NEPA, the wish to involve private investment and management and the appointment of an independent regulator are important steps to a long-term solution in which Nigeria's power disadvantage is turned into a competitive advantage for business. However, it is questionable whether the unbundling model that has been adopted will attract the volumes of private investment that are so urgently required. The proposed separation of generation and distribution, in particular, is likely to be an obstacle to foreign investment outside the special case of industrial users:

- Private investment in generation relies on power purchase agreements with distributors. The distribution system requires comprehensive investment and not just strong commercial management to restore it to a reasonable standard. Reputable operators might be attracted to a management concession. But given the size of investment required, and the inherent risks, it is unlikely that foreign investors of sufficient stature will be attracted to provide reliable power purchase undertakings;

---

[80] Only 36 of the country's 78 generating installations are operating at present. Nigeria, a country approaching 140 million people, produces only 3,000 MW a day, compared to the 40,000 MW per day for South Africa, with a population of 46 million. Also, a high proportion of energy produced does not reach consumers due to transmission and distribution losses.

[81] It is reported that payment to the IPPs for supply to the State-owned system is guaranteed permitting the IPP owners, the oil producers, to net such charges off against oil revenues owed to the Government. This appears to be a useful short-term solution until the distribution companies are creditworthy offtakers.

- Conversely, private investment in distribution will be difficult to secure unless there is confidence that there will be sufficient investment to regularize and expand power supply;

- Power producers and distributors are too interdependent for a successful separation to be workable at this time in Nigeria.

The Government should consider instead a system of regional vertically integrated production and distribution entities, served by a common grid (in which the regional entities had consortium ownership).[82] This allows the power producers to directly access their customers as in the successful expansion of mobile telephony. The B2C model of mobile telephony is more likely to attract investment than the B2B model proposed for electricity. Of course, this does not introduce competition from the outset. However, the existence of several regional utilities will provide valuable benchmarking information for the regulator to set tariff and quality standards for the industry. And, in the longer term, it would be possible to build competitive options into the system.

c. Rail

At present, the sector is entirely owned and operated by the Government. The 1955 Railway Act established the National Railway Corporation, which acts as both operator and regulator across the country's Central, Western and Eastern railways. The rail network is reasonably large (table II.7) but is severely under utilized because it is poorly run and maintained. Currently, the National Railway Corporation accounts for only 1.2 per cent of Nigeria's total freight market. This can be compared to Uganda, where approximately 10 per cent of domestic freight and 30 per cent of external freight is transported by rail, even though the Ugandan system and its seaport transit routes are also dilapidated (UNCTAD, 2000b).

The BPE has decided on the vertically integrated concession of operations and the outright sale of non-core assets. By way of build-operate-transfer (BOT) and public–private partnership PPP agreements, concessionaires will be responsible for infrastructure maintenance, expansion, upgrade and train operations (passenger and freight). Legislation is being drafted to create a rail regulator and a National Rail Development Authority. In addition to granting concessions and receiving concession fees, the authority will determine public service obligations, payment of subsidies for passenger services and monitor concessionaire obligation compliance. The rail regulator will (a) oversee tariffs and fare structure; (b) set and monitor service, quality and delivery standards; and (c) arbitrate disputes. The BPE has committed to the pilot concession of Central Railway in 2006.

Table II.7. Comparative rail networks and usage, 2003

	Network, km	Goods hauled, million ton-km	Passengers, millions
Nigeria	3,557	39**	973**
South Africa	20,041	105,725	9,960
Kenya	2,634	1,538	288
Ghana	977	242	85
Egypt	5,145	4,188*	40,837

Source: World Bank Development Indicators.
Notes: *2002 ; **2004.

---

[82] Generation capacity need not all be located within a given distributor's region. Regional utilities would be able to build or buy capacity from anywhere in Nigeria.

d. Roads

Nigeria's road network is reasonably extensive and compares well with other African countries in the proportion of paved roads. Approximately 90 per cent Nigeria's passenger freight is carried by road. Road conditions are often poor (potholes, inadequate drainage, fallen bridges and washed away pavements are common) and overweight vehicles are not adequately policed. Additional vehicle operating costs associated with bad roads have been estimated at the equivalent of almost $500 million per annum (Central Bank of Nigeria, 2003).

Currently, local Government is responsible for 67 per cent of the road network (urban and rural access roads), federal Government for 17 per cent (major roads and highways) and State Government for 16 per cent.

The importance of better management and expansion of the road network is recognized in NEEDS and reforms are being undertaken. The initial phase is to strengthen public institutions and tackle rehabilitation. The beleaguered Federal Roads Maintenance Agency is to be strengthened. Further proposed reforms include establishing a Federal Highway Authority and other institutions. It is proposed that the Federal Highway Authority would be empowered to award BOT concessions to private operators. It would certainly be useful to see if private operators would be attracted to rehabilitation concessions (which entail fewer political and commercial risks). For the foreseeable future, the bulk of funding is likely to be public.

Table II.8. Road network, 2002

	Nigeria*	Kenya	Ghana**	South Africa	Egypt
Total network (km)	194,394	63,942	46,179	275,971	64,000
Paved road (%)	31	12	18	21	78
Paved road (km)	60,262	7,673	8,312	57,953	49,920
Paved road (km per 1,000 people)	0.4	0.2	0.4	1	0.7

Source: World Bank Development Indicators.
Notes: *1999; **2001.

e. Ports

Nigeria's eight ports became, under State ownership and management, a byword for underinvestment, corruption and poor service. Corrective action began in 1999 with the passage of the Nigerian Ports Authority Act. This act permitted private sector port operations and created a new regulator, the Nigerian Ports Authority. A proposed new law, the Ports and Harbour Authorities Bill, makes more explicit provision for the encouragement of private sector operations under appropriate regulation. The bill proposes the creation of two "landlord" authorities (in Lagos and in the Niger Delta) which will own port infrastructure but will be empowered to concession terminal operations and issue service licences. The split is designed to introduce an element of internal competition. In addition, they would be responsible for technical regulation and the provision of certain essential services and infrastructure e.g. ensuring road and rail access to ports and providing off-shore cargo handling. However, economic regulation will be the responsibility of the proposed National Transport Commission, which is the subject of an eponymous bill now before the National Assembly. The commission's powers include tariff determination for the relevant entities, public and private. For example, while the authorities may levy tariffs on concessionaires for certain services, e.g. towage, this will be subject to commission approval.

Concurrently with the development of new legislation, the BPE has put into effect plans to commercialize operations within the sector. Overall, 25 concessions are underway. An important feature is that intra-port competition will be promoted where practicable by offering multiple concessions for individual terminals within single ports (for instance, six terminal concessions are available in the Apapa Port Complex, four in Tin Island Port, three in Onne Port and two in Port Harcourt). Tariffs are currently regulated but, when the National Transport Commission is in place, it can decide to open tariffs to competitive forces. Tariff regulation will probably remain in smaller ports, where competition is less likely.

By July 2006, 20 port concessions had already been decided upon, while the remainder were at the bidding stage. For example, AP Moller S.A. of Denmark, part of the Maersk Group, will "operate and manage" Apapa Port container terminal. It has a 25-year concession for a reported fee of $1.061 billion (net present value over the concession life). The ENL Consortium – which includes Haastrup Line WA; GSI, a South African logistics equipment supplier; Dublin Ports Company; and ENL of Nigeria – was the preferred bidder for Apapa Port terminals C and D. The consortium was awarded a 15-year concession agreement for the two terminals in June 2005.

The structuring of concession contracts in the larger ports relies heavily on competition to govern tariffs and service quality. Importantly, the concessions offered did not stipulate capacity expansion.[83] Competition will be relied upon to stimulate investors to meet the demands of the market. This is a bold approach but is well conceived. At this early stage of Nigeria's re-emergence, it would be unrealistic and self-defeating to mandate large investment obligations.

Nevertheless, foreign investment is being solicited directly for infrastructure improvement, through concession schemes. For example, the Grimaldi Group of Italy will construct a new port in Lagos under a 25-year BOT concession.

f. Telecommunications

Nigeria made an early start in the liberalization of the telecommunications market. The telecommunications system was separated from the postal service in 1985. The National Communications Commission was inaugurated in 1993 to initiate the sector's liberalization. In 2003, the commission was given full regulatory control including regulation of entry, licensing, spectrum management and implementation of developmental objectives such as promoting universal access. The national telecommunications policy unequivocally encourages private sector participation, within a competitive environment and provides for interventions to achieve greater network coverage.

Until quite recently, the liberalization had little practical impact. The sector was dominated by the State-owned incumbent NITEL, which offered a small network, a long and expensive process to obtain fixed line connections and poor technical quality. The National Communications Commission did not regulate NITEL but focused on some fringe services where competition was permitted.

However, liberalization has taken off in the last four to five years, with some impressive results (table II.9). A viable second national operator, Globacom, was introduced in 2002 to the market and already has more subscribers than NITEL. Nevertheless, the combined subscriber base is tiny (table II.10). Two additional GSM licences were awarded by auction in January 2001 to compete with the NITEL mobile phone monopoly. These went to MTN and V mobile (formerly Econet Wireless). Globacom also obtained

---

[83] However, operators will be required to comply with investment plans submitted with their bids.

a GSM licence as part of its second national operator status.[84] Mobile subscriber numbers have expanded enormously (Table II.10). MTN alone claims to have invested in excess of $1.8 billion in the development of mobile telecommunications infrastructure in Nigeria since 2001, while V mobile reports investment of $650 million. Celtel, a large pan-African mobile operator, has recently acquired a controlling interest in Vmobile and intends to invest heavily in network expansion. GSM operations are expanding fast and are highly attractive investments.[85] The new GSM licensees were permitted to operate international gateways for their own traffic. Also, many VSAT operators were licensed including at least four that were permitted to offer international access.

Table II.9. Telecom sector operators and investment

Number of operators and service providers by category	1999	2000	2001	2002	2003	2004	2005*
National carriers	1	1	1	2	2	2	2
Mobile (GSM) telephony	1	1	3	3	4	4	4
Fixed telephony	9	16	16	17	20***	24***	24***
VSAT networks	n.a	n.a	n.a	n.a	51	52	52
Internet services	18	30	30	35	35	35	35
Cumulative investment all categories ($ million)	50	150	1,200	2,100	4,000	6,080**	n.a

Source: Nigerian Communication Commission, Presentation to the National Political Reform Conference Committee on Social Infrastructure for Development, 7 April 2005.
Notes: *March; **September; ***Including 3 Fixed Wireless Access operators.

Clearly, the liberalization of the sector has revealed a substantial market that was poorly served by NITEL and has induced a burst of private investment from both national and foreign sources. Competition has been beneficial especially in the GSM market in lowering local call costs (figure I.6). International charges have also fallen dramatically.[86]

Important challenges for the future remain in areas that are key to business competitiveness and to Nigeria's development objectives:

● The fixed line network is tiny and rural areas are underserved; and

● Broadband access is not a developmental focus.

In fixed-line services, a second national operator has been introduced and is providing competition. To this extent, Nigeria is ahead of South Africa, where the incumbent remains dominant, although this is also a reflection of the weakness of NITEL. But there is competition in a small market. Fixed-line coverage is still extremely low and does not serve developmental aims. The introduction of Globacom has helped, but it appears that it will fall well short of its obligation to roll out 1.4 million fixed lines within five years. NITEL is financially incapable of providing a significant network expansion as well as funding its GSM infrastructure needs. Three attempts to divest NITEL to a credible private investor failed.

---

[84] The auction, which included payment by NITEL raised $855 million, which when adjusted for national income exceeds that of the United Kingdom 3G auction per MHz. *Source*: ITS Regional Conference, *On the design and implementation of the Nigerian GSM auction in Nigeria*.

[85] Celtel, owned by MTC of Kuwait, bought a majority stake in Vmobile for over $1billlion in June 2006.

[86] The average cost of a three-minute call to the United States fell from $2.47 in 2002 to $0.84 in 2004, but continues to be higher than in South Africa ($0.58) and in Ghana ($0.39). *Sources*: NCC (2005), World Bank *World Development Indicators*, UNCTAD (2005).

It appears that NCC may now abandon fixed-line network expansion obligations as a condition of according national carrier status. This is perhaps a practical recognition of its inability to enforce these obligations on existing operators or impose them as conditions on the privatization of NITEL. In part, it is also because the NCC is moving to a policy of unified licences to recognize technical convergence in the industry. "Universal service" will now be pursued through a universal service fund to be created from the levy of 2.5 per cent on the revenues of licensees.

Low broadband access is a direct reflection of the poor fixed-line network. But even if fixed-line networks are induced or subsidized to expand, it is unlikely that market forces alone will facilitate rapid deployment of broadband. The market for international voice telephony is still lucrative and operators have no incentive yet to risk their core business by facilitating voice over Internet protocol telephony. There may be a case for offering a separate class of licences to broadband providers, including for WiMax technology, that will permit wireless termination to computers. WiMAX could overcome the fixed-line constraints and be an effective tool for Internet connection for data and voice, including in rural areas. This may have implications for the scope of the proposed unified licences because there are spectrum constraints in the licensing of WiMAX.

Table II.10. Growth in telecom subscribers and teledensity

Service category	Number of subscribers/teledensity						
	1999	2000	2001	2002	2003	2004*	2005***
Fixed							
NITEL	450,172	497,019	540,662	555,466	555,466	524,596	525,000*
PTOs	23,144	56,355	59,659	146,534	333,068	515,173	568,925**
Subtotal	*473,316*	*553,374*	*600,321*	*702,000*	*888,534*	*1,039,769*	*1,093,925*
Mobile	35,000	35,000	266,461	1,569,050	3,149,472	8,500,000	9,950,000
Total	*508,316*	*588,374*	*866,782*	*2,271,050*	*4,038,006*	*9,539,769*	*11,043,925*
Teledensity	0.42	0.49	0.72	1.89	3.36	7.77	9.2

Source: Nigerian Communication Commission, Presentation to the National Political Reform Conference Committee on Social Infrastructure for Development, 7 April 2005.

Notes: *Estimates; **Includes estimates for some companies; ***January.

12. Summary of recommendations on the investment framework

Table II.11 presents a brief overview of the status of Nigeria's regulatory framework for FDI, by policy area and by Government's initiative for reform.

Table II.11. Nigeria, summary of main FDI policy issues

Policy area (last revised)	Current status	Comment/recommendation
FDI entry (1995)	***	Open entry to FDI, solid legal basis.
FDI establishment (2006)	**	OSIC recently introduced and CAC incorporation efficient. NIPC registration barriers need administrative reform.
FDI treatment and protection (1995)	**	BITs closure and negotiation needed, national treatment needs to be formalized.
Taxation (2006 proposed)	**	Deliver on VAT and zones tax reforms. Consider low flat corporate tax for all and eliminate the pioneer scheme.
Labour (2006)	***	Standards are currently good and will improve with adoption of new legislation.
Entry of foreign workers (1990)	*	Both temporary visas and entry of foreign workers regimes badly in need of reform.
Land (1978)	*	Anachronistic and discretionary land title allocation system in need of reform.
Technology transfer regulations (1998)	*	Old regulatory approach to technology transfer, shift in focus needed.
Competition (2006)	**	Competition regime and authority are being introduced, but there is room for improvements.
Sectoral regulations (2005)	**	Major improvements achieved. Reconsider electricity unbundling. Address fixed-line and broadband expansion in telecoms.
Rule of law (2006)	***	Sustained anti-corruption drive, need communication strategy targeted at international business.
Court system (2006)	**	Serious questions of speed and fairness of the system. Improvements underway, including State-level initiatives.
Intellectual property protection (2006)	*	Organization, staffing and enforcement are major problems, a new Internet Protocol framework is being devised – not made available for assessment.
Environment (2003)	***	Modern legal framework but enforcement a problem. Funding and staffing issues need to be addressed.

Source: UNCTAD.
Key: * = poorly developed; ** = solid development but room for improvement; *** = high standard regulation.

The main suggestions on policy options emerging from the review of the legal and regulatory framework for FDI are the following:

Entry and establishment

- Remove NIPC from its current "gatekeeping" functions, including business permitting, expatriate quota and pioneer status approval. These are contrary to the NEEDS' objective to make the NIPC a facilitator of investment and make establishment unnecessarily complicated. The creation of the OSIC is a significant step in the direction set by NEEDS, and the relevant agencies within the OSIC (immigration desk, FIRS desk, labour desk) are better positioned to perform licensing function.

The NIPC, as supervisor of the OSIC, should monitor the efficiency of the various desks in responding effectively and in a timely fashion. in responding effectively and in a timely fashion.

- Entrench good practice within the OSIC by negotiating protocols of cooperation between NIPC and all participating agencies, spelling out the extent of empowerment of the officers located in the OSIC desks, the NIPC oversight arrangements, the quality and number of staff assigned and service delivery expectations. Progress is being made on this.

- Utilize the NIPC desk at the OSIC to register all foreign investment for statistical purposes and introduce an "investor tracking system". Remove the administrative practice of setting a Naira 10 million threshold for FDI registration, which is not prescribed by the NIPC Act and creates confusion on the treatment and protection available to smaller foreign investors.

- Integrate an electronic OSIC (e-OSIC) within the physical office in Abuja to provide an information technology-based service to investors outside Abuja and to enable monitoring of customer service standards. The NIPC has stated its commitment to establish this service within three years.

Treatment of FDI

- Given the risk perception of Nigeria, adopt a proactive BIT closure and negotiation approach with the NIPC as lead agency, to seek: (a) ratification of negotiated BITs; and (b) negotiation of new BITs with countries that are emerging as potentially large investors to Nigeria in the short to medium run. These should constitute the building blocks of broader instruments of economic diplomacy with strategic partner countries.

- Consider revising the NIPC Act to include an explicit provision guaranteeing "national treatment" to foreign investment, although this is currently a low priority given that national treatment is extended for almost all practical purposes.

Taxation

- Consider introducing a flat 15 or 20 per cent tax rate on corporate income for all non-extractive businesses whilst maintaining and rationalizing the current attractive capital allowances. This approach would provide internationally competitive taxes for all investors (not just SMEs or those eligible for the pioneer scheme) and would be a simple and powerful investment promotion message. The proposed corporate tax reduction to 25 per cent does not go far enough as a "low, flat" regime to obviate recourse to major incentives.

- Eliminate the pioneer industry scheme as a consequence of the above recommendation. It is overly generous and limits competitive tax arrangements to the few eligible businesses rather than all.

- Eliminate the current caps on utilization of capital allowances and the limitation of loss carry forward to four years. The current restrictions are technically muddled and in any event need not apply as a corollary to introducing a low flat tax and rationalizing capital allowances.

- Remove the minimum requirement of $500,000 to invest in the free zones. The removal of domestic sales restrictions on zone companies is sensible and the proposed dual basis of taxation by income source is a natural consequence.

- Restructure VAT into a genuine VAT system to remove the bias against exports.

- Abolish the excess profits tax, which could operate as a burdensome second-tier minimum tax when applicable to turnover.

- Clarify the tax treatment of services payments to non-residents and bring it in line with standard practice.

- Pursue more energetically the conclusion and ratification of DTTs with key investment partners.

Labour

- Adopt the proposed new labour acts, which will further improve the already modern labour regime.
- Eliminate the uncertainty involved in the current formulation of redundancy provisions by drafting a regulation on redundancy compensation to accompany the Labour Standards Bill when it passes into law.

Employment and residence of non-citizens

- Remove the "immigration responsibility" requirement for business visa applicants, currently an impediment to business visits from potential investors. Further improve the short-term visas system by introducing a fast-track "Green Channel Business Visa", where NIPC endorses the "bona fide" of the applicant.
- Streamline the entry procedures for key expatriate personnel, currently highly discretionary, by adopting an "automatic EQ scheme", which would allow investors to recruit for a select number of positions without the requirement to justify the need to hire abroad or to engage understudies.
- Maintain the current BP/EQ scheme (including its understudy requirement) for allocation of additional EQ positions, but extend the BP requirement to all investment (including domestic) above $50,000 in order to assess the risk of the employer hiring unnecessary foreigners and not being able to cover for "immigration responsibility".
- At a later stage, move towards international best practice and introduce an open list of skills shortages to be reviewed annually and allow investors to recruit foreign employees with the required competences subject to verification of their credentials by the immigration authorities and to commitment of the company to a training programme for the advancement of local staff.

Land

- Eliminate the need for Governors' approval of land transactions as it is a source for delays and rent-seeking. Governors should allocate new land lease titles, but title transfer and encumbrances should be simply registered by the deeds' registry.
- Remove the incentive for land expropriation intrinsic to the current regime by instituting full compensation at market value for land resumed by public authorities.
- Outsource land surveying and the administrative support to land registries to specialized commercial enterprises to reduce delays.
- Encourage the transformation of free zones into multi-facility zones so as to provide ready-to-use plots of land for investment. While the need for a broader administrative reform is strong, this can offer a temporary palliative.

Technology transfer requirements

- Complete the transition of NOTAP from a regulatory to a monitoring and promotion agency by removing it from registration and screening of technology transfer agreements and address regulatory concerns related to such agreements (tax avoidance, anticompetitive behaviour) in the appropriate tax and competition regimes.
- Switch NOTAP's focus to providing training to Nigerian SMEs on licence agreements negotiation.

Competition policy

- Apply a minimum threshold to the M&A notification requirement so as to avoid overworking the Competition Commission with minor mergers with no relevance to competition.

- Define clearly the concept of "public benefit" in the Competition Bill. As this can lead to approval of otherwise illegal M&As, a clear definition is necessary to avoid abuse of discretionary power.

- Revise the current definition of monopolies, which does not correspond to either economic theory or competition policy standards and could hamper progressive firms. Make monopolization illegal.

Sectoral regulations

- In electricity, reconsider the proposed separation of generation and distribution in favour of a system of regional vertically integrated entities, served by a common grid. Power producers would directly access their customers and this is more likely to attract private investment in the short term. Later, more competitive options can be built in the system.

III. FDI GENERATION AND DEVELOPMENT

A strategy of supported market forces

Nigeria's broader development goals, as set out in NEEDS, must entail dynamic investment growth beyond the oil sector. In this context, this chapter is a strategic review of how FDI can contribute to this objective, with a focus on manufacturing, including the agro-allied industries.

The evolution of foreign affiliates in Nigeria affects their commercial prospects and also their contribution to the development of a manufacturing sector able to compete regionally and globally. For the time being, foreign affiliates in Nigeria are at the least dynamic stages of a development ladder whose end point for many industries is a role in sophisticated international value chains (section A). To reach this end point, a strategy of supported market forces is proposed to induce and support foreign affiliates to progress along the development ladder. It comprises big picture issues of trade policy, infrastructure support, skills development and regulatory change supported by selected measures (section B). As a result of such strategy, the improving investment climate will attract more FDI for Nigeria's large market even with the present low level of investment promotion activity. At that state, it will become important to make a special effort to promote and attract FDI that will be most beneficial (section C). The attraction of future FDI would benefit from institutional re-organization and from establishing coordinated federal-State investment promotion relationships (section D).

A. Nigeria on the TNCs development ladder

In the past 20 years, the nature of cross-border business has changed fundamentally. The worldwide trend to liberalized markets, allied to other globalization drivers such as the information and communications technology revolution, are leading to a new global economic transformation and division of labour. TNCs are at the forefront of this process, with the globalization/regionalization of production networks and the emergence of global/regional supply chains, now key dimensions of firm-level international strategy. TNCs in many industries seek competitive advantages by dispersing activities in the supply chain around the globe where each activity can be performed most cost-effectively, and product quality can be increased. Successful countries are not necessarily those that host manufacturers of finished goods for the domestic market, but host efficient segments of global supply chains. These could be partially processed raw materials, manufactured components or indeed finished goods based on assembly of mostly imported components from elsewhere in the TNC's global supply chain.

The dispersion of production is more pronounced in some industries than in others. In this regard, bulky, highly perishable or commodity-type goods have less integrated global supply chains within TNCs. However, goods with high value added manufacturing content depend on specialization within regional or global networks. Against this background, an FDI strategy for manufacturing should have the long-term goal of helping to position Nigeria to participate successfully in the enormous opportunities that this international landscape represents.

Figure III.1. Development ladder of TNC affiliates

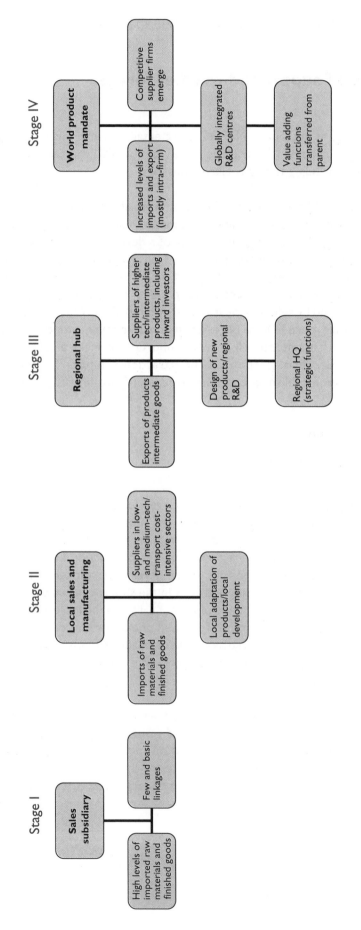

Increasing value added to host-country economy

Source: UNCTAD.

Note: The figure refers to manufacturing industry. It can be adapted to represent the service industry.

Figure III.1 presents a schematic representation of the evolutionary processes of a TNC subsidiary in an emerging economy along the development ladder. The progression highlighted essentially indicates increased sophistication and hence a greater contribution to the host economy. At the early stages, the foreign affiliate moves from a sales/assembly function towards local manufacturing, thus increasing use of local supplies. To enhance a competitive position in the local and perhaps regional market, increased emphasis begins to be placed on securing more competitive supplies, including nurturing local suppliers. Another response to competitive opportunities and pressures of local manufacturing is to adapt products to local market needs and later to design new products for local and regional markets. Local and regional product adaptation is done through a local R&D capacity, including use of local science and technology institutions. The search for competitive local supplies and the development of local R&D capacity are both important outcomes for upgrading local industrial and technological capacity in the host economy.

Further affiliate development (stages III and IV) requires an important leap in capacity – the ability to export to regional or world markets. This can take the form of exporting finished products, providing selected components to the global supply chain of the TNC or even outsourcing particular functions such as R&D. Moving from the stage of building the affiliate and its value chain and achieving globally competitive performance to that of having a role as a hub for regional/global operations will be determined by the TNC parent. In the Nigerian context, this might, for example, see a foreign affiliate acting as a pan-African hub for a specific product area.

To attain advanced stages of manufacturing, the host country's industrial and technological base has to exhibit competitive advantages over other locations. In this regard, a high-cost local market supported indefinitely by import protection, as is presently the case of Nigeria, is not an option. If foreign affiliates are to progress to stage IV within the host economy, it is important to focus on a coherent application of a long-term strategy to build competitive infrastructure, foster good governance and reduce import protection.

As highlighted in chapter I, there has been no transformational manufacturing development in Nigeria over many decades and, as a corollary, foreign affiliates have played a minor role. The interviews conducted at the company level during the UNCTAD fact-finding mission to Nigeria corroborate this picture. These interviews were conducted with six large foreign affiliates who employ a total of 12,500 persons in the manufacturing sector. All except one have been operating in Nigeria for several decades. The results of the interviews are reported in table III.1.[87]

Affiliate development has mostly been modest – generally stuck at stage II. This is not surprising given the volatility in the economy, the import substitution policies prevailing in the past, and the relatively recent arrival of regionalization/globalization pressures. Furthermore, existing concrete plans to progress to stage III or IV remain so far modest. In this regard, only company "C" saw itself evolving as a stage IV operation. The affiliate managers pointed to the likelihood that by end of 2006, the Nigerian operation would be bigger than that of South Africa. This would make it the largest business in Africa. The next level in the company's regional structure is the Africa, Europe and Middle East area: here Nigeria is currently tied for the fourth largest operation with Ireland. A different case is that of company "B", where pan-African integration is forecast to lead to the loss of marketing and R&D in Nigeria for one product area to the regional headquarters in South Africa. As company "E" noted, however, much depends upon the development of the Nigerian economy (and by implication, the competitiveness of the affiliate).

---

[87] To ensure confidentiality, names of the companies interviewed are not disclosed.

Table III.1. Survey results based on company interviews on potential TNC affiliate development up to 2011[1]

TNC affiliates[2]	Affiliate role in 2006	Development by 2011
"A"	Stage II (primarily). Some exports as part of group regionalization (stage III) but no local development/ R&D (stage I)	None
"B"	Stage III (primarily) with regionalization and regional HQ in Nigeria, local R&D, exports to regional markets, and local suppliers providing higher technology intermediate products	Marketing and R&D for one product line will move from Nigeria to South Africa
"C"	Stage III/emerging Stage IV	HQ for West and Central Africa; prospects for exports beyond the region and for the emergence of regionally competitive supplier firms (stage IV)
"D"	Stage II/III	None, except emergence of regionally competitive suppliers
"E"	Stage II	None, unless significant growth in Nigerian economy; in latter case, company will play a regional role
"F"	Stage II (largely)	Some evolution to stage III with local R&D and some exports

Source: UNCTAD, Survey of major foreign affiliates in Nigeria, 2006.
Notes (1) Affiliate development stage defined as in figure III.1; (2) Company names removed to ensure confidentiality.

B. Obtaining more developmental value from FDI

For Nigeria, building a robust presence of TNC affiliates would:

- Help to bridge capital, management, skills and technology gaps where they are most severe;

- Help to develop the competence of local companies and the workforce towards world standards;

- Help them be dynamic and competitive in a world where TNC headquarters are under incessant pressure to shift group operations to the most efficient locations; and

- Enable, within 20 years, Nigerian manufactures and service companies, foreign and national alike, to stand with the best in supplying local, regional and global markets.

In brief, the objective is for Nigeria to better utilize FDI to support the development of local productive capacities. To this end, a more systematic government strategy is required. This should work at two levels that can affect positively the business responses of foreign affiliates. The first is acting upon the competitive envelope of major issues of trade, infrastructure, skills and regulatory quality (section B.1) that both push and support foreign affiliates to attain competitiveness in regional and global markets. The second comprises more specific measures to support foreign affiliates to move up the development ladder (sections B.2 to B.5). These measures should work together. In particular, there is little point in developing specific support measures if the competitive envelope presents serious obstacles to more dynamic affiliate performance. So far, there has been a distinct lack of success of such measures in Nigeria, but the country is by no means alone in this respect. Furthermore, these measures should not be limited to investors already established in

Nigeria. They should also influence Nigeria's programme to attract new investors. An important thrust of this programme should therefore be an effort to target world-class TNCs that have the ability to get their affiliates up the development ladder (Section C).

The government strategy as introduced above and detailed in the following sections should guide the formulation of an explicit and comprehensive National Investment Policy of Nigeria. This would spell out the policy thrust of Government in respect to investment attraction, and represent an investment-friendly guide that is implementable, predictable and promotes policy consistency. But it should also contain concrete objectives and targets for the improvement of Nigeria's business competitiveness and formulate Nigeria's expectations regarding the role and contribution of FDI towards achieving its development objectives.

1. The competitive envelope – pressures and support to improve competitiveness

The competitive envelope in manufacturing is an interplay between the external pressures and external support to be competitive (external in this sense means external to the firm). The competitive pressure is exerted by the degree of import protection while the competitive support is determined by the quality of infrastructure (both physical and human capital) and of the regulatory environment.

Other things being equal, the prospect of substantial and indefinite import protection exerts low pressure on foreign affiliates to become more efficient and innovative. In this case, investors can stay in business by performing simple assembly, finishing or packing activities. In this sense, there is no outside pressure to adapt products, develop quality suppliers or reach out to more competitive regional markets in order to remain in business.

Setting a strategy that in tandem increases competitive pressure and delivers support is easier said than done. It requires difficult policy decisions and the ability to provide a planning horizon for businesses to evolve. In this regard, NEEDS sets out the position for Nigeria as follows:

- "While the Government is reducing the cost of doing business in Nigeria, it will use restrictions on imports as part of a strategy to ensure orderly restructuring of the industrial sector. The Government will aggressively promote exports and general commercial policy to attract foreign direct investment and it will pursue export orientation as a deliberate policy."[88]

This statement recognizes the relationship between competitive pressures and support. It needs, though, to be more forcefully and precisely linked. To this end, this report proposes the creation of an International Trade Commission to bring a systematic approach (section B.1c). But first, it is useful to see how Nigeria compares to other countries on these key competitive envelope parameters.

Figure III.2 provides a conceptual development path for Nigeria.[89] It illustrates where Nigeria is and compares it to other economies, including the industrially-advanced countries that should be Nigeria's long-term models. The top line of the figure shows the weighted average applied tariff on imports, while the bottom two lines are indicators of the relative regulatory and infrastructure quality pertaining to business in the selected countries.

Among the selected countries, with the exception of Kenya and Brazil, Nigeria had the highest average tariffs and the poorest infrastructure and skills until the 2005 reform. Moreover, the tariff index does not take into account Nigeria's extensive import bans. The adoption of the ECOWAS external tariff in 2005

---

[88] National Economic Empowerment and Development Strategy (NEEDS) (2004). National Planning Commission, Abuja: 54.
[89] Annex II provides the details on the construction of the wedge.

substantially reduced Nigeria's average tariff, although the loss of protection has been heavily cushioned by import bans on around 200 sensitive products.

India closely rivals Nigeria in the extent of its trade protection and poor state of infrastructure. On the other hand, Nigeria imposes less of a regulatory burden on business than other large countries such as Brazil and Kenya. This might be surprising, but it is consistent with the improving story on the investment framework related in chapter II. Nevertheless, among the largest African economies, South Africa ranks well ahead of Nigeria, and Egypt is quickly improving. With respect to infrastructure and skills competitiveness, Nigeria is the least advanced compared with peer countries. This suggests where future strategic attention could have the highest payoffs.

In comparison, China, a leading manufacturing exporter, is well-advanced along the wedge. Strong competitive pressures through low tariff protection are coupled with relatively good infrastructure. The apparent regulatory burden is substantially mitigated by conditions offered to investors within China's extensive free zones.

Figure III.2. Industrial development path of Nigeria and comparator countries – the "wedge" 2005

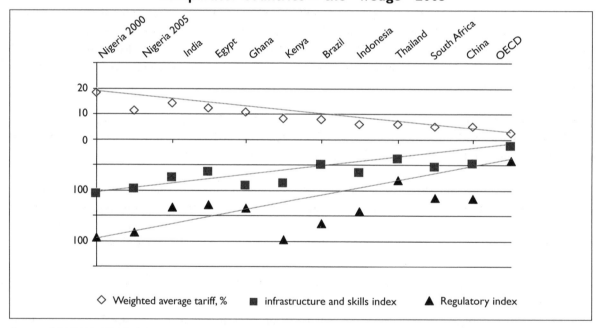

Sources: UNCTAD, TRAINS database; World Bank WDI 2006 and UNCTAD's Investment Compass Database 2006; World Economic Forum, Global Competitiveness Report 2005–2006.
Notes: For each country, the infrastructure and skills index is measured by the distance between the horizontal axis and the respective index marker. The regulatory index is determined by the distance between the infrastructure and the regulatory index markers. Latest available data (2005) unless specified. Regulatory index for Nigeria 2002 and Nigeria 2005 is the same due to lack of comparable data for 2002. Descending weighted average tariffs determine the countries' order along the horizontal axis. Annex II provides details on the construction of the wedge.

Brazil is arguably 20 years ahead of Nigeria in the scope and depth of foreign investment.[90] Yet it struggles to turn that investment from serving a large and protected market to becoming an innovative and export-oriented force that is fully integrated into the global supply chain. The extent of protection and the lack of competitiveness of the regulatory environment militate against this objective. Egypt has more of the major TNCs than Nigeria, but faces similar strategic hurdles as Brazil. On the other hand, South Africa appears to be strategically well positioned, at least in the auto industry. The Egyptian auto industry (e.g.

---

[90] Eighty per cent of Fortune 500 companies have a presence in Brazil.

General Motors) has small production runs for the domestic market (with some exports to neighbouring countries), while large segments of the South African auto industry are integrated into the global supply chain of their groups (e.g. BMW).

a. Nigeria's competitiveness: views of investors

Fieldwork undertaken for this report identified some of the competitive implications for TNCs of operating in the Nigerian environment (box III.1). As part of global groups, world class TNCs are routinely benchmarked against sister affiliates elsewhere in Africa and worldwide, as well as against TNC competitors within Nigeria. The cost disadvantage of operating in Nigeria varied from 15 to 25 per cent in the companies surveyed.

All firms pointed out cost disadvantages arising from poor infrastructure and regulation. The requirements for investment in human capital were also identified. Some alluded to their dependence on protection from imports although all the firms interviewed enjoyed substantial protection from competitive pressures. Electrical power was singled out as the most challenging area, in particular cases adding up to 10 per cent to operating costs. Other cost impediments derived from corruption, poor transport infrastructure, arbitrary taxation and problems of security. Companies indicated that they are responding to these challenges in areas at least partially within their control, such as electrical power. The comments of company E are an explicit illustration of non-dynamic behaviour of a firm that has been in business in Nigeria for 40 years.

Through a strategy of supported market forces, the Government could have an opportunity to induce and support foreign affiliates to make a dynamic contribution to the economy. This would require revisiting the way the competitive envelope is shaped. The key elements of the strategy should be:

- Improving costs and quality of physical infrastructure and human capital in areas of most concern to business;

- Achieving high standards in business regulation and taxation, and in regulatory administration; and

- Designing a consistent and well-timed opening up of markets to trade that moves in step with cost and productivity improvements achieved through better infrastructure and regulation.

b. Improving infrastructure and human capital

Nigeria has an outstanding opportunity to make decisive improvements in infrastructure and human capital over at least the next decade. This arises from two sources:

- The transformation in the outlook for public expenditures deriving from higher oil prices and the cancellation of the external debt; and

- The liberalization of the regulated backbone services, which provides opportunities for private investment and management that were hitherto unavailable.

Both sources will be important, but public expenditures will make the biggest difference to the scale of forthcoming investment. The challenge will be to achieve a beneficial interface between public and private investment. Figure III.3 illustrates the transformation in public fiscal outlook for 2007–2010, compared with a decade earlier.[91] Based on these estimates, public expenditures are expected to quintuple. This result is due to increased oil prices and also to debt relief and repayment (which have cut public external debt outstanding from $35 billion to $5 billion).

---

[91] Projections are based on IMF (2008). Projections beyond 2010 are not available.

Box III.1. Cost structures and corporate benchmarking

Company A: 15 to 20 per cent below international competitiveness benchmarks, because of cost impediments derived from corruption, electricity, poor transport infrastructure, problems of law and order and of arbitrary taxation. The Nigerian affiliate is also benchmarked on product quality which is adversely affected by an unsatisfactory road system.

Company B: 20 per cent cost disadvantage compared with an average operation within the Africa, Middle East and Turkey region. This is in spite of the fact that manufacturing control costs are lower than in South Africa due to labour costs, and lower than in Egypt, where transaction costs are problematic. The company benchmarks its factory performance. Excluding power, Nigeria was reasonably competitive, but power was a major factor which added 10 per cent to costs. Plans are now afoot to outsource power completely and to install tri-generation power equipment which, on a like-for-like basis, will save 5 per cent on costs.

Company C: Nigeria is benchmarked against other subsidiaries in Côte d'Ivoire, Ghana and Senegal. The group operates global benchmarking in areas where best practice norms have been established for particular areas of activity. The Managing Director/Chief Executive stated that the company operated an integrated business model and, therefore, its cost structure was better than those of local competitors (including TNCs). By international standards, power produced a significant cost disadvantage, although it was suggested that, with efficiency improvements, this could be brought under control. Unsatisfactory regulation was regarded as a key barrier, mention being made of multiple forms of taxation. The company was locally traded, which was considered to help reducing corruption.

Company D: Successor to a 100 per cent foreign-owned company, following the indigenization decrees of the 1970s. Costs are estimated to be about 25 per cent higher than in India and East Asia, where labour costs are often lower and infrastructure is better. Energy and logistics (e.g. ports and warehousing) costs are much higher in Nigeria. Consideration is being given to investing in gas in the medium term (although gas prices have begun to rise). The company is currently investing ₦10 million in energy-saving equipment.

Company E: This is the case of a company that has been protected by high tariff barriers. The company's fortunes, since it started business in 1963, have been closely linked to government policy direction, prospering during periods of protected markets and suffering during times of open markets. The 40 per cent tariff on finished products was to be reduced to 20 per cent as part of the ECOWAS tariff reduction programme. At this level, the company stated it could not compete against imports. The Government apparently accepted this argument, and an exemption was obtained which provided for 50 per cent tariffs until the end of 2007. The company argued that its competitiveness problems also stemmed from 50 per cent average import tariffs on imported raw materials and intermediate products, tariff levels that have risen from 15 per cent in earlier years. Infrastructural difficulties led to a policy of "just-in-case" as opposed to "just-in-time". The company considered it could compete if the infrastructural deficiencies – power, water and security – were addressed. At the time of the interview, the company was in the process of outsourcing many peripheral activities (including e.g. truck drivers), for estimated cost savings of 5 to 7.5 per cent.

Source: UNCTAD interviews.

Figure III.3. Nigeria fiscal outlook

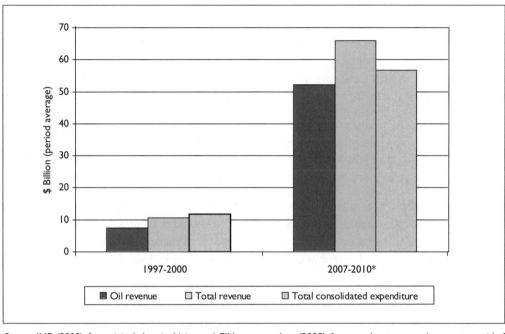

Source: IMF (2008) for original data in Naira and EIU country data (2008) for annual average exchange rates with $ (actual and 2008-2010 estimates).
Notes: * Nigerian authorities and IMF staff estimates and projections.

On the basis of a more positive fiscal outlook, the former Government had embarked on an infrastructure upgrade which had been a theme of the 2005 federal budget (Federal Ministry of Finance, Building of Physical and Human Infrastructure for Job Creation and Poverty Eradication, Budget, 2005). From a business standpoint, giving priority to improving electricity supply is an appropriate decision (box III.1) and should have a major economic payoff. In this regard, the Government had plans to invest $3.9 billion in seven power plants and associated gas development in the Niger Delta. After the 2007 elections, large infrastructure projects were put on hold for review by the new administration. It is encouraging that the new Government's medium-term fiscal strategy for 2008–2010 provides for an adequate spending envelope to begin addressing the infrastructure gap (IMF, 2008).

With respect to infrastructure services, the major strategic challenge in the next few years will be to correctly blend public and private investment. Private investors will not commit large amounts of money until the reality and perception of risks and difficulties in the commercial environment are firmly turned around. Furthermore, confidence in the new regulatory structures needs to be built. Notwithstanding the impressive reform efforts underway and the New Partnership for Africa's Development (NEPAD) initiatives on infrastructure (box III.2), this will take many years.

Given the scale of infrastructure rehabilitation needed, the Government should not wait for private investment to take the lead. It should, however, seek ways to partner with private investors so that public investment benefits from their discipline (market assessment, cost effective construction, well-managed operations and asset maintenance). In a sense, Nigeria should be developing concepts in which private investors are initially minority investors but with secure management rights. Thus, it should develop concepts of reverse BOT projects (with initial funding principally from public investment and eventual sale of the public interest to the minority private investor) or more generally, a specific type of PPP that involves small initial private equity.

Box III. 2 Bridging the infrastructure gap – the role of NEPAD

NEPAD is an African initiative designed to address the current challenges facing the continent. It arose from a mandate of the Organization of African Unity (OAU) to develop an integrated socio-economic development framework in Africa and was formally launched in July 2001. Nigeria has taken a leading role as one of the five initiating States, together with Algeria, Egypt, Senegal and South Africa.

NEPAD's main priority is the promotion of regional integration. This is to be achieved through a number of initiatives on agriculture, market access, human resources development, infrastructure and environment. In this regard, one of the most advanced projects of NEPAD is the infrastructure development initiative on energy, water, transport, and information and communication technologies.

In this regard, an infrastructure Short-Term Action Plan (STAP) was launched in 2002. STAP stresses the importance of creating a suitable environment to attract investment in infrastructure and thus the need for a sound legal and regulatory framework for PPPs. One concrete action of NEPAD through the STAP is to help African countries assess existing laws affecting PPPs and provide assistance in drafting new PPP laws, regulations and contracts.

One of the key regional infrastructure initiatives being pursued by NEPAD is the West African Gas Pipeline (WAGP) project, which has received the financial assistance of the World Bank and of the African Development Bank. Others include electricity inter-connectors in West and Southern Africa, high-priority road networks and a number of feasibility studies. The amount committed to NEPAD infrastructure projects, including those in the pipeline, is more than $5 billion. NEPAD is assisting with solutions to the main commercial and contractual issues involved.

Source: www.nepad.org.

As the largest country in Africa, Nigeria is endowed with an abundant supply of labour. However, to build a workforce that meets the requirements of the twenty-first century, the Government will have to overcome the challenges of the education sector. In spite of the fact that Nigerian data on education are not complete or reliable, table III.2 shows distinct underperformance in enrolments at the secondary and tertiary levels. Furthermore, the legacy of the military era is a decline of quality of education in universities as well as a reduction of research output. This is concomitant to a declining real value of Government allocations for education and deteriorating facilities. The poor results achieved by the education sector were also highlighted during the interviews with TNC executives.

At the tertiary level, only a minority of students is enrolled on the basis of academic performance, while dropout rates are high. Lecturer quality has declined due to shortages of qualified staff and problems of recruitment and retention, a consequence of low academic salaries and poor conditions. Furthermore, lack of availability of textbooks had led to abuse by staff, who sold their own notes as compulsory reading. This practice is now banned. In the meantime, criticism has been leveled at the weak governance of universities As a consequence of all these factors, Nigerian degrees lack recognition by overseas universities.

Responding to these challenges, the federal Government's budget for universities has been substantially increased in recent years. For example, between 2002 and 2004, the budget for universities rose by almost 40 per cent, to a level that represented over half of the total budget for the education sector. Figure III.4 shows that the funding of universities has therefore tripled compared with a decade ago. As the very valuable Monday Memos from the National University Commission show, increased efforts are being made to evaluate the performance of universities, through assessment of the quality of teaching, research, community service and internal efficiency. The analyses are notably based on dropout rates, overcrowding, graduate output, and corruption in respect of admission and grading.[92] In spite of recent improvements on a number of measures, there is a huge catch-up process required following, for instance, the six-month strike in 2003 and irregular payments to staff. Moreover, the quality of research remains poor.

Table III.2. Educational profile of Nigeria and selected comparator countries, 2002/2003

	Nigeria	Egypt	Ghana	South Africa	Brazil	China	India	Indonesia
Literacy rate (>15 yrs)	..[3]	56[1]	54.1	82	88	91	61	89
Gross enrolment ratio[4]								
Primary	119	97	79	106	147	115	108	112
Secondary	36	85	39	89	110	70	53	61
Tertiary	8	29	3	15	21	16	12	16
Expenditure on education (%GDP)	n.a	n.a	4.1	5.3	4.2[2]	2.1	4.1	1.2
School life expectancy (ISCED 1 - 6)	10	n.a	7	13	8	9	9	9
Compulsory education (years)	9	8	9	9	15	11	10	11
Pupil teacher ratio (primary)	42	n.a	31	34	24	21	41	20

Source: United Nations Educational Scientific and Cultural Organization (UNESCO) UIS database.

Notes: (1) 1996; (2) 2001/2002; (3) Literacy rates data for Nigeria not reliable; (4) The number of pupils enrolled in a given level of education, regardless the age, expressed as a percentage of the population in the theoretical age group.

Figure III.4. Nigeria, total university grant in real terms

(deflated by the consumer price index, 1995=100))

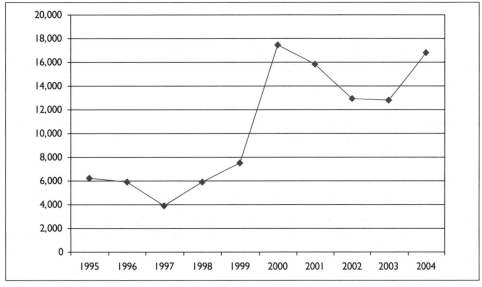

Source: National Universities Commission

---

[92] The term "sorting" is commonly used to describe the process of obtaining grade improvements in exchange for money, gifts or sexual intercourse.

The deficiencies in human resources capabilities and the lack of capacity at the managerial level represent a significant barrier to economic development in Nigeria. Overcoming these shortcomings requires a long-term, wide-ranging reorganization, restructuring and upgrading of education in Nigeria. This will require top-to-bottom reform and a 15- to 20-year plan, along with massive investment. This chapter will further elaborate on more specific measures to boost the quality of people available to business.

c. The tariff regime

Nigeria's adoption in October 2005 of the ECOWAS tariff regime (with the exceptions as detailed in box III.11) has led to a substantial reduction in tariffs and an associated compression of tariffs escalation within the supply chain of all industries. Table III.3 shows both the weighted average applied tariff on agricultural and industrial goods. If Nigeria removed the exceptional rates of 50 per cent on sensitive products and adhered to the full ECOWAS Common External Tariff (CET), there would be further reductions in average tariffs, especially on agricultural goods.

Table III.3. Nigeria tariffs on industrial and agricultural goods
(Weighted average applied tariff, %)

Goods	2002	2005	ECOWAS*
Agricultural	32.9	19.5	10.7
Industrial	15.3	9.1	8.0

Source: UNCTAD TRAINS database. Weights based on 2003 trade data.

* Projections based on the application of full ECOWAS Common External Tariff.

The ECOWAS tariff regime sharply reduces tariff escalation, as shown in figure III.5. This compression of protection within the supply chain puts increased competitive pressure on Nigerian suppliers of raw materials and semi-finished goods to domestic users. The tobacco industry is the starkest illustration of the change from 2002 to 2005 and to the full ECOWAS CET. But the effect is evident in all the product lines shown in the figure. Indeed, there is some evidence of negative escalation occurring, for example in fruit and vegetable processing.

The reduction of tariffs in Nigeria since 2005 was counterbalanced by bans imposed on importation of over 200 products. These bans significantly reduce the competitive pressure that would otherwise be exerted by the ECOWAS-led tariff regime. The import bans were due to be removed by January 2008. However, after carrying out an impact assessment of the affected industries, the authorities have decided to maintain the import ban, but reduce the number of items on the list (box III.11). No clear date is offered regarding the phasing out of these import bans.

The process by which the tariff strategy will evolve in the long term and the import bans are phased out in shorter term needs to be more adequately formalized. This would help investors to make the required changes over a determined horizon to adjust to the competitive landscape that they will face. Furthermore, the strategy needs to be linked to progress achieved in improving the competitiveness of infrastructure and regulatory environment affecting business. The ECOWAS process has, in recent years, driven long-term tariff strategy. An ad hoc body, the Tariff Review Board, has handled industry requests for specific protection in Nigeria. It is difficult to avoid the conclusion that the Tariff Review Board is focused more on helping industry, including TNC affiliates, to avoid competitive pressure rather than defining the timing and conditions under which the industry will need to adjust to competitive pressure (Tsikata, 2000; and WTO, 2005).

Figure III.5. Nigeria, tariff escalation in 2002, 2005 and projections to full ECOWAS CET
(selected products)

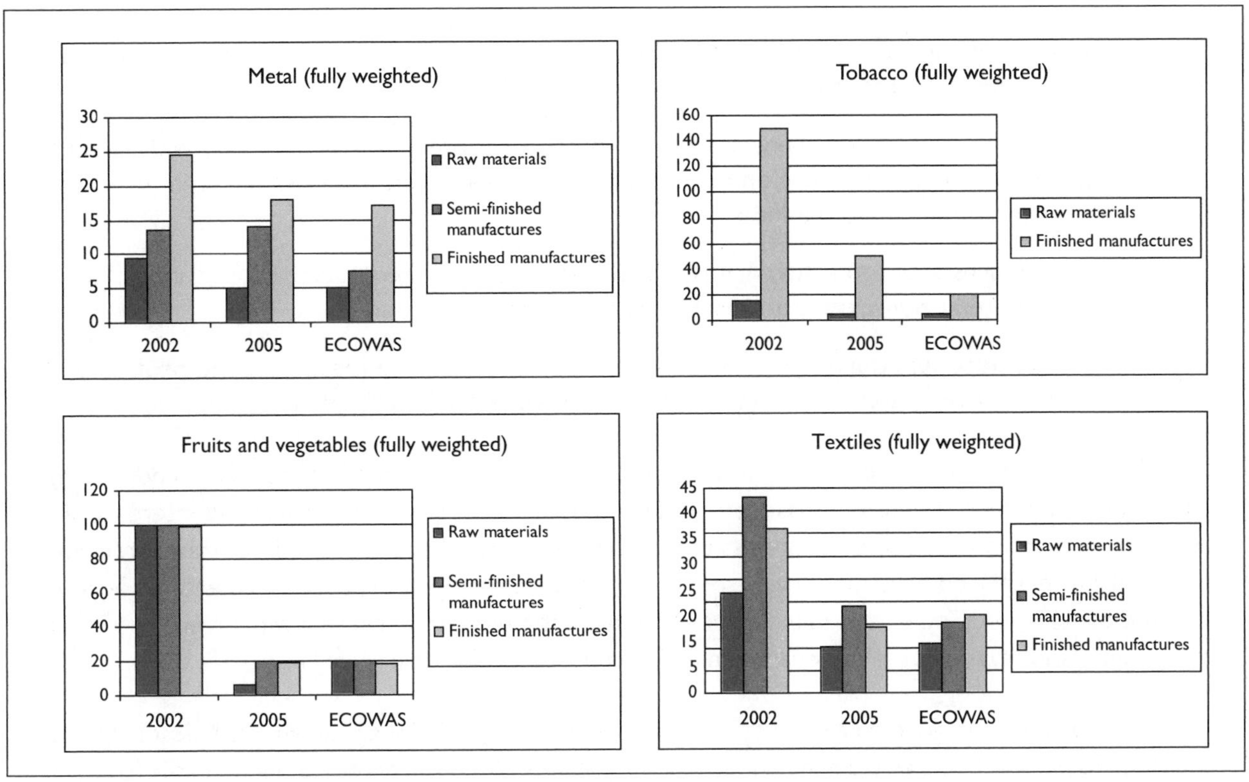

Source: UNCTAD TRAINS database.

In order to design and implement a systematic approach to move towards international levels of competitiveness, this report recommends that Nigeria establish an International Trade Commission. The commission should be charged with analyzing the long-term path of tariff reduction in line with improving competitive conditions for business and advising the government on the pace and strategy for liberalization. In proposing the timing and sequencing of the liberalization, the commission would also examine the merits of individual industry requests to depart for a time from the general regime so as to allow for sufficient adjustment time for those companies with good long-term prospects. This is particularly important for local companies, which lack the support of internationally advanced parent groups (box III.3).

d. Internal competition

Improving business competitiveness is also a function of competition within the Nigerian market. It is recognized that a small number of TNCs substantially control manufacturing in some sectors and subsectors such as cement, beer, soft drinks, other beverages, motorcycles and tyres. Their market dominance is partly a reflection of the length of time the companies have operated in the country, including periods of military Government, when competitors divested or simply ignored Nigeria. Furthermore, a number of local companies have similar market dominance. As an illustration, the Nigerian Dangote Group of Companies dominates in a number of the food (flour, rice, pasta and sugar), cement, transport and agriculture industries in which it operates (Economist Intelligence Unit, 2006). When markets are liberalized and stabilized, and policy consistency prevails, new domestic and foreign competitors will emerge to challenge the dominant position of the large existing players. Chapter II discusses the current gaps and proposals to upgrade the competition regime.

Box III.3. The Nigerian International Trade Commission

The proposed commission would be an independent and expert body, set up by statute, that would advise the Government on three matters:

* The pace and strategy for liberalization of the import protection regime in line with national objectives for industrial development and taking into account progress made in improving competitive conditions for business;

* Industry requests for protection that is above general norms or requests to pause the application of a general reduction in trade protection to a particular industry; and

* The application of safeguards, anti-dumping and countervailing measures. The professional application of safeguards is important throughout a process of liberalization.

The experience of other countries shows that a trade commission would not be a small undertaking. The commission must examine issues from an economy-wide perspective, not just the interests of a particular sector. Its work should be professional and evidence-based, and its procedures transparent and fair to all parties. The commission's advice should be published and open to public comments. To achieve this, the commission should have an independent status, and report to a ministry with a wide economic remit, such as, for example, the National Planning Commission or the Ministry of Finance.

The commission's governing body can include part-time commissioners drawn from academia and industry. To be credible, it would need enough full-time staff – a well-run commission can easily have 200 staff. In Nigeria, a start can be made with seconded economists, accountants and customs specialists from existing ministries.

Potential models for Nigeria are South Africa's International Trade Administration Commission (established in 2003 to replace the former Board on Tariffs and Trade) and Australia's Productivity Commission (established in 1996, originally the Tariff Board and thence the Industries Assistance Commission). The evolution of the names of these bodies reflects a broadening of their ambit, from examining specific industry requests to advice on enhancing productivity and international competitiveness of all industry.

Source: UNCTAD

2. Developmental affiliates programmes

The foreign affiliate development ladder presented in figure III.1 characterizes the long-term path towards world-class manufacturing.

Of course, there have been initiatives in the past to deepen the contribution of foreign affiliates, including efforts to stimulate local sourcing. Local content policies were operated during the late 1970s and early 1980s, but these were a constituent of the import substitution policies operated at the time, and not part of a strategy to enhance affiliate competitiveness. Indeed, the thrust was possibly the reverse. Companies could not obtain import licences unless they showed evidence that they had tried to obtain supplies locally. Unilever, for example, launched a number of initiatives to comply with Government demands in the areas of packaging, the production of scourers, bleaching earth, oil mills and palm oil extraction.

But a number of the ventures failed because of (a) working capital and management problems in the supplier firms; (b) inability to meet Unilever's volume demands; and (c) difficulty, in the case of oil mills, because demand outstripped supply. Problems experienced by other TNCs related to government failure to take an integrated approach to the local content programmes including tariff and tax policy: hence, some initiatives failed because of smuggling. With local content policies now banned under WTO rules, and the prevailing philosophy of liberalization, building a local supplier industry or local R&D is still feasible but only within the context of improving competitiveness.

In this regard, specific, planned and integrated policy initiatives can play an important role, as the experiences of other countries have shown. Issues of regional integration and market access, and the development of management capabilities and capacity, are identified as separate FDI programmes. The emphasis here is upon public policies to move affiliates up the development ladder through two programmes concerning R&D and product development and supplier linkages.

a. R&D and product development programme

While R&D has historically been highly centralized within TNCs' headquarters, recent evidence reveals a growing share being undertaken abroad. The benefits to host economies relate to the move up the value chain and the generation of dynamic comparative advantage. Specifically, R&D can bring in new knowledge and research know-how, and create knowledge spillovers to domestic enterprises and other organizations. In addition, research skills and the quality of human resources are enhanced, and industrial upgrading is stimulated.

In developing countries, the early stages of R&D will, in most cases, take the form of local adaptation (stage II in the affiliate development ladder). Box III.4 shows how the evolutionary process can change in respect of R&D, using the example of General Motors in Brazil. The driving forces for these developments were partly the technological capabilities of the affiliate itself and parent TNC decision-making. However, Brazilian government policy also played a role.

To date, Africa has been largely excluded from the process of internationalizing R&D centres (stage IV, the most advanced stage in the development ladder), except for isolated cases in Morocco and South Africa. For example, Morocco has attracted R&D centres in software and electronics, while in South Africa there are state-of-the-art R&D facilities in autos, aerospace and healthcare (UNCTAD, 2005 and 2006). In the case of Nigeria, UNCTAD interviews found no evidence of foreign affiliates engaged in stage IV R&D, except in an isolated case where a Nigerian affiliate was involved in product testing for its group R&D effort.

There are 54 research institutes comprising government research institutions, private sector research companies, international research centres and universities and colleges in Nigeria. There are also examples of ad hoc collaboration in R&D (box III.6). However, one study indicated that only 25 per cent of research institutes interacted with industrial firms in terms of information, knowledge flow and materials/equipment usage. So, generally, R&D is largely divorced from commercial utilization, although there has been no empirical assessment of the effectiveness of past policies (Aju, 2003; and Oyewale, 2003). This might be partly due to the lack of reliable data on total expenditures on R&D in Nigeria and its split between the public and corporate sectors. Furthermore, it is also probable that the publicly funded R&D effort has been driven by an import substitution model (a search for local raw materials to replace imports) rather than for local materials and products that give competitive advantage to Nigerian producers. Apart from its funding of research institutes, the Government has also provided a plethora of tax incentives to encourage enterprise R&D (Chapter II and below).

Box III.4. The evolution of R&D at General Motors in Brazil

General Motors (GM) has an important R&D centre at its São Caetano plant in southern Brazil. Established in the 1960s as a small unit to adapt GM autos and parts to Brazilian conditions, it became a large laboratory by the end of the 1980s, focusing on a variety of projects for the host country market (stage II in the affiliate development ladder).

The Brazilian Automotive Regime launched in 1995 was designed to attract FDI but also to upgrade products and manufacturing processes. In addition, a series of Information Technology Laws from 1991 stated that, in order to be eligible for fiscal incentives, TNCs were required to undertake R&D investments and establish partnerships with local universities and research centres.

By the late 1990s, GM Brazil had accumulated technical expertise in designing local versions of GM models, and became involved in the development of a new GM model (stage III). After 1996, GM changed the mandate of its Brazilian R&D centre from local to global: GM Brazil was allocated responsibility for designing a new vehicle – the Meriva minivan – for world markets (stage IV). These increased responsibilities have meant expanded product and process development for both local and global applications. Approximately 1,000 employees are engaged in product development and 500 in process engineering work.

GM in Brazil currently competes with GM affiliates in the United States, Europe and Asia for mandates to design and build new vehicles and undertake other core projects for the global corporation.

Source: UNCTAD, *World Investment Report 2005.*

According to UNCTAD's Innovation Capability Index,[93] Nigeria was ranked 96th of 117 countries in 2001 compared with the rankings of South Africa (48) and Egypt (56).

In respect of R&D activity by *foreign affiliates in Nigeria* to date, this largely takes the form of adaptation (stage II in the development ladder) as suggested by the interviews reported in chapter 1 (box 1.3).[94] Nevertheless, the potential for higher value added, new product R&D (stage III in the development ladder) is shown in the case of Neimeth Pharmaceuticals Plc. (box III.5). This company was established through a management buyout of a former TNC affiliate Pfizer and is now wholly Nigerian-owned. It has made significant advances in developing its own product range in the area of natural products of plant origin.

Against this background, although there is insufficient formal evidence, it seems reasonable to conclude that:

- Only some foreign affiliates undertake R&D locally and their efforts tend to be confined to product adaptation or, in the past, to meeting local content obligations. There is little evidence of systematic new product design or of progression to participation in group R&D work;

- There has been substantial Government support to local R&D in the form of publicly funded institutions and tax incentives. Its commercial impact has not been significant and it has been misdirected towards a search for local substitutes rather than sources of competitive advantage;

---

[93] Derived from measures of technological activity, including R&D personnel, patents and publications, and of human capital, represented by literacy rates and school and university/college enrolments.

[94] Of the six large foreign affiliates interviewed, only three have R&D departments, which employ a total of only 28 staff. The other three companies conduct no R&D in Nigeria.

- Some Governments, including in Nigeria in the past, have sought to mandate R&D activity through performance requirements as a condition of FDI entry. There is little evidence that such forms of compulsion are successful and very few countries apply them now (UNCTAD, 2005); and

- Thus, there is no systematic progression by foreign affiliates R&D up the development ladder or of well-conceived Government policy to support it.

Box III.5. R&D in Neimeth Pharmaceuticals Plc.

Pre-1997 (date of management buy-out) R&D-related activity was mostly clinical work with researchers to evaluate the efficacy of new drugs. However, since 1997 the company has had its own R&D department. This R&D operation has 12 people led by a medical doctor and has three roles:

(a) Improvements of existing products: product extension and adaptation to preferences of consumers;

(b) More fundamental R&D on natural products (of plant origin). This is considered the company's key competitive advantage. The principal product from this research to date is Ciklavit (Nutritional Supplement for Sicklers). The company is now working on two or three other products derived from natural substances;

(c) Collaborative research (also part of (b)), where the company's in-house team collaborates with other institutions in Nigeria. An example quoted was work with a Nigerian biochemistry professor in the area of the management of anaemia, where R&D is progressing towards product completion and subsequently marketing. Neimeth is also working with the Nigerian Medical Research Council.

The group of products (Neimeth Products Group (NPG)) derived from in-house R&D comprises 30 per cent of turnover. The balance is made up of licenced products from Pfizer (Pfizer Products Group). Exports (mainly to Ghana, Sierra Leone and Gambia) from the NPG represent 10 per cent of turnover, as part of a strong commitment to the ECOWAS market. The managing director saw ECOWAS as "one country" potentially. In terms of business in ECOWAS, Neimeth products were not subject to the same competitive pressures, while the economic situation was considered to be improving.

Source: Company interviews.

In this context, a new approach to stimulate innovation activities by TNCs in Nigeria is required and should be based on three principles:

(a) *Increasing competitive pressure.* The historically difficult investment climate attracts many low-quality foreign investors with little capacity to innovate. The commercial imperative for innovation in product adaptation and design must be strengthened. Increased competitive pressures from imports and well-enforced openness to internal competition – elements of the competitive envelope – are drivers of commercial innovation to maintain market share and profitability. The current protective environment encourages *de minimis* activity.

(b) *Strengthening management to promote Nigeria's production.* Local management of foreign affiliates is a key change agent and should be supported. Local managers need to convince their global or regional headquarters that investing in product innovation in Nigeria is worthwhile, given the ability of HQ management to shift production elsewhere. Put another way, unless the products of

Nigerian foreign affiliates can become more specific to the demands and tastes of the local, regional and pan-African market, the decision to produce in Nigeria rather than elsewhere becomes an efficiency contest in which the Nigerian affiliate is greatly handicapped until infrastructure and regulatory improvements come through.

(c) *Improving government support.* The extent and kind of direct government support to R&D must produce a proportionate public benefit.

How can these principles be put into effect?

The implementation of the ECOWAS common tariff, coupled with the removal of exceptional tariff rates and import bans on sensitive goods, sharply increase the commercial imperative for R&D in product innovation. A supportive trade strategy will exert longer-term competitive pressure (principle I). How can local managers of foreign affiliates best be supported to invest in sustainable operations to maintain their competitiveness (principles II and III)? Although basic R&D in product adaptation (stage II of the development ladder) presumably internalizes most of the benefits, there is widespread acceptance that public financial support for R&D is warranted because spillovers and other externalities are extensive (OECD, 2002). A practical way to enhance spillovers is to facilitate greater collaboration between foreign affiliates and research institutes so as to build their competence in commercially relevant skills.

Box III.6. Successful collaborations between research organizations and enterprises in Nigeria

- The Raw Materials Research and Development Council, in collaboration with universities and other research centres, developed small-scale dryer insecticide from local plant extracts as an anti-corrosion agent for cast-iron components, anti-ulcer and anti-snake bite remedies.

- A livestock raising and livestock feeds production firm in Ibadan, the Hope Industries Ltd., has gone into fruitful collaboration with the Cocoa Research Institute of Nigeria (CRIN) in Ibadan. The objective was to gradually replace maize (which is expensive and usually scarce) with cocoa husks, kola pod husks, sweet potatoes and cassava leaves in the production of livestock feeds. The R&D activities of CRIN have also yielded positive results in the production of cocoa wine, chocolate, cocoa bread and cocoa butter. These activities have also contributed to the fabrication of extraction machine for a cottage cashew juice factory.

- The Federal Institute of Industrial Research fabricated the equipment for yam processing into instant flour, and for essential oil distillation to extract oil from lemon grass and eucalyptus. It has also contributed to technology for high-protein garri and baby food formulation from local materials, among others.

Source: Company interviews.

Whilst government support for corporate R&D is warranted, there is no settled opinion on how best to deliver it. Among the OECD countries (which have the most experience of supporting corporate R&D) some favour fiscal incentives and some prefer Government-administered financial assistance. Many countries do both. Fiscal incentives are easier for Government to administer and are more market-driven in their application. However, the lower corporate taxation is, the less impact these incentives would have. Direct financial assistance is administratively more burdensome. While it enables Government to more closely target expected spillovers, it can also lead to a "picking winners" approach (OECD, 2002).

However, it is recognized that effective interactions among key stakeholders are crucial for the effectiveness of the National Innovation System. In Nigeria, as in most African countries, weak interactions exist among universities, research institutes and enterprises. For instance, as discussed above, this is the case in Nigeria, even though there is a specific tax incentive to encourage corporate contributions to research institutes.

It is suggested that a grant-supported programme be designed to stimulate affiliate R&D in collaboration with research institutes. Its design would recognize some of the reasons why foreign affiliate R&D, including collaboration with public sector research institutes, has been weak so far. Key features of the programme design are set out in box III.7.

Box III.7. Proposed collaborative R&D programme for foreign affiliates

The objectives of the collaborative R&D programme should be to:
- Localize/regionalize the product range of participating TNC's;
- Increase use of competitive raw materials in manufacturing; and
- Encourage greater private sector orientation and funding by public sector research institutes.

The features of the programme should include:

(a) Moving up the development ladder:
- Each participating TNC should aim, in the short run, to move one step up (e.g. II to III) and two steps up within 10 years (e.g. III to IV);

(b) Joint funding approach:
- Government grants will be provided on a joint funding basis with participating affiliates;

(c) Operating in a competitive environment:
- Affiliate participation is voluntary and projects will be proposed by the affiliates. However, participants must be operating within the general tariff regime, without exceptional rates or import bans, or moving in that direction. This ensures that competitive pressures are in place;

(d) Maximizing spillovers:
- Appropriate public sector partners (from the range of universities and research institutions in the country) should be involved to maximize spillovers. These should be selected by the affiliates on the basis of their research specialization and evidence of previous success with private sector partners;

(e) Favouring public–private interaction:
- Evidence from India and elsewhere indicates that interaction of public research institutes with the private sector can be increased by limiting the public financing of research institutions and setting targets for the generation of returns from selling research and other services to industry. This principle should be considered in Nigeria;

(f) Management role for the NIPC:
- The programme should be managed by the NIPC as part of a specialized foreign affiliates development unit. Some staff could be transferred in from NOTAP as part of its reorientation from a regulator of technology transfer to a promoter of local R&D.

Source: UNCTAD.

b. Supplier linkages programme

International experience reveals a wide range of policy initiatives to stimulate local sourcing and promote the local supply base. These include information and match-making, technology upgrading of local firms, human resource development programmes with local suppliers and other forms of training support, financial assistance and cluster-oriented programmes. Linkage programmes have become more difficult in an era of globalization because of TNC demands for globally competitive suppliers. On the other hand, the involvement of TNCs enables local supplier cost and quality to be benchmarked internationally and thus provides targets for linkage programmes.

The experience of previous Nigerian local sourcing initiatives highlights problems relating to suppliers' inability to meet cost and quality standards, to be able to supply in sufficient volumes to avoid production gaps among customer TNCs, and to maintain stable relationships in areas such as pricing policies. Past difficulties have also derived from failures of complementary policies in respect of tariff measures. This is reflected in Nigeria's poor ranking among the countries chosen as comparators in the "wedge" (figure III.2 and table III.4).

Table III.4. World and Africa ranking of suppliers in Nigeria and comparator countries

Rank in world (in Africa)	Nigeria	Egypt	Ghana	South Africa	Brazil	China	India	Indonesia	Thailand
Local supplier quantity	67 (6)	75 (9)	70 (8)	21 (1)	27	37	5	81	32
Local supplier quality	89 (11)	85 (9)	73 (6)	25 (1)	36	68	27	83	32

Source: World Economic Forum, Global Competitiveness Reports 2005–2006.
Notes: Total countries ranked: 117. Total African countries ranked: 23.

For Nigeria, the emphasis should therefore be upon developing an effective linkage programme, which means learning from past experiences within the country and from best practice elsewhere. Box III.8 presents successful examples from Ireland and Malaysia, where the selection of suppliers and their training/mentoring is stressed. South Africa's introduction of a systematic benchmarking programme to assist the upgrade of local suppliers to world-class manufacturing standard in the auto industry is also a useful case study. However, it is important to note that Nigerian manufacturing is less a restructuring story (as suggested by NEEDS) than a development one.

The proposed Nigerian programme is therefore critically important to the successful rebuilding of the manufacturing sector and especially the food and agro-business value chain. But there will be other opportunities derived from the large prospective infrastructure spending. The outline of the features of a partnership linkage programme are set out in box III.9.

3. Regional integration

Nigeria's large internal market is and will remain its primary asset to attract FDI. The strategic aim of foreign affiliate progression along the development ladder, nevertheless, is to position Nigeria as a base for pan-African sourcing and/or integration within the global supply chains of TNCs. Figure I.5 in chapter I showed that, over the last 40 years, Nigeria's manufactured exports have stagnated in absolute terms and have halved on a per capita basis. In this sense, there is little evidence that foreign affiliates have made a dynamic contribution; thus, this is a long-term aim given Nigeria's starting point.

Box III.8. Successful supplier linkage programmes

Ireland's National Linkage Programme

The current National Linkage Programme (NLP) was introduced in 1998. It was focused primarily upon potential suppliers to TNCs in the electronics, engineering and – more recently – healthcare industries. The NLP cooperates with foreign affiliates and their parent companies to identify specific parts and components that may be supplied domestically, and to identify domestic firms showing the best potential. Realistic supply opportunities were identified in metal and plastic components. A key criterion for selection of local supplier companies is a forward-looking, ambitious and dynamic attitude. The NLP then works with its selected firms on an individual basis to deliver tailored solutions. Lessons to be drawn are that:

* Matchmaking requires accompanying measures to upgrade the capabilities of potential and actual suppliers;
* Supplier development efforts should be selective;
* Close collaboration with foreign affiliates and their parent TNCs is crucial; and
* Close coordination amongst the various government agencies involved in assisting local suppliers is important.

National and regional linkages in Malaysia

The Small and Medium Industries Corporation (SMIC) launched a Global Supplier Programme in 1999, aimed at strengthening the competitiveness of Malaysian SMEs. The objective was for local SMEs to become suppliers to foreign affiliates of TNCs, and also potentially to evolve into global suppliers. The programme has two initiatives – training in critical skills and building linkages with TNCs. The training initiative focuses on helping participants acquire competencies to adopt and use new technologies. Under the linkage initiative, foreign affiliates "adopt" local companies and guide them for upgrading in leadership skills and technology. In most cases, there would be a long-term commitment with regular reviews between affiliates and suppliers.

In a related programme, the Industrial Linkages Programme of SMIC offers a number of incentives. Large companies participating can claim tax deductions for supplier-related support activities – e.g. training, product development and testing, or quality assurance of vendors' products. Approved suppliers are eligible for a full tax exemption at statutory income tax levels for a period of five years under the pioneer status or an investment tax allowance of 60 per cent on qualifying capital expenditure incurred within a period of five years.

Firm-level upgrading in South Africa

At the beginning of the 1990s, the South African auto industry appeared to be in terminal decline with low volumes and proliferation of models. Within a decade, it became a strong performer and has made significant strides as an exporter of both autos and components. A number of factors drove this restructuring, including the Government's Motor Industry Development Programme, and the demands of the foreign-owned assemblers for quality improvement and cost reduction. An important contributing factor in the sector's growing competitiveness was the formation of Benchmarking Clubs in which suppliers initially benchmarked against each other and then against the world's best. Through its Sector Partnership Fund, the Government provided two-thirds of the cost of starting and running this learning network. Combining a benchmarking programme with structured activities for continuous improvement assisted firms to make spectacular progress in upgrading their performance. As a side effect, the consulting group that set-up the Benchmarking Clubs has developed skills that have led to their providing benchmarking services to other industries.

Source: UNCTAD, *World Investment Report 2001*. UNCTAD, *Investment Policy Review of Kenya (2005)*.

Box III.9. Proposed Partnership Linkage Programme for Nigeria

(a) Specific objectives: to move participating TNC affiliates one step up the development ladder in 5 years (stage I to II) and two steps up in 10 years (stage II to III).

(b) Programme components will include elements of technology transfer and upgrading, provision and sharing of information, financial support, training and benchmarking. TNCs will take the leading role in delivery with outside consultancy support.

(c) Selection of industries should be determined by country priorities (the agro-business value chain should be the first priority) and the potential to achieve local supply. The latter depends upon factors such as the actual or potential supplier base, technological capability required of suppliers, and actual or potential quantity and quality of raw material supply.

(d) The selection of foreign affiliates should be voluntary and based on their willingness and potential to establish valuable linkages, and to work with and mentor partner suppliers. Preliminary discussions with companies showed a significant level of interest.

(e) Supplier selection should be determined by suppliers' commitment and capabilities to meet the requirements of TNCs and their motivation. Criteria to be used include self-improvement requirements, technological and skill audits, production capabilities, ISO certification and commitment of the CEO and key managers.

(f) Foreign affiliates and suppliers must be committed to adherence to the ECOWAS tariff regime (i.e. without exceptional rates or continued import bans).

(g) It should be managed by the proposed affiliate development unit of NIPC and involve interested parties such as the Lagos Chamber of Commerce, the Manufacturers Association of Nigeria, industrial development centres and research institutes.

(h) It should be funded by the Government but also be financially supported by TNCs and suppliers.

(i) A supportive set of policy measures must be considered, particularly concerning tariff measures for raw materials and finished products. In addition, their impact upon related industries and suppliers, as well as taxation provisions (e.g. tax credits or tax reductions for provision of funds to suppliers) and financial support (e.g. direct support to suppliers, incentives for R&D cooperation with Nigerian institutions/universities and affiliates) should be taken into account. Ready access to visas for industry training specialists should be included.

Source: UNCTAD.

Nigeria has preferential trade access to the North American market under the AGOA agreement. It is also negotiating, as part of ECOWAS, a new economic partnership agreement with the European Union to replace the Cotonou agreement, which came to an end on December 31, 2007.[95] However, an important intermediary step to reach the goal set above is to focus initially upon the export opportunities within ECOWAS since this will be the objective of TNCs' integration strategies.

---

[95] Economic partnership agreement negotiations are set to conclude by mid-2009. Discussions are ongoing on sensitive issues such as excluded sectors and specific provisions related to competition, trade in services and intellectual property.

Discussions with companies indicated that ECOWAS is the market area allocated to Nigerian affiliates by their parent TNCs, as part of regionalization within Africa as a whole. What is also important is that product specialization allied to regional integration may be significant in encouraging affiliate upgrading – for example, product development to cater to different customer tastes and requirements in the wider ECOWAS market. ECOWAS is thus important in beginning the process of mindset change and creativity, which is necessary for successful export orientation. Neimeth Pharmaceuticals Plc. (box III.5) is a good example of what can be achieved within ECOWAS. The competitive stimulus from participating within ECOWAS will, however, be constrained by the relatively low levels of economic and presumably corporate development. Nevertheless, Ghana is a competitive threat, particularly as a headquarters location for pan-ECOWAS operations. This is confirmed in the competitiveness rankings for selected ECOWAS countries presented in table III.5. Also, Côte d'Ivoire, not shown in the table, accounts for a higher share of ECOWAS manufacturing value added than Nigeria.

Table III.5. Competitiveness rankings in ECOWAS

Competitiveness rankings	Nigeria	Ghana	Mali	Gambia	Benin
Growth competitiveness index 2005	88	59	90	94	114
(Growth competitiveness index 2004)	(93)	(68)	(88)	(75)	(n.a.)
Macroeconomic environment index	76	66	97	107	101
Public institutions index	98	51	72	77	110
Technology index	90	69	103	97	116

Source: World Economic Forum 2005.

Notes: Growth competitiveness rankings shown are the overall rankings for 2005 (with 2004 comparisons in brackets) and the constituent rankings for the macroeconomic environment, public institutions, and technology. The ranking is over 117, where 1 is best, 117 is worst.

Because of small populations and limited purchasing power, infrastructure problems, such as poor road systems and both tariff and non-tariff barriers to market access, there is little evidence to date of new FDI having been attracted to Nigeria to supply the wider ECOWAS market. However, there is evidence among existing TNCs of early commitment to regional integration and the establishment of regional supply chains, and to ECOWAS' market opportunities. In this regard, a number of TNCs have now begun to take cautious steps to implement regional integration policies and regional supply chains (box III.10). One investor even suggested that "regionalization will gather pace and momentum".

Despite its longevity, progress on trade matters, let alone harmonization of economic and financial policies and the creation of a single monetary zone, has been painfully slow (box III.10). Adoption of the Common External Tariff (CET) was due to be completed by end-2007. However, by June 2007, it became clear that Nigeria would not agree to eliminate its exceptions to the ECOWAS CET (box III.10). Early in 2008, the Ministry of Finance of Nigeria announced that "The five-year tariff regime 2008–2012 would, as much as possible, be harmonized with the ECOWAS CET, while at the same time protecting the interests of the manufacturing sector in particular and the Nigerian economy in general".[96] Aside from tariff structures, non-tariff barriers (NTBs) continue to represent major obstacles to trade. NTBs include poor communications infrastructure, bureaucracy and corruption in customs, numerous road blocks and general harassment, and payments' difficulties. There are also language barriers with the Francophone block, the countries that are more closely integrated amongst themselves.

[96] Address by Dr. Shamsudden Usman at the sectoral hearing of the ECOWAS tariff 2008–2012, held at the Manufacturers Association of Nigeria, in Lagos as reported in Vanguard, 3 April 2008.

Box III.10. Regional integration and regional supply chains among world-class TNCs

Company A: The group operates global supply chains as part of a worldwide integration strategy, with China, India and Indonesia representing important supply locations. An ECOWAS-based regionalization strategy, with Nigeria as its hub, was initiated in 2004 and hence is still in its early stages, with exports representing about 10 per cent of turnover. The recognized advantages include economies of scale from larger factory size and in machinery and utility design and utilization, speed in the transfer of technology and know-how to one rather than several locations. Conversely, logistics and customs clearance are very real and large challenges. The first pan-regional decision was to transfer responsibility for one entire product line to Ghana, which now exports to Nigeria. The decision was taken in part because of the need to access one basic input of production at competitive prices. The three factories in Nigeria facilities have a role in supplying to specific household products for regional markets.

Company B: At the global group level, the entire supply chain is globalized, but this has yet to occur in West Africa because of tariff structures which hamper multi-country supply chains. However, supply chain integration is planned for West Africa going forward, with particular locations specializing in specific products, and some factories being closed. Recently, production of one of the group's product has ceased in Ghana and has been concentrated in Nigeria to achieve consistency across the region. Marketing strategy for the region is developed from the hub centre in Lagos. Exports are valued at $16m per annum, 7 per cent of revenues. Imports represent 50–60 per cent of input costs by value (including high-value items) and 30–35 per cent by volume. Challenges for the company's regional integration strategy include the insularity of the Francophone block (although opportunities in some small outlay products had been identified); tariffs, especially in Nigeria, given that an integrated ECOWAS required free movement of goods and people; and problems of corruption at the border posts. The last is being circumvented by the use of sea freight.

Company C: While this company espouses the notion of an integrated ECOWAS market, it is still at the stage of "looking for opportunities". No proactive policies have yet been pursued to implement regional supply chains, although there appear to be good possibilities given that the company has eight factories in ECOWAS. In Nigeria, the company manufactures a full product line, with the exception of one product which is imported from the plant in Côte d'Ivoire. The new CET regime means that the tariff on one of the specific imported inputs will be raised from zero to 20 per cent which may lead to a cessation of importing. The company does not export at present. Barriers to regionalization to date include lack of capacity, reflecting the rapid expansion of domestic sales in Nigeria, and fluctuations in laws which will necessitate back-up plants. There is a West African management structure in this company, with headquarters in Ghana (formerly in Côte d'Ivoire). Ghana is considered to be the most stable and safest place to locate a headquarters, as security in Nigeria is still considered problematic.

Source: Company interviews.

Because of such factors, Nigeria's trade with ECOWAS countries represents a very small share of total trade. In 2003, for example, ECOWAS accounted for only 2.7 per cent of Nigerian non-oil imports and 5.5 per cent of Nigerian non-oil exports. Nevertheless, ECOWAS was Nigeria's fourth-largest export destination.

Box III.11. Nigeria and ECOWAS

The Economic Community of West African States (ECOWAS), established in 1975, is composed of 15 West African countries: Benin, Burkina Faso, Cape Verde, Côte d'Ivoire, the Gambia, Ghana, Guinea, Guinea-Bissau, Liberia, Mali, Niger, Nigeria, Senegal, Sierra Leone and Togo. Nigeria is the largest member of ECOWAS, accounting for 60 per cent of the population and 47 per cent of GDP (but only 24 per cent of manufacturing value added, smaller than that of Côte d'Ivoire at 26 per cent). ECOWAS' mission is to promote cooperation and integration within the West African subregion through the removal of customs duties and taxes having equivalent effect, the establishment of a common external tariff, the harmonization of economic and financial policies and the creation of a single monetary zone. Some efforts are also being made to develop a West African Common Industrial Policy (WACIP).

ECOWAS members have been implementing a trade liberalization scheme since 1990, with the objective of establishing a free-trade area by 1 January 2000. By 2001, eight countries had lifted tariff barriers in respect of unprocessed products under the scheme. Furthermore, only Benin had removed tariff barriers to trade in industrial products. As of December 2004, the free-trade area component was being implemented fully by only 7 of the 15 members (i.e. Benin, Burkina Faso, Côte d'Ivoire, Ghana, Guinea, Senegal and Togo). Nigeria has lagged behind: as of December 2004, it had only removed tariffs applying to unprocessed goods, but had maintained import prohibitions on some products, including those originating from ECOWAS member States.

A common external tariff (CET) was to be accepted by 1 January 2004, but due to implementation delays, adoption of the CET was rescheduled to start on 1 January 2005 and to be completed by 1 January 2008. However, this objective was further postponed, as national exceptions to the common tariff continue, as is the case for Nigeria. The ECOWAS CET consists of four bands (0, 5, 10 and 20 per cent), similar to those already being applied by West African Economic and Monetary Union (WAEMU) member States (WAEMU comprises the francophone countries which already shared a common currency). During the transition period (2005–2007), non-WAEMU ECOWAS countries should therefore gradually align their tariffs on the WAEMU CET. In October 2005, Nigeria introduced the ECOWAS CET, the main changes being as follows:

(a) Nigeria's tariff bands are reduced from 19 to 4 (0 per cent on necessities, e.g. anti-retroviral drugs, industrial machinery and equipment; 5 per cent on raw materials and other capital goods; 10 per cent on intermediate goods; and 20 per cent on consumer goods);

(b) A 50 per cent band applies to strategically designated products, e.g. tobacco and rice. The Government has, however, indicated that this "fifth band" will be reduced to 30 or 35 per cent by the end of 2009;

(c) The import ban list is still in effect; 2006 data indicated 59 items on the prohibition list; and

(d) A wide range of exceptions to the CET rates are applicable. Where the Nigerian duty rate is higher than the CET rate (commonly a rate of 50 per cent applies), the reasons put forward to explain the discrepancy are support to: domestic industries or domestic assembly plants or FDI: agriculture or local packaging industry: or because of excess capacity. By contrast, for example, the Nigerian duty rate is 5 per cent for juices and concentrates, compared with the CET rate of 20 per cent, to encourage the local packaging industry.

In a bid to further accelerate subregional integration towards common market status, Nigeria and six other ECOWAS member States (Benin, Burkina Faso, Ghana, Mali, Niger and Togo) are engaged in a programme, launched in 2002, which seeks, inter alia, to remove all physical and non-physical trade barriers (including remaining tariffs), eradicate rigid border formalities, enforce the application of ECOWAS prescribed customs procedures and adopt a common ECOWAS passport.

WACIP was launched in 1994 (following a series of earlier initiatives) to promote accelerated industrialization. Ten strategic focuses have been defined, including the promotion of private investment, development of entrepreneurship, development of microenterprises and SMEs, patents and R&D, technology transfer and innovation, export funding, promotion of intra-community trade, infrastructure development, information and communication technology, export promotion and market research, and integration into the multilateral trading system (WTO, AGOA, EU/ACP). Progress appears to have been limited so far.

Sources: WTO 2005; ECOWAS 2008; Nigeria Customs Service; UNCTAD.

Improving the workings of ECOWAS is a stated priority of Nigerian government policy, although this is often couched in terms of Nigeria contributing to regional development and stability. This review suggests that accelerated regional integration could also benefit Nigeria as an intermediate step towards the evolution of foreign affiliates in the pan-African region and global supply chains of their TNC groups. This suggests that, at the strategic level, there should be a more concerted drive to accelerate regional integration within ECOWAS. At the implementation level, improvements in trade facilitation to assist TNC export and supply chain operations within the West African region take on greater priority.

Regional integration has not necessarily been high on the agenda of successive Nigerian Governments. This is understandable given the political and economic problems throughout the region. The time, however, is now right to give regionalization much higher priority at top levels in Government. The principle is recognized in the NEEDS Report, which asserts that the Government will "aggressively work" towards the attainment of an integrated market. What is now required, therefore, is the setting of specific and actionable priorities with time-scales for the short, medium and long term in respect of the free trade area, customs union and common market (progress towards free movement of factors of production).

On *trade facilitation*, the NEEDS Report speaks generally of removal of all NTBs to trade. One major NTB concerns impediments to the free movement of goods, especially at border posts. Measures to improve trade facilitation for FDI supply chains (as well as for trade more generally) are thus essential. One TNC suggested that it could take a truck up to two weeks to drive to Ghana from Nigeria, whereas the CEO himself could drive the route in 12 hours. Efforts must thus be made to reduce delays and arbitrary taxation at the borders. The United States Agency for International Development in Ghana is taking the lead in a West African trade hub project, in collaboration with ECOWAS, to train customs officers. This project should be expanded and widened to include Nigeria and other countries. In addition, the volume of trade is quite limited at present, and it should be possible to provide greater security to truck movements and particularly truck convoys.

4. Free zones integration

Free zones have multiplied around the world to achieve various objectives, including increased attraction of FDI, promotion of linkages with local suppliers, promotion of export-oriented production, employment creation and income generation. Recent studies on their worldwide impact indicate that zones have played an important role in the export performance of many countries, while their impact on employment has generally been marginal, although exceptions exist.[97] As for the promotion of linkages, experience is also mixed. International evidence points to a number of clear lessons relating to their success or failure (World Bank, FIAS (2004a); BearingPoint, 2004). In respect of success, the following lessons have been learned:

- Zones need to be integrated within host economies, as the static and dynamic impacts are very limited when zones are operated as enclaves;

- Zones should not be viewed as a substitute for a country's larger trade and investment efforts;

- The regulatory framework should provide streamlined procedures for business registration; and

- Private rather than public development of zones increases the chances of success and zones operation should be undertaken by private sector groups on a commercial basis.

---

[97] In Taiwan Province of China and the Republic of Korea, for example, essentially all manufactured exports were either produced in a zone or used duty exemption/drawback schemes. In countries such as China, the Dominican Republic and Mauritius, a very high share of manufactured exports are produced in the free zones. In countries such as Mauritius, the Dominican Republic and the United Arab Emirates, zones are a major source of employment.

By comparison, factors inducing failure include bureaucratic policy frameworks, uncompetitive fiscal incentives, subsidized rent and other services, poor locations (e.g. in remote locations), and inadequate coordination between private developers and Governments in infrastructure provision.

The key objective in Nigeria's zone development is to broaden their integration into the economy rather than treat them as export-processing enclaves.

The act establishing the Nigeria Export Processing Zones Authority (NEPZA) came into effect in 1992. However, the first free zone – the Calabar Free Trade Zone – was not fully completed until 1999 and commissioned in 2001. The history of free zones in Nigeria is therefore very recent. Ostensibly, growth progression has been rapid, since there are now are 22 free zones. However, only nine of them are operational (including three in the oil sector).[98] Of the operational non-oil zones, three are owned by the federal Government, four are private, while the others are sponsored by State Governments. There are also plans to privatize the zones, leaving NEPZA to handle marketing and regulation activities.

To date, growth within the non-oil zones has been moderate because Nigeria has not been able to provide three of the conditions needed for these zones to succeed:

- A staple of export processing zones is assembly and further processing for re-export of imported raw materials and components. Excellent shipping and customs clearance of imports and exports (especially those that are time-sensitive) are essential. The Nigerian non-oil zones are not located at sea ports and do not have dedicated trade facilitation arrangements.[99] Given the present state of trade facilitation services, and of transport infrastructure, it is not reasonable to expect inland zones to succeed as export platforms. An exception to this general rule is zones that are dedicated to the processing of local raw materials for export and which are best located near the raw material source. The NEPZA gives the Maigatari zone as an example;

- Zone infrastructure is either not first class or expensive. In addition, electricity and telecommunications services are dependent on unreliable national providers; and

- Zones have not been convincing as portraying themselves exempt of red tape and corruption problems associated with doing business in Nigeria.

Gradually, the profile of zones is being changed from pure export-oriented facilities to multi-facility zones (free zones). In this context, free zone producers will no longer be required to export 75 per cent of output. They will be able to sell either locally (up to 100 per cent of their output) or abroad. Export income will be subject to zero corporate tax (as at present) and domestic sales income subject to standard taxation.[100] Import duties will be paid or relieved dependent on the final destination of sales. Investment promotion will now be on the basis of high quality infrastructure, reduced bureaucracy and elimination of corruption. In addition, investors can be attracted without being limited in accessing the local market.

Reports indicate that the Calabar Zone – located in the south-east of Nigeria, 2 km from a container port and 20 minutes drive from Calabar Airport – is modern, with excellent facilities in a small, clean and modern town. The United Nations Industrial Development Organization (UNIDO) concluded that this

---

[98] Some reports suggest that a new category of export-processing factories has been established in which individual factories can qualify as private or virtual zones, provided the 75 per cent export requirement is met. Such entities are used in many other countries. However, the Federal Revenue Service states that such factories have never been permitted in Nigeria.

[99] It is worth noting that the first free zones around the world originated as free ports. In modern times, some zones have exclusive ports and customs' facilities and a large hinterland for industry and settlement, e.g. the Islamic Republic of Iran's free trade industrial zones on the islands of Kish and Qesm.

[100] The corporate tax change is subject to adoption of proposed legislation. See the review of taxation in chapter 2.

and other zones could provide the basis for establishing an export-oriented ready-made garments industry (box III.12). Costs in Calabar, for example, were estimated to be 20 per cent lower than for an equivalent ready-made garments plant in Lagos.

Box III.12. Ready-made garments industry in Nigeria: some recommendations

* Introduce new policies to reduce smuggling;

* Introduce anti-dumping protection against import competition of yarns and fabrics;

* Establish export incentives for 10 years that are not subject to any change;

* Develop further the zones, with regulations designed to meet the needs of dynamic, export-oriented companies and to satisfy the demand of buyers for quality products supplied with short delivery times;

* Address the education needs of the industry for trained, skilled workers and effective management; and

* Develop a marketing/promotional programme to attract foreign investors, focusing upon China, the Republic of Korea, Taiwan Province of China, and the United States. Special incentives should be offered to initial investors.

Sources: UNIDO/Federal Ministry of Industry, FGN (2003).

From international evidence and the experiences with free zones in Nigeria to date, a number of recommendations are proposed to enhance their effectiveness and potential development impact:

* Reorient the zones to Free Zones with unlimited domestic market access.
* Move to private development of zone facilities and privatize existing zones. Private developers are more likely to take a realistic view of the prospects for attracting investors. Also, they have a commercial incentive to build appropriate facilities in favourable locations and to promote the zones to investors. There may sometimes be a case for public subsidy for zone development, under public–private partnership (PPP) arrangements. However, the commercial disciplines should be paramount. NEPZA should concentrate on assisting private zone developers to secure good locations, to obtain development permits and to provide excellent administrative services to zone industries.
* Consider adopting policy measures to encourage investors in free zones to assist value chain integration in target sectors. In principle, well-conceived free zones could provide a short- to medium-term stimulus to the attraction of foreign-owned SMEs in manufacturing industry (where the costs associated with poor infrastructure are a particularly important inhibiting factor).
* Target investors in agro-processing. It is consistent with development objectives and current constraints in Nigeria. It has export potential and is less dependent than other manufacturing on imported inputs and thus on the quality of import facilitation services.
* Encourage supplier development by a deemed export scheme. Suppliers of processed inputs which enter into zone manufactures would have the same incentives as the manufacturers themselves (including zero corporate tax on export-related income).

Alongside these overall objectives, the Calabar Zone should continue to be developed and expanded as an exemplar for zone strategy in Nigeria.

5. People quality programme

Restoration of education standards to improve Nigeria's position within the competitive envelope will require heavy investment over a long period. At the tertiary level, there have recently been substantial rises in federal budget expenditures on universities and measures taken to improve quality (section B above). Nevertheless, for business, there are deficiencies in human resources capabilities at the managerial level. Problems with low educational standards apply at the tertiary level as well as at the school and technician levels (Moja, 2000). These are mirrored almost exactly in the responses of TNCs interviewed, all of which commented on the declining skill levels at the tertiary level. Several pointed out that the problems began at the primary school level, and were also critical of technician level training (as compared with, for example, South Africa).

Some companies resolved the problems of education standards through increased investment in training. Others began to look at ways of obtaining managerial and professional staff by recruiting from the Diaspora (box III.13).

Box III.13. TNCs' responses to the decline in education standards

Company A: There had been an observable decline in the level of skills, especially at the tertiary level and to a lesser extent at the technician level. The company had around 6,000 applicants for the 10 management trainee positions offered annually. Because of the education deficiencies of even these high-level staff, this large manufacturing company put them through a redesigned training programme which started with a six-month "finishing school" (mini MBA) after which they had to pass an exam. It was only after this that the conventional two-year management training programme was implemented.

Company B: This service provider was faced with the challenge of labour shortages during its start-up and growth phase, when it required hiring experienced staff. One solution was to recruit "repats" (as they are termed) from the Diaspora. As part of a planned approach, the company visited the United Kingdom, Continental Europe and the United States to head-hunt staff from various sectors. A meeting of repats was held in 2004. Only 25 to 30 people turned up, a relatively small number for a company employing 2,000 people. However, the company is encouraging repats to use their networks to recruit more. Among some of the difficulties raised by the company are the need for motivated staff (some repats want a more luxurious lifestyle and return) and some discrimination of repatriates by local Nigerians (which may partly be due to salary differentials). However, the main advantage to the company remains the experience gained elsewhere that repats bring with them.

Other experiences: Some other companies had begun to experiment with Diaspora recruitment by participating, for example, in job fairs in the United Kingdom. The need for commitment was a common theme.

Source: Company interviews.

The Government has the capacity to boost long-term public investment in education as part of driving improvement in the competitive wedge. The Government can also take more specific steps to accelerate the supply of executive talent in the medium term and reduce the transactions and training costs for TNCs. Two specific initiatives are proposed: improving executive level business education and training through the establishment of world-class business schools, and supporting Diaspora recruitment. The aim of these programmes should be to make an identifiable difference to the availability of managerial talent for the Nigerian private sector within a four- to five-year period.

a. Establish a joint venture world-class business school

Management education is globalizing rapidly, although the expected growth, for example, from e-learning has not been realized to date. The senior executive education business is dominated by a small group of elite business schools from the United States and Europe, while in the next tier of entry- and middle-level management education providers, providers from the United Kingdom and Australia are also prominent. Some emerging market universities are beginning to expand abroad. In respect of modes of entry into global markets, there are a variety of models of management education (table III.6) with differing advantages and disadvantages.

The Government should enable Nigeria to participate more forcefully in international management education. In addition, the country should address criticisms about the marketing of a global product, when the requirement is for localization, to meet specific market needs, for instance, emerging market rather than developed country market conditions. Although there have been developments within the country itself, infrastructural weaknesses are a major barrier at present to the foreign provision of *distance learning*. In this sense, a report for the World Bank (Col International, 2001) indicated that only two (Abuja and Lagos) of the 30 federal universities offered dedicated distance learning courses at the degree level. However, the National Open University of Nigeria (NOUN), established in 1983 but then suspended a year later, was relaunched in April 2001. Presently, NOUN has 32,400 students enrolled on a variety of degree and diploma programmes, including business education, with 20 study centres around the country.

In respect of *collaborative modes*, IESE (a well-known Spanish Business School) has an association agreement with the Lagos Business School.

Concerning business education provision from within Nigeria itself, the best-known institution is the Lagos Business School. It was established in 1973 and became private in 2002 as the first school of the newly-formed Pan-African University. It launched executive and full-time MBA programmes in 2002 and 2003. In the National Universities Commission 2004 rankings of universities in Nigeria, the Lagos Business School was ranked first for the quality of administration/management science programmes, for the percentage of foreign staff, and for student/personal computer ratio; fourth for the percentage of foreign students (still very small at 1.6 per cent); and fifth for that of successful graduates. The International Finance Corporation (IFC) has launched an initiative called the Global Business School Network to enhance management skills in emerging markets by partnering with leading international business schools to build local capacity. The Lagos Business School was involved in designing and organizing one of four Global Business School Network African pilot programmes on teaching the practice of management in 2005.

Given the Nigerian context, there is an urgent requirement to improve the quantity and quality of management education to support FDI attraction and development over the short-to-medium term. However, accessing the distance learning programmes of foreign universities is a long-term objective because of, among other things, infrastructure deficiencies. The reform of Nigerian universities is again a long-term goal. Lagos Business School shows what can be done in building a highly reputable business school using private funding and – despite an expansion in the number of private universities – additional capacity is undoubtedly needed at the leading edge of management education.

This report proposes to establish a new privately-funded world-class business school with competitive entry, in collaboration with an internationally-renowned overseas partner. As is the case with the current private university system, the new business school can operate outside the constraints imposed by the present structures and regulations for public universities. The key issue is the selection of a partner institution: an obvious target is one of the elite United States or European business schools, a number of which are active globally, and should at least be considered. There is, however, an argument for evaluating a world-class business school based in an emerging country as the desired target for collaboration, given the greater familiarity with business practices in the Nigerian context.

Table III.6. Management education modes of entry into global markets by foreign universities*

Entry mode by foreign university	Nature of education activity	Significance for Nigeria
Export modes	Distance learning products differentiated: by: • Provision of learning materials – hard copy, e-learning • Lecturer/tutor support – none, local support, staff support from foreign universities • Degree award – host country university, foreign university, joint degree	• Variability in quality of foreign providers • Potential for corruption as in existing university education system • Introduces new knowledge and thinking, learning methods, books and materials • Opportunities for fairly large-scale provision in future to meet unsatisfied demand for higher education • Inadequacy of essential services and infrastructure
Collaborative modes	Range of association/partnership agreements, of greater or lesser commitment. Greater commitment associated with stronger contribution by foreign universities, e.g. classes taught by foreign professors, similar curricula and books, degrees awarded by overseas partner or jointly	• Many different types of arrangements • Strong commitment by foreign universities, desirable, combined with training of local staff • Introduction of interactive teaching methods important • Greater localization desirable, e.g. local case studies • Joint degrees and dual country study offer major multicultural benefits
Joint venture and wholly-owned subsidiary modes	Differentiated from collaborative modes by establishment of campuses in host country. Plus greater degree of commitment, extending to, for example, training of host country faculty abroad; and writing of case studies for the host country market Some joint ventures established by intergovernmental agreements e.g. between foreign university (acting on behalf of the foreign Government) and host country Government	• Similar advantages as advanced collaboration • Resident foreign staff may increase spillover benefits • May lead to opportunities for student (and staff) exchanges

Source: UNCTAD.

* Relates primarily to MBAs and management masters' degrees (full-time, part-time and executive (EMBA)) mainly in Western universities.

Various options should be investigated. One possibility is the National University of Singapore (NUS) Business School. It has been teaching business since 1961 and has a faculty of 160. Furthermore, it is ranked in the top 100 MBA programmes worldwide by various organizations and in the top 30 for its Executive MBA (EIU and Financial Times rankings). NUS has extensive experience in international collaboration through its dual degree programmes with the University of California–Los Angeles (UCLA, United States) and Beijing University (China). The former is the UCLA–NUS Executive MBA taught by faculty from both business schools, with classes held in Singapore, Los Angeles, Shanghai and Bangalore. With regard to the NUS–PKU (Beijing University) International MBA, students spend approximately half of their time and study an equal number of courses in both institutions. If this model were to be replicated in Nigeria, it would require a Nigerian partner, where Lagos Business School is the obvious candidate.

Another possibility is the attraction of an Indian business school. The Indian Institutes of Management (IIMs) are the top-rated business schools in India, with IIM-Ahmedabad ranked number 1. Established in 1961 with Indian Government funding, IIM-A collaborated with Harvard to launch the case study teaching method in India. It has the highest ratio of applicants to enrolments of any business school in the world, and an impressive array of global alumni. Nevertheless, factors such as the low proportion of international faculty and international student base, as well as low staff salaries and starting salaries for graduates, mean that IIM-A is not listed in the top 100 business schools globally. Its internationalization was limited historically because of Indian Government restrictions, but permission to internationalize has been granted as of 2006.

Such a large cooperation project with Nigeria would be premature for IIM-A, at least on its own. However, in February 2006, IIM-A and Ecole supérieure des Sciences économiques et commerciales (ESSEC) Business School–Paris signed a strategic partnership arrangement, after 20 years of less formal collaboration. This relates to double-degree programmes for MBAs, exchanges of students and faculty, and common research projects. Furthermore, in May 2006, ESSEC (a major player in international management education) established an Asian Centre in Singapore, and executive programmes involving both IIM-A and ESSEC faculty. Therefore, an ESSEC–IIM-A campus in Nigeria might be feasible, with the support of both French and Indian Governments (as with the strategic partnership).

A further approach is to consider the foreign business schools currently running programmes with leading universities in China. In this respect, American universities are particularly prominent, including MIT's IMBA with Tsinghua University in Beijing, Rutgers University's EMBA with Shanghai Jiao Tong University, and Washington University's EMBA with Fudan University in Shanghai. Further study is thus recommended, but approaches should be made to the institutions highlighted above, beginning with NUS and ESSEC–IIM-A.

The business school would be a joint venture between a leading Nigerian university and an international business school. It would be run as a private venture and would require Government seed funding. It might also be a candidate for an aid programme in the context of developing closer ties with a country such as India.

b. Support for Diaspora recruitment

The efforts within the Nigeria in the Diaspora Organization (NIDO) to develop a network of talented and entrepreneurial Nigerians willing to invest in the country were highlighted above. Explicit links should be forged between NIDO and companies seeking to recruit Diaspora staff. These efforts could be supported by two sets of measures: pre-departure orientation programmes and tax support. The aim is to facilitate Diaspora recruitment by reducing its costs and risks to employers and by assisting the individuals to make an easier transition.

1. Pre-departure orientation

Employers are keen to recruit members of the Diaspora, but there is a need to support them to overcome the problems currently experienced with Diaspora employees. These include a lack of understanding of the challenging Nigerian environment, and also cultural and management skills issues (box III.13). In conjunction with NIDO, pre-departure orientation programmes could be established in key source countries such as the United States and the United Kingdom to fill these gaps. These programmes could be available to support recruitment in all sectors or could be industry-specific, emphasizing rapid-growth sectors such as telecommunications, where skill shortages are most acute.

2. Tax support

In order to keep up with schemes adopted in other countries to encourage Diaspora recruitment, the Nigerian tax code should be examined to ensure that, at the very least, it does not discourage Diaspora recruitment from the standpoint of both the employer and the employee. Some countries go even further and provide incentives to encourage such recruitment. The issues to be considered in Nigeria are set out in box III.14.

Currently, passive income (such as dividends and interest) derived overseas is fully tax-exempt in the hands of a Nigerian resident. This is favourable treatment. A useful incentive (provided that it could be administered simply) would be to provide a stability certificate to appropriately qualified Diaspora recruits. Such a certificate would guarantee that any adverse change in the general law on taxation of foreign source passive income for a period (say 10 years) would not apply to the designated Diaspora recruit.

All these measures would be designed to simplify the choice and ease the transition of the Diaspora back to Nigeria for productive employment. Some additional public cost is involved (by way of funding the pre-departure programme or by means of tax incentives). This is justified by the remedial element in publicly funded education and by the potential long-term relocation of skills and their diffusion within the economy.

C. Generating FDI with development potential

Nigeria has underperformed in FDI attraction (chapter I). This relates to the challenging investment climate, the background of military rule and the country's image problem. With the reform agenda progressing, Nigeria will attract more FDI in non-extractive industries, drawn principally by a large and growing market. This will occur even if no further improvements take place in specific programmes to promote FDI and facilitate its entry. What, then, is the appropriate role for active investment promotion, including investor targeting and image raising?

Currently, investment promotion comprises a mixture of overseas missions to selected countries, together with business forums abroad. These and related activities are designed to rebuild Nigeria's image in the outside world as an investment destination. Efforts are also being made to attract investment from Nigeria's substantial Diaspora.

Box III.14. Issues in the taxation of returning Nigerian Diaspora

<u>For the employer</u>

- Specified costs of recruitment and relocation. The Diaspora employees could be entitled to more than 100 per cent deductibility. Singapore, for example, allows a double deduction.

- A Nigerian employer could continue to make contributions to an existing overseas pension fund held by a Diaspora recruit and have these fully deductible on the same basis as for domestic schemes. Continued active participation in an overseas pension fund would be the choice of the employee. (In some cases the advantages of a continued contribution would fall away if the Nigerian becomes non-resident in the source country).

<u>For the employee</u>

- The cost of passage back to Nigeria continues to be treated as a fringe benefit and thus subject to personal taxation. This seems an undue handicap and no countries that actively encourage the return of the Diaspora apply this approach.

- Annuities from foreign pension funds have the same exemption from personal tax as has applied to Nigerian source annuities since 1996. This treatment extends to capital withdrawals.

- The tax treatment of employee stock options is favourable. Stock options help to mitigate the "tax shock" of moving from a developed country where the higher marginal tax rates on personal income apply at much higher income thresholds.

- There is scope for higher personal allowances and for favourable import duty treatment of personal effects for the Diaspora. Some countries (e.g. Mauritius) have such schemes to encourage returning Diaspora investors in specified high-priority industries. However, this is likely to be cumbersome and more open to abuse in a large country such as Nigeria.

Source: UNCTAD.

There is room, without undue budget cost, to further shape Nigeria's FDI stimulation programmes, both to accelerate FDI inflows and to target areas of FDI that will have the greatest developmental impact. The suggested strategy to meet this objective is anchored on five key elements:

- Targeting of world-class TNCs aimed at notable divestors and absentees;
- Targeting of investors in two key development niches – the agriculture/food value chain and in the building supplies and services industry;
- Supporting FDI by Chinese, Indian, South African and other non-traditional investors;
- Attracting Diaspora investment; and
- Raising long-term positive awareness.

Element 1: Targeting of world-class TNCs

The presence of world-class TNCs in a country is of major significance. Not only are these firms global leaders in their fields, but they also have a strong demonstration effect in terms of encouraging other investors. The TNC divestees and absentees are recommended as first targets for investment generation in Nigeria. To this end, a well-researched and implemented attraction programme is essential and is the objective of element 1.

Divestees: Many well-known TNCs divested from Nigeria during the years of military rule. These include world-class TNCs in power and infrastructure development (e.g. General Electric), pharmaceuticals (e.g. Sandoz, Roche), agro-business (e.g. Cargill), and even packaging (e.g. Smurfit). The packaging sector has recently seen significant investments by second-tier TNCs, such as Nicapaco of China/Brazil and local firms, but there are still gaps in areas of higher technology packaging. Some TNCs, such as General Electric, have re-entered Nigeria on a project basis or with sales subsidiaries, as is the case for some of big pharmaceutical companies.

Absentees: Attracting such firms will be no simple task. For example, the nature of the automobile industry has changed dramatically with globalization. In the current context, small-scale completely knocked down/assembly operations are no longer likely to be considered by the global automakers. This is due in part to their low volume and high-cost output, which derives from such activities. Nigeria's interests are therefore to establish whether it can attract FDI into segments of the auto industry, including suppliers, where such investment will represent a step onto the development ladder.

For other TNCs, their African strategy is well established, and the companies may simply establish marketing affiliates in Nigeria, as is the case with Pfizer Inc. in pharmaceuticals. Nevertheless, recent evidence indicates that there is need to improve confidence in the pharmaceutical sector in Nigeria, related to NAFDAC's effective attack on dumping and counterfeiting, as well as tax and tariff reform (chapter II). In response, a number of TNCs have either expanded existing manufacturing (GlaxoSmithKline) or replaced importing by local manufacture (Reckett Benckiser Ltd., Tura International).

Element 2: Targeting of investors in selected manufacturing sectors

Sectoral investment targeting can be expensive and requires specialized expertise. The choice of targets should therefore reflect both FDI potential and a view of where FDI is likely to have the largest developmental payoff. In that regard, two areas of manufacturing stand out:

- The agro-allied industries; and
- The building supplies and services industries.

Of course, there are likely to be potential niche markets in other areas of manufacturing. Considering opportunities for targeted FDI, textiles and clothing is an intensely competitive global industry, and increasingly so since the ending of the Multi-Fibre Agreement. There may thus be some limited prospects for FDI in clothing. But here and in a miscellany of fairly small-scale manufacturing industries, opportunities in Nigeria can be highlighted in country-investment missions and forums, leaving manufacturers abroad to decide upon specific sectoral prospects (element 3).

The same is broadly true in services. For example, it is likely that the commercial bank recapitalization programme will lead to the entry of more foreign banks, probably through acquisitions. Greater foreign involvement in other financial services – capital markets and insurance – will occur in due course. There is no pressing need to accelerate this process through an active FDI generation campaign. In other services, especially information technology and tourism, it would be premature to establish active FDI generation programmes, since specialized infrastructure needs are not in place. On the other hand, FDI opportunities in general business and professional services will grow organically with the rise in overall business activity and improvements in the investment climate. In all these cases, the investment promotion activity should focus on investor facilitation rather than active investor targeting.

Within the agro-allied industries, the focus should be on attracting TNC affiliates with developmental capabilities. The importance of agricultural investment in Nigeria is manifold: it has strong social implications in terms of rural poverty reduction and employment, but it can also be a powerful engine for economic growth. Possibilities exist throughout the agro-business supply chain, from commercial farming through to processing for home and export markets and in support sectors such as fertilizers. Targets should include private farming interests (where the investment activities of a number of Zimbabwean farmers can provide a model for the future), large-scale commercial agricultural investments and big agro-processors. Agriculture is a NEEDS priority, and FDI should be sought to help underpin it.

Examples of specific priorities include several industries that have demonstrated export potential:

- **Vegetable oils and seeds.** In 1970, Nigeria was the world's largest producer of palm oil seeds, fats and products. Historically, Unilever processed palm oil in Nigeria. But since then, the decline has been dramatic. In rebuilding this subsector, other more profitable crops such as soybean may offer better opportunities. In this sector, FDI may take the form of estate agriculture or contract farming involving TNCs.

- **Cocoa and products.** In the 1970s, Nigeria produced more than 20 per cent of world production, a figure which has declined to around 5 per cent by 2005.[101] Some limited processing continues to take place, including TNC involvement. In 2004, Cadbury Nigeria Plc. reported making a major investment to establish a cocoa processing facility.

- **Fruit and vegetable products.** A wide range of fruits is grown, but losses through spoilage are considerable. Nigerian exports of these products remain very limited, in contrast to other African countries, including Kenya, Morocco and South Africa. Opportunities may exist for collaboration with major developed country TNCs in respect of contract production, processing and marketing.

- **Leather and leather products.** Nigeria has the third-largest livestock population in Africa. However, quality levels of products are low, and the industry is poorly organized and integrated across the value chain. For example, studies have shown weak linkages between firms and research institutions such as the National Research Institute for Chemical Technology.

- **Rubber and products.** This is also an industry in decline due to supply constraints.

In all of these cases, the focus has to be upon the further processing of basic agricultural products and/or their utilization as inputs into processed foods. In 2000, for example, Nigeria exported nearly $30 million of seeds for vegetable oil. In comparison, it exported only $1.1 million of vegetable oil itself, because of the necessity to rebuild the capabilities of vegetable oil processing companies (Albaladejo, 2003). Building competitive industry value chains also requires a strengthening of agro-related engineering industries. Hence, FDI targets should include processing machinery and equipment as well as agricultural-related equipment for production, irrigation, storage and transportation.

The building supplies and services industries are the other priority. Nigeria has both the need and resources for a major upgrade of public infrastructure, including transportation, education, health, backbone business services in electricity and telecommunications, and other areas. This will create demand for:

- Building materials – cement, steel, other metals, timber and glass among others; and
- Building services – construction and allied building industry services.

---

[101] UNCTAD, based on the data from International Cocoa Organization, quarterly bulletin of cocoa statistics, 2006.

Historically, strategic building materials industries were State-owned. This has changed and, recently, many more such industries have been privatized. Active targeting of new FDI is warranted to help build capacity and maintain competition in these industries as the infrastructure upgrade accelerates.

Some of the sectoral baseline information on potential manufacturing sectors has been developed from the partnership work of UNIDO to plan joint projects. Based on this information, it is clear that an integrated approach involving relevant ministries, agencies and organizations is essential for a holistic, coordinated approach, in which FDI is a crucial but not the sole driver. However, further study is required of specific opportunities in manufacturing and other subsectors before targeted promotions are launched. Finally, to ensure an effective implementation of the approach selected, it will also require a buildup in the capacity of the NIPC.

Element 3: Supporting FDI by non-traditional investors

The trickle of FDI into Nigeria in the recent past has mainly comprised second-tier and non-conventional TNCs from countries such as China, India, the Russian Federation, the Republic of Korea, Egypt and Lebanon. These companies are used to operating in challenging and volatile environments. Many such enterprises have been primarily attracted in the past by the prospects of rent-seeking offered by the vagaries of government policy, with investments being opportunistic and short-term oriented. As the prospects for rent-seeking diminish, Nigeria will see less of such investment.

For several reasons, there could now be an opportunity to take a more formal approach and attract higher quality corporate investors from non-traditional sources. Outward FDI from larger developing countries is expanding rapidly. With the rapid economic growth observed in China and India in particular, flows of FDI into Africa will expand. Data are limited, but work by the World Bank (World Bank, 2004b) indicates 450 Chinese FDI projects in Africa in 2001, and perhaps as many as 700 in 2004. Of these projects, 46 per cent are estimated to be in manufacturing and engineering to utilize low wage labour, and 9 per cent in natural resources. In respect of India, the FDI presence is smaller, but the above source suggests growth since 2002 with greater sectoral diversity, including information technology, autos, energy, steel, pharmaceuticals, garments and financial services.

In the case of China, there are prospects for efficiency-seeking FDI in the manufacture of cheap medium-quality goods, as well as resource-seeking export-oriented investment. In this regard, the Nigerian free zones may be attractive to many of the medium-sized Chinese companies. In respect to India, there are also likely to be a variety of potential investors. NIPC data on the pioneer status offered to investors over the period 2002–2005 indicates that 25 per cent of projects involved Indian investors, mostly in joint ventures. Metals processing and food/agriculture were the most prominent sectors.

Nigeria has signed several cooperation agreements with China and is in discussion with India. China and Nigeria have signed bilateral investment treaties and double tax treaties, and parallel agreements are under discussion with India. It would, however, be premature to try to evolve these important relationships into formal economic integration agreements. On the trade side, presumably both China and India would not be willing to grant non-reciprocal market access. On the investment side, Nigeria already has an open regime for FDI entry and is willing to enter into BITs for the mutual good treatment and protection of FDI. Nevertheless, there could be value in formalizing and energizing these relationships in the following manner:

- Appointing of a high-level steering body to progress the relationships;
- Prioritizing the conclusion and ratification of BITs and DTTs;
- Developing specific investment promotion cooperation mechanisms, including, for example, organized visits by investors or special VIP channel for business visitors;

- Devising an enabling work permit programme for Chinese and Indian skilled personnel;

- Developing with each country's financial support a signature project. For China, it could be a multi-facility zone for Chinese investors, while for India it could take the form of support for the establishment of an Indian management school.

Another significant phenomenon in the recent past has been the rapid expansion of South African TNCs within Africa. One database indicates 921 investment projects in Africa by 287 South African companies (including non-South African affiliates) (Gelb, 2006). The sectoral breakdown includes the following: information technology/telecoms 14 per cent, mining 15 per cent, agriculture 3 per cent, manufacturing 13 per cent, infrastructure/construction 16 per cent, tourism and hospitality 9 per cent, and trade and other services 13 per cent. With respect to host countries, 17 per cent of projects are in West Africa.

Element 4: Attracting Diaspora investment

Many countries have now recognized the potential of their overseas Diaspora. A major objective historically has been to access hard-currency flows, but new programmes are also designed to facilitate investment, including joint ventures between host-country SMEs and Diaspora-owned enterprises abroad, and the promotion of specific sectors particularly information technology.

It is estimated that there are between 2 million and 5 million Nigerians in the Diaspora worldwide, a consequence of a persistent outflow of talent to developed countries. There are indeed large concentrations in the United States and United Kingdom, and to a lesser extent in countries such as France and Germany. NIDO represents a highly innovative approach to capitalizing upon the wealth, talent and entrepreneurial potential of this group. NIDO is in the early stages of building a network of Diaspora organizations in countries such as the United States and the United Kingdom.

A starting point for most of these organizations is to develop an accurate database of the Diaspora population and its characteristics. The aim is also to identify business backgrounds and investment/ entrepreneurial potential. Allied to this are the establishment of online and in-country services to promote investment, and sector-specific advisory councils aimed at supporting industrial development in the mother country. As noted, NIDO is still in its very early stages. In this sense, building a database of overseas Nigerians in the private sector (and particularly those owning and running businesses) should be an early objective, which can then be followed by specific initiatives to attract FDI.

The efforts of NIDO should be supported by a careful examination of taxation issues that affect the decisions of the Diaspora to start businesses in the mother country, especially where they have an active role in the business and thus become tax residents of Nigeria. Section V ("People quality programme") discusses these in the context of Diaspora staff recruitment, but similar issues apply to investors who become residents in Nigeria.

Element 5: Raising long-term positive awareness

The NIPC had begun to take steps to raise awareness on the basis of "come and see for yourselves". However, the efforts have been small-scale and ad hoc. Most expenditure has been directed at media campaigns and advertisements in local and international print and electronic media. These were designed to raise the profile of the country as a preferred investment destination and investment summits. NIPC data indicate that close to 13 per cent of the 2004 budget – approximately $275,000 – was spent on image-building. As a share of the total budget, this is broadly similar to Sweden and Costa Rica, and well above countries such as Ethiopia and Lesotho (although as noted above, comparisons depend upon how image building is defined).

Nigeria's improving fundamentals, and poor current perceptions, justify an enhanced awareness-raising programme. The programme must be professionally executed. It should be targeted at business and political opinion leaders with specific outputs in terms of positive perspectives and attitudes towards the country. In other words, it should be an expansion of the "come and see for yourself programme". Expensive paid advertising is less appropriate at this particular stage of development of Nigeria.

Industry experts suggest that an annual expenditure of at least $1 million is required to make an impact, but clearly this depends upon the specific objectives. It should also be a sustained campaign. Many such campaigns in other countries stop after a year or so, and for Nigeria a sustained approach is vital: this means an initial five-year period for the campaign, with extension for a further five years subject to results.

D. Strengthening FDI-related institutions

The functions of strategy setting, policy advocacy, country marketing and investor support (aftercare) are generally accepted as important constituents of FDI policy. The establishment of NIPC in 1995 was an early recognition of the importance of these investment-related activities. Following the restoration of democracy in 1999, the need to attract FDI took on an added urgency. Recommendations to strengthen the investment environment by reducing the obstacles to doing business were developed in studies at the beginning of the millennium.

In its desire both to improve consultation with the private sector and overcome barriers to FDI, a Presidential Inter-Ministerial Committee on Investor Problem-Solving was also inaugurated in May 2005. Special advisers to the President (e.g. the Special Adviser to the President on Manufacturing and the Private Sector) were appointed as troubleshooters.

As a result of the growing importance of FDI in government strategy, NIPC has undergone a number of internal reforms in the recent past, including a reengineering of the management team through a vigorous selection process by private consultants. In March 2005, the Governing Council of the NIPC was established with a significant representation of private investors. In March 2006, the One Stop Investment Centre (OSIC) was established within NIPC. The locus of NIPC within Government, including its reporting channels and its coordination with other agencies dealing with investment promotion at the federal and State level, has also been object to much attention in recent years. Originally reporting to the Ministry of Commerce and Industry, NIPC was placed under the direct responsibility of the President's Office during the administration of President Obasanjo. It has been relocated under the Ministry of Commerce and Industry by the current Government.

The internal reorganization of NIPC has contributed to streamlining the way the agency works. Additional functions are proposed in this section which would enable NIPC to better target its investment promotion activities and extract more benefits from FDI. At the same time, this section recommends that the institutional setting for investment promotion be revised to ensure synergy among the agencies involved in investment promotion at all levels of Government, supported by a specialist ministry with a policy and strategic coordination role.

With respect to the institutional setting for investment promotion, there are two key and related issues for consideration: (a) the role and functions of NIPC; and (b) the overall institutional structure for foreign investment. Nigeria's size and the scale of development needs, its improving profile for attracting non-oil FDI and the importance of maximizing the contribution of FDI to industrial development require a heavyweight political and operational response. The current arrangements do not add up to this. Why not?

- The role of NIPC is not clear at the federal level. For instance, it is not the sole or first point of contact for investors. Also, prospective investors may go initially to the Special Adviser on Manufacturing and the Private Sector instead of NIPC to resolve potential blockages. Similarly ambiguous is the relationship between NIPC and NEPZA: the two collaborate and compete for FDI. On occasions, they undertake joint missions abroad, and on others, they promote FDI independently.

- The role of the federal agencies (NIPC and NEPZA) in relation to State government efforts to promote and facilitate investment is not up to the formal standard needed in a large federal system. Relationships are cordial, notwithstanding some overlapping of effort in investment promotion. But the working relationships are not systematic to the extent needed to promote FDI as positive force for regional development within the country. Moreover, there is ample opportunity for the States to compete with each other to attract investment. This can lead to undue incentives (as in the well-known case of Brazil's fiscal dispute between the States to attract the auto industry). Nevertheless, the lack of clear relationships is not too alarming due to the fact that the overall investment promotion effort remains low for now. When FDI attraction moves into higher gear, however, a seamless professional promotion effort to the international investment community will be needed.

- With regard to the operations of NIPC, the organization has been in an almost constant state of review and reform for several years. Discussions at the time of UNCTAD's fact-finding mission (October 2005) revealed an institution with shortages of funding, weak managerial capacity and uncertainties about the future. Since then, there have been changes at the management level, designed to strengthen the organization. However, NIPC would need further strengthening and resources to take on the additional programmes proposed in this report. For example, it is proposed that NIPC would implement the Developmental Affiliates Programmes, a very significant and high-level activity that is central to improving the dynamic impact of FDI in Nigeria.

- With respect to the overall institutional structure for FDI, interviews revealed concerns with the feudalism of government ministries and authorities. In a sense, this is inevitable, since FDI policy is so wide ranging. And the solutions involving the Inter-Ministerial Committee on Investor Problem-Solving and the Special Advisers, while valuable and investor-friendly, can only be short-term palliatives because of their ad hoc nature.

1.   Strengthening investment-related institutions

The strategic focus of this report does not include a thorough assessment of the institutions dealing with investment, both at the policy and promotion levels. However, it is considered necessary that Nigeria embark on a review of the effectiveness of its current setting in order to fully benefit from the FDI strategy proposed in this report.

In particular, the analysis underlying the preparation of this report identified the need for an institutional mechanism to ensure effective coordination of the different government agencies with an investment mandate. Also, the current institutional setting does not give sufficient prominence to the investment policy advocacy function, which is recognized in other countries as a key element to attract and benefit from FDI.

Under the proposed new setting, the head of the entity responsible for investment policy advocacy and coordination would be a member of the Cabinet and of the economic reform team. This would ensure that he/she had adequate clout in dealing with cross-ministerial investment issues. In addition, this new entity would take on the responsibilities of the Inter-Ministerial Committee on Problems of Investors in Nigeria.

The entity should control BPE, NEPZA, the Small-Medium Enterprise Development Agency of Nigeria (SMEDAN) and NIPC, as all these agencies have a direct investment mandate. It should have a relatively small but high-level team that would be responsible for advocacy and policy reforms, and for monitoring progress in respect of the business climate improvement objectives set forth in the proposed National Investment Policy. The aim is to ensure powerful advocacy for investment in Nigeria, and one head that would have respect from all investors – small and large, domestic and foreign-owned. In this context, NIPC would no longer have a regulatory or advocacy function. Its principal role would be operational – to handle investment attraction and support, and to take on the important developmental affiliates activity.

Against this background and based on international experience, this report therefore proposes three alternative options for the new entity:

- Establishing a Ministry of investment;
- Empowering the Vice-president as the main investment policy advocate; and
- Extending the mandate of the Chief Economic Adviser to the President to include investment policy advocacy or creating a new post of Senior Advisor to the President with responsibilities for investment.

While the creation of a Ministry of Investment could entail, in the particular case of Nigeria, important administrative reform, the two other options are seen as potentially easier to put in place. Box III.15 sets out experiences elsewhere that can be drawn upon.

2. Continued transformation of NIPC

NIPC is a relatively large investment promotion agency, with about 120 staff and an annual budget of about $2 million. It is organized conventionally, with three key operating departments, namely Investment Promotion, Policy Advocacy, and External and Investor Relations. It handles both national and foreign investment. In March 2006, Investor Relations was strengthened by the inauguration of the OSIC. Regional outreach is expressed through five "zonal offices", each containing representatives of the key operating departments. Its current structure is designed to transform the NIPC from "a controlling organ to a marketing one" (NIPC, 2004). This will also require a corresponding change in attitudes and skills of staff. The private sector is represented in the governing council of NIPC. In October 2004, the President initiated an Investment Advisory Council of international business and political leaders to advise on improving Nigeria's profile. This is serviced by NIPC.

A detailed review of the mandate, structure and performance of NIPC is not a task of this report. So far, NIPC's impact has been low-key. Should the Government accept the findings of this report, there would be many implications for NIPC. These are in line with its declared aim of becoming more prominent as an investment promoter and facilitator. The key implications are:

a. Its *regulatory role* should be confined to the pro-forma registration of foreign investors. It could have delegated powers to approve automatic expatriate quotas and to grant fiscal incentives that require prior approval;

b. Its *investor support* function should extend to administering the proposed foreign affiliates' development programme. This will entail helping foreign affiliates to match-make with local companies under a linkages programme and with Nigerian research institutes under an affiliates R&D programme. It is proposed that a specialized unit for foreign affiliates development be created within NIPC;

c. Its *investment promotion* function should extend to some more active investor targeting in niche areas as described and to an expanded awareness-raising programme;

d. The excellent *OSIC* initiative should be progressed to an e-enabled centre;

e. The new entity responsible for investment policy advocacy and coordination should take over primary responsibility for the *advocacy* function with NIPC, providing a supporting role of channelling investors concerns to Government based on its day-to-day interaction with them;

f. In the event that NIPC does limit its regulatory role, it may consider changing the name of NIPC to Nigerian Investment Promotion Agency to better reflect its mandate.

Box III.15. Experiences with IPA reporting

Having investment promotion agencies (IPAs) reporting directly to the office of the President or Prime Minister was once highly favoured and is still often recommended by experts (OECD, 2005). It is seen as a means of obtaining high-level decision-making to resolve the cross-sectoral issues that bedevil the investment climate (investment policy advocacy). Direct reporting to the Head of Government is an option selected by Ghana and others. While it may increase the status of the agency, it can also have certain disadvantages. Some experiences in South America suggest that the Head of Government is just too busy to give sufficient attention to private investment. In response, direct reporting to a Head of Government seems to be less in vogue today.

IPAs more often report to ministers or ministries – typically ministries of economy, commerce or trade and industry – as is currently the case in Nigeria. It is still rare to have a minister dedicated solely to investment. However, in Algeria, Benin and Egypt, there is a dedicated investment minister. Since 2004, there has been a Minister of Investment in Egypt (who also has privatization responsibility). The IPA reports directly to this minister and the minister also has a small ministry of policy experts. The minister has cabinet rank and has been active in supporting investment-related policy reform, appointing key persons in the IPA, receiving VIP investors and delegations, and promoting Egypt's profile in high-visibility events abroad.

In several cases, including leading IPAs, there is a middle ground. In Thailand, there is a dedicated minister, attached to the Office of the Prime Minister, while in El Salvador the head of the IPA is the Vice-President. In other cases, there is a Vice Minister in charge of Investment within a larger ministry. For example, in China the IPA reports directly to a senior vice minister.

The Office of the Investment Ombudsman of the Republic of Korea constitutes an example of an institutional entity in charge of investment policy advocacy with access to the highest level of Government. Appointed by the President, the Investment Ombudsman is an integral part of KOTRA, the national IPA, and works in close cooperation with the investment promotion team of the agency. The ombudsman encourages reinvestment through grievance resolution (aftercare) and investment climate improvement (policy advocacy).

Having a dedicated Minister of Investment has the obvious merit that the minister has the specific mandate to devote his or her time to investment issues, meet investors and lead important promotional events. There are also conceptual merits in having a dedicated Minister and Ministry of Investment. Furthermore, the minister is well positioned to engage with his or her ministerial colleagues on key cross-cutting or key issues (infrastructure, skills, taxation, red tape problems, etc.) that affect the investment climate.

Source: UNCTAD.

It is important to note that the R&D and supplier linkages programmes require a totally different strategic and developmental approach to TNC support within NIPC. Until now, the FDI aftercare function has been, at best, a routinized, troubleshooting activity, in a situation where NIPC has little detailed knowledge or understanding of the stock of investors in Nigeria. By contrast, in some other countries (e.g. Ireland), this has been replaced by a strategic function focused upon affiliate development.

The proposed developmental affiliates' team is not an aftercare team as traditionally understood. Strong emphasis is placed upon the need to build close relationships with and detailed strategic information concerning TNCs in Nigeria. This relationship-building should take place not only at the affiliate level, but also with parent TNCs. The latter have a major role in permitting and facilitating quasi-autonomous initiatives by their affiliates. More importantly, if Nigerian affiliates are to integrate within pan-African or global strategies, this is a decision to be taken by TNC headquarters.

It is a challenging task for the developmental affiliates' team to add value in the process of affiliate evolution and upgrading. This will require the establishment of an appropriate structure and capacity-building for its staff. The team must be skilled and knowledgeable if they are to be credible with TNCs, and, therefore, be able to establish a reputation for competence with both affiliates and group headquarters. The team members must have had relevant experience with TNCs and salary structures will need to reflect this. Despite the challenges and costs, the benefits of this strategic approach in terms of the economic contribution to the country will be very substantial.

In the context of the proposed increased responsibilities of NIPC, it is key for Nigeria to review the resources, both financial and human, made available to the agency to ensure that it has the capacity to deliver on its mandate.

3. Establishing coordinated federal–State investment promotion relationships

Sooner or later, a model will need to be agreed between the federal and State levels on their roles in foreign investment promotion and facilitation. The choices are between a decentralized model (such as in Brazil and the United States), where States take the lead, and a collaborative model (such as in Australia and the United Kingdom) where both levels work to define roles. There are pros and cons of each. For example, a decentralized model makes best use of local dynamis[102] but runs the risk that poorer States will get insufficient support. On the other hand, a collaborative model in which federally run overseas marketing is combined with local facilitation can be more cost-effective and less confusing to foreign investors faced with multiple, competing approaches. An important corollary to this is helping States to establish ground rules among themselves to avoid excessive competition in the granting of incentives to foreign investors who have already made the country-level decision.

NIPC's zonal offices provide "eyes and ears" for NIPC outside its Abuja headquarters, but obviously do not tackle the fundamental matters described above. Helping the federal and State levels to arrive at mutually satisfactory roles and ground rules in FDI attraction and facilitation should be on the agenda of the proposed new entity responsible for investment. Once the choice is made between the decentralized and the collaborative model, the details of the federal–State cooperation need to be formalized. This requires the federal and State agencies to work out protocols of cooperation as to the contribution of each to achieving positive investor decisions (the United Kingdom is one example). Meanwhile, experience could be gained by NIPC through engaging in some pilot projects with selected States. A good place to start would be in the promotion of foreign investment in agriculture/food chain industry as this naturally lends itself to stimulating investment outside of the major population centres.

---

[102] The State-level initiative to attract Zimbabwean farmers illustrates this.

IV. WORKING TOWARDS AN EFFECTIVE FDI STRATEGY: CONCLUSIONS AND RECOMMENDATIONS

In recent years, Nigeria has attracted increasing levels of FDI, essentially concentrated in the oil sector. Beyond this sector, FDI has, however, remained low and not played a significant role in industrial development. As articulated in its home-grown strategy, the Government of Nigeria is promoting a private sector-led approach to achieving its national development objectives. In this regard, NEEDS emphasizes the central role of broad-based investment and focuses on the need to attract FDI in a variety of economic activities. Based on the philosophy presented in NEEDS, the role of the Government is therefore evolving towards one of regulation and facilitation of investment rather than direct involvement in business. This was reiterated by the current Administration. Against this background, the authorities have removed virtually all restrictions to FDI entry and are currently extending the scope of FDI by inviting private investment into areas such as public infrastructure and utilities. As economic fundamentals further strengthen and new measures are put in place to improve the investment environment, greater volumes of FDI will undoubtedly enter Nigeria.

In this context, the investment policy review of Nigeria prepared by UNCTAD considers what needs to be done to enable FDI, outside the oil sector, to make its full contribution to the orientation set by the Government. According to the analysis presented in this report, the conclusions call for the adoption of a National Investment Policy based on an FDI strategy that would lead to dynamic investment growth with a focus on a strong manufacturing sector, including the agro-allied industries. In this regard, Nigeria should adopt policies that induce and support foreign affiliates to focus on high value added as a necessary condition for reaping and maximizing the potential benefits of FDI to the economy. The report also emphasizes the need to improve the overall environment for doing business and to adopt an effective investment promotion approach. Against this background, the report makes the following recommendations:

a. Designing and implementing a strategy to attract non-oil FDI

The proposed FDI strategy needs to be consistent and coherent with the economic and social objectives set out by the Nigerian Government in its national development strategy. To meet these objectives, Nigeria should tap its comparative advantages, including its abundant oil resources. Thus, the revenues generated by the exploitation of the oil resources will remain significant. In this context, and if the fiscal responsibility demonstrated in recent years persists, Nigeria is well positioned to implement an ambitious programme to fully develop its economy. This would entail the reconstruction and modernization of key infrastructure, including transport, electricity and telecommunications. This in turn will contribute to enhance the competitiveness of Nigerian enterprises and increase their ability to take advantage of the larger market opportunities provided by ECOWAS.

The worldwide trend towards liberalized markets has enabled TNCs to lead a process of globalization and regionalization of production networks. As a result, country-level operations within global/regional supply chains are now a key dimension of corporate strategy. Components of the supply chain are thus located in the country where their activities can be performed best. On the basis of the analysis of this report, it is recommended that Nigeria adopt a strategy to induce and support foreign affiliates, both existing and new ones, to be able compete regionally and globally in activities with high domestic value addition.

Increased competition will most likely increase the need to place more emphasis on securing more competitive supplies, including nurturing local suppliers. To this end, free zones could be converted into economic development zones where businesses will have access to excellent facilities, including high quality services. These zones could then be used as incubators for the development of local industrial capacity and insertion into the global value chain.

Against this background, the proposed strategy is articulated around a set of key measures which aim at:

- Improving the regulatory framework;
- Investing in physical and human capital;
- Taking advantage of regional integration and reviewing external tariffs;
- Fostering linkages and local industrial capacity; and
- Strengthening institutions dealing with investment and related issues.

b. Improving the regulatory framework

The Nigerian authorities fully appreciate the serious difficulties investors face in their day-to-day dealings with the country's rules and administrative processes. While in some areas reforms have been remarkable, challenges remain. Some of the proposed measures to address them include:

- **Enhancing foreign investor legal protection.** Nigeria has negotiated many bilateral investment treaties (BITs), but only few have been ratified so far. A more comprehensive network of BITs, including with countries emerging as potential sources of FDI, should be negotiated and ratified. In addition, double tax treaties should be energetically pursued to support inward and outward investment in ECOWAS.

- **Streamlining procedures for business visas and entry of foreign workers.** The requirements for obtaining business visas are onerous and difficult to fulfil. At the same time, working permit regulations are discretionary and discriminate against foreign investors, especially small sized investors and start-ups. It is proposed to streamline the procedures to make them more flexible and hospitable so as to support FDI attraction.

- **Reforming land policy and administration.** The problems affecting the land system in Nigeria include (a) lack of adequate occupancy protection; (b) undue incentives for public expropriation and limited compensation; (c) Governors' approval for all title transfer procedures, including straightforward ones; and (d) a backlog of unresolved land disputes. To remedy them, the report proposes to compensate expropriated land at market value and remove State Governors' approval for certain types of land transactions that could be registered by the deeds' registry. The measures also include the outsourcing of land surveying and administrative support to land registries to specialized commercial enterprises.

- **Speeding up and deepening tax reforms.** Several aspects of the taxation system would require attention. For example, VAT arrangements act in part as a sales tax and disadvantage exporters. Also, the tax system is characterized by high corporate tax rates together with overly generous incentives. Therefore, the zero rating of exports for VAT should proceed along with a restructuring of the VAT. More fundamental reform should also be considered, in particular the introduction of a lower corporate tax rate compensated by the elimination of over generous and selective pioneer industry scheme.

- **Improving the administration of environmental protection.** Though the legislation seems to be adequate, its enforcement remains an issue. The creation of a special agency to oversee oil industry practices (NOSDRA) will fill a gap, but comprehensive regulatory coverage is still required.

- **Enacting the proposed new labour law.** While Nigeria already has a liberal labour regime, the new act will fully modernize it by codifying fundamental principals and minimum standards of treatment that comply with internationally agreed labour standards. For example, it will bring to best practice standard the dispute resolution mechanism.

- **Adopting the proposed new competition law.** This law is long overdue. However, the proposed text appears overly cumbersome and bureaucratic. UNCTAD, following a request made by the Government, stands ready to provide assistance to revise it before its presentation to Parliament.

c. Investing in physical and human capital

Nigeria cannot depend on private investment to provide sufficient funds to secure the required levels of improvement in infrastructure, particularly within the power sector. As indicated above, the improved fiscal outlook, resulting notably from high oil prices and debt relief, provides Nigeria with the opportunity to significantly boost public **investment in infrastructure.** Public sector investment should still benefit from private sector discipline. Therefore, in promoting public–private partnerships in critical infrastructure, the Government should:

- Lead initial construction with public expenditures; and
- Seek private investment in management and operations to impart commercial discipline.

Firms operating in Nigeria face an acute **human capital** deficit, particularly at the managerial level. For policymakers, the challenge is to address this immediate shortfall, while making improvements to the overall education system. Against this background, the budget priority set by the Government on education should be maintained. At the same time, some additional measures should be envisaged and these comprise, among others:

- Establishing joint ventures with renowned international business schools; and
- Supporting measures to attract skills from the Diaspora by notably providing tax support and pre-departure orientation programmes.

d. Taking advantage of regional integration and reviewing external tariffs

To fully tap the potential of its regional market, Nigeria should aim at becoming a base for pan-African sourcing and focus, as a first step towards the global market, on export opportunities within ECOWAS. In this regard, the country needs to play a more prominent role in moving forward the ECOWAS agenda, with a view to accelerating integration in the region. In this regard, the Government should deal, among other things, with the existing tariff structure, including import protection policies. This would promote the evolution of Nigeria's foreign affiliates in the pan-African supply chain of their TNC groups. In this context, Nigeria should aim at becoming a regional hub to attract domestic and foreign investors in sectors other than oil. To this end, specific recommendations include:

- Setting specific and actionable priorities with timescales for the short, medium and long term with respect to free trade area, customs union and common market;
- Defining a long-term path of tariff reduction, mainly on the import protection regime necessary to exert competitive pressures on businesses; and
- Reviewing individual industry needs for temporary departure from the general tariff regime.

e. Fostering linkages and local industrial capacity

So far, foreign affiliates outside the oil sector have played a dismal role in Nigeria's economy, as their operations have had little interaction with local enterprises. Previous Nigerian local sourcing initiatives highlight problems relating to suppliers' inability to meet cost and quality standards, to be able to supply in sufficient volumes, to avoid production gaps among customer TNCs, and to maintain stable relationships in areas such as pricing policies. Special consideration should therefore be given to policy measures aimed at encouraging foreign investors to assist value chain integration and linkages with the local productive sector. In particular, this report recommends to:

- Convert free zones from export-oriented facilities to multi-facility zones (or economic development zones). The key objective is to broaden their integration into the economy rather than letting them operate in closed circles. To this end, the Government should grant them unlimited domestic market access (with domestic sales income subjected to standard taxation), upgrade the infrastructure facilities made available, allocate permits and provide state-of-the-art business facilitation services. In addition, it should encourage industrial clustering and supplier development by means of fiscal incentives to zones' suppliers.

- Design a supplier linkages programme to stimulate and promote local sourcing and the local supply base. Programme components will include elements of technology transfer and upgrading, provision and sharing of information, financial support, training and benchmarking. International best practices show that selection, training and mentoring of potential local suppliers are key to motivating them to attain world-class manufacturing standards. The programme should be carried out by NIPC.

f. Strengthening institutions dealing with investment and related issues

A solid institutional framework is a necessary condition for achieving the ambitious development objectives set by the Government. This IPR identifies several shortcomings associated with the institutional framework in charge of issues related to investment, including promotion. Among those are problems of funding, weak managerial capacity, lack of coordination mechanisms as well as unclear division of labour between institutions dealing with investment, in particular FDI. The report recommends changes to existing institutions and the creation of new ones. Furthermore, these institutions, to be fully effective, will need to rely on adequately trained staff members who have the capacity to deal with the broad issues related to investment, including FDI. The report therefore recommends to:

- **Establish a new entity responsible for investment policy advocacy and coordination.** The entity should be supported by a small policy team and have responsibility for policy advocacy. It could take the form of a Ministry of Investment, or a policy team reporting to the Vice-President or to a Senior Policy Advisor to the President. It should oversee key investment related institutions, including NIPC, BPE, NEPZA and SMEDAN.

- **Further strengthen NIPC.** The primary role of NIPC would be to attract and support investment. In this sense, the promotion function should be more active at targeting investors in niche areas with higher developmental impact and at raising awareness about the potential benefits of FDI. Furthermore, its investor support function should administer the supplier development and the aftercare programmes.

- **Create an independent international trade commission.** Its role would be to advise the Government on (a) the pace and strategy for liberalization of the import protection regime; (b) extraordinary requests for protection from selected industries; and (c) the application of safeguards, anti-dumping and countervailing measures.

- **Revise the mandate of NOTAP.** NOTAP is currently involved in regulating the entry of foreign technology in Nigeria while the international practice has evolved from regulation to facilitation in this domain. Therefore, the report recommends that the mandate of NOTAP focus on providing training to Nigerian businesses, especially SMEs, in accessing foreign technology, including the negotiation of favourable terms. The regulatory matters would be better handled by the tax and competition authorities.

- **Establish coordinated federal–State investment promotion relationships.** At the moment, though interaction is cordial, the relationships between the various entities dealing with the attraction and facilitation of investment at the State and federal levels are not systematically defined. Joining forces at all levels of Government would contribute to ensuring that promotion messages are consistent, information asymmetries are addressed and prospective investors get the same quality of treatment. This exercise should be coordinated by the proposed Ministry of Investment.

To reap the expected benefits of the FDI strategy proposed in this IPR report, a coordinated and consistent approach to implementing the recommendations is key. This requires the commitment of the Nigerian Government at the highest level, the involvement of the private sector and the support of the international community. As the report recognizes the needs for capacity-building on various issues related to investment and FDI in particular, the Government of Nigeria may call upon the expertise of UNCTAD to develop a joint follow-up programme to assist in the implementation of selected recommendations. In this regard, UNCTAD has started work, with the financial support of the Japanese Government, on the preparation of an action plan – the Blue Book – which will contain practical investment-related measures that can be implemented within a 12-month period. In addition, the follow-up programme may, upon the Government's request, include capacity-building and institution-strengthening activities.

ANNEX I: FDI STATISTICS IN NIGERIA

The need for reliable data

Reliable and timely statistics are essential tools to properly track FDI flows and assess their role and impact on host and home economies, and formulate sound FDI policies. However, measurement of FDI still constitutes a problem in many countries, particularly in the developing world. In the case of Nigeria, the analysis of FDI trends is seriously handicapped by the quality and availability of data.

An example of the lack of reliability of statistics is illustrated by the following example. While total FDI inflows as reported to the IMF and UNCTAD by the Central Bank of Nigeria (CBN) conform to the Balance of Payments Manual (BPM 5) methodology of the IMF, data on the sectoral distribution of FDI within the country or its origin though available are not reliable. For the year 2003, for instance, the share of non-oil FDI inflows in total inflows was less than 5 per cent according to the CBN and more than 75 per cent according to NIPC (figures below). Their magnitude is also significantly different.

FDI inflows estimates from CBN

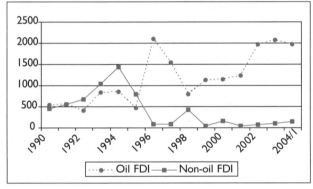

FDI inflows estimates from NIPC

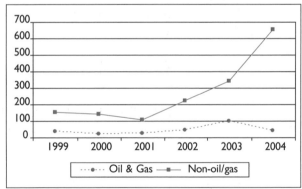

Other issues include the lack of systematic data collection on other aspects of TNCs' activities in the country (such as employment, R&D and tax payments). This is due in part to the lack of cooperation of the international private sector with the CBN's surveys, and also to the lack of coordination between the different Government agencies. These reasons were identified by NIPC as the cause for the country's inability to produce accurate FDI statistics.[103] In addition, the CBN reports that FDI announcements are frequently over-hyped, and not only by the companies themselves. This contributes to an undercurrent of dissatisfaction with foreign investors on this score which is one more reason to produce reliable statistics.

The Nigerian authorities, aware of these problems, have started to take corrective measures. An inter-agency committee including representatives of NIPC, CBN, the Bureau of Statistics and other agencies was recently set up, and CBN is receiving technical support from the IMF to carry out annual FDI surveys.

International experience can be very helpful in this respect. UNCTAD has supported a number of countries in strengthening their FDI data collection systems. In Algeria, for example, UNCTAD has established an "Investor Tracking System" and trained the investment promotion agency on its use. The same system could be readily implemented in Nigeria.

---

[103] NIPC, Annual Report 2004, available online at www.nipc.gov.ng.

ANNEX II: CONSTRUCTION OF THE NIGERIA "WEDGE"

A) The "Infrastructure index" in the wedge is a composite of the World Bank WDI indicators appearing below, normalized following UNCTAD's Investment Compass procedure (i.e. all indicators are normalized to a 0–100 scale and country aggregates are obtained via a simple average of the normalized indicators). For each county, the most recent available data is used. Data on literacy rates for Nigeria were not included because of reliability issues. Nigeria's "infrastructure" underperformance compared to large African and other developing countries is evident for most indicators, but more so in respect to the energy infrastructure, the telecommunications network and its tertiary education levels. It must be noted, however, that virtually all indicators have improved since 2002.

Indicator	Nigeria (02)	Nigeria (05)	India	Egypt	Ghana	Kenya	S.Africa	Brazil	China	Indonesia	Thailand	OECD
Infrastructure and skills Index	84	76	58	50	71	68	39	52	30	42	38	10

The indicators used for the construction of the "Infrastructure index" are:

Indicator	Nigeria (02)	Nigeria (05)	India	Egypt	Ghana	Kenya	S.Africa	Brazil	China	Indonesia	Thailand	OECD
Literacy rate, adult total (% of ages 15 and above)	..	..	61	..	57.9	73.6	82.4	88.6	90.9	90.4	92.7	98
School enrollment, tertiary (% gross)	8.2	10.2	11.5	28.5	3.14	..	15.3	20.1	15.4	16.2	41	68.7
Improved water source (% of pop. with access)	60	60	86	98	..	62	87	89	77	78	85	99.4
Electricity production, ratio of kwh/GDP (PPP)	12.6	10.9	22	23.6	11	13.6	42.7	23.5	30	16	19.2	35
Electric power trans. & distr. losses (% of output)	37.8	33.4	27.1	11.7	12.42	19.4	9.9	16.6	6.5	16.3	7.3	6.4
Telephone mainlines (per 1,000 people)	5.8	8	40.7	130.3	14.46	8.9	105.2	230.5	241.1	45.9	106.7	550.9
Internet users (per 1,000 people)	3.5	13.8	32.4	53.7	16.99	44.8	78.4	119.6	72.5	66.7	109.5	562.7
Mobile phones (per 1,000 people)	13.4	71.1	43.8	105.2	78.24	76.1	428.5	356.7	258.3	137.9	429.9	769.8
Phone av. cost, call to United States ($/ 3 min.)	7.1	1.5	1.2	1.5	0.39	3	0.8	0.7	2.9	2.8	0.7	0.8
Air transport, freight (million tons per km)	8.7	10.1	689.4	248	16.63	193.5	930.5	1,499.5	8,188.2	434.1	1,868.6	93,660.8
Roads network (tot. network in km surface area)	0.2	0.2	N.A.	0.2	0.203	0.1	0.3	0.2	0.2	n.a.	0.1	0.1
Roads, paved (% of total roads)	31	31	57	78	17.92	12	21	6	..	58	99	78

Source: World Bank, World Development Indicators 2006.

B) The "Regulatory index" in the wedge is derived from a subset of indicators from the World Economic Forum (WEF) Growth Competitiveness Report 2005-2006. The indicators are "property rights", "diversion of public funds", "public trust of politicians", "judicial independence", "favouritism in decisions of government officials", "wastefulness of government spending", "burden of government regulation", "reliability of police services", "business costs of crime and violence", "organized crime", "efficiency of legal framework", "extent and effect of taxation", "number of procedures to start a business" and "time required to start a business". The indicators are aggregated following the WEF procedure to obtain a world ranking for each country in the wedge. The resulting rankings utilized for the wedge are:

Indicator	Nigeria	India	Egypt	Ghana	Kenya	S.Africa	Brazil	China	Indonesia	Thailand	OECD
Regulatory Index	70	49	54	37	90	50	94	55	62	35	24

Note: the OECD ranking was obtained by computing the average of its high-income members' rankings.

ANNEX III: METHODOLOGY OF INTERNATIONAL TAX COMPARISONS

The Comparative Taxation Survey compares taxation on investment in several sectors in Nigeria with taxation in other selected countries – neighbours and countries elsewhere that have succeeded in attracting FDI to the industries concerned. These comparisons enable Nigeria to assess the competitiveness of its taxation.

Corporate taxation affects the cost of investment and its profitability, and thus the return on investment. This impact is not just a question of looking at the headline rate of tax on profits. The tax burden on the investor depends on a number of factors and their interaction, including expenses allowed, rates of capital allowances (tax depreciation), the availability of tax credits, investment allowances and tax holidays, the loss-carry-forward provisions and the taxation of dividends, among other things.

Comparative tax modelling is a method of taking into account the most important of these variables in the fiscal regime in a manner that facilitates comparison between countries. The tax variables included in the analysis are:

- Corporate income tax;
- Rate of tax, including tax holidays, if any;
- Loss-carry-forward provisions;
- Capital allowances, investment allowances and investment credits; and
- Tax on dividends (withholding rate on dividends paid abroad).

Financial models of project investment and financing, revenues and expenses are utilized for a hypothetical business in each industry. These are based on typical costs and revenues experienced in such businesses in a developing economy. A standard set of costs and revenues is employed so that the impact of taxation on investor return can be isolated. The business models cover a selected business within each industry.

The fiscal regime in Nigeria and of the chosen comparator countries for each industry is applied to the standard business model for each sector over 10 years commencing from the initial investment. The financial models calculate net cash flow to the investor, assuming that the company pays out all residual profits after tax (100 per cent dividend pay out) and that the investor gains the residual value of the company, which is sold after 10 years for an amount equal to its balance sheet value.

The impact of the fiscal regime is presented as the Present Value of tax per cent (PV tax per cent). PV tax per cent is the total of taxes and duties collected by Government over the 10 years as a percentage of the project cash flow pre-tax and post-finance where both cash flows are discounted to a present value at a rate of 10 per cent per annum. PV tax per cent thus measures how much of an investor's potential project return is taken by Government in taxes. The higher the PV tax per cent, the more the fiscal regime burdens investors and reduces the incentive to invest.

REFERENCES

Aju JO (2003). *Technology investment in pollution control in sub-Saharan Africa: evidence from Nigerian manufacturing.* In *The Developing Economies:* 39(4), 395–431.

Albaladejo M (2003). *Industrial Realities in Nigeria: From Bad to Worse.* QEH Working Paper, Number 102, Queen Elizabeth House, London, February.

Asouzu AA (2001). *International Commercial Arbitration and African States.* Cambridge University Press.

BearingPoint (2004), *Free Zones: Performance, Lessons Learned and Implications for Zone Development.*

Biersteker TJ (1987). *Multinationals, the State and Control of the Nigerian Economy.* Princeton, New Jersey.

Business in Africa (2005). Nigeria woos S.A. investors. 30 August.

Central Bank of Brazil (2001). *Censo de capitais estrangeiros no país.* Brazilia.

Central Bank of Nigeria (2003). *Highway Maintenance in Nigeria: Lessons from other Countries.* Abuja.

Central Bank of Nigeria (2004a). Ilory B. *The Role of Government in the Development of Basic Infrastructure.* Occasional Paper, JOS 02-3.

Central Bank of Nigeria (2004b). *Annual Report and Statement of Accounts.* Abuja.

Central Bank of Nigeria (2005). *Annual Report.* December, Abuja.

Col International (2001). *Building Capacity to Deliver Distance Education in Nigeria's Federal University System.* Report prepared for the World Bank, Vancouver, Canada, August.

Deininger K and Binswanger H (1999). The evolution of the World Bank's land policy: principles, experience and future challenges. *The World Bank Research Observer .* Vol. 14, #2: 247–76.

Dung-Gwom Y (2004). Recent developments in EIA, environmental assessment in Nigeria. In *EIA Newsletter.* No. 12, EIA Centre.

Echefu N and Akpofure E (2002). *Environmental impact assessment in Nigeria: regulatory background and procedural framework.* In *EIA Training Resource Manual.* Case study 7, United Nations Environment Programme.

The Economist (2006). Nollywood dreams. 27 July.

Economist Intelligence Unit (2006). Country Commerce Nigeria. New York: EIU, March.

Edge Institute and University of Witswatersrand (2006). South–South FDI: an African perspective. Presentation to World Bank/IFC PSD Forum, 4 April.

Energy Information Administration (2003). Nigeria environmental issues. Country analysis brief.

Federal Ministry of Finance, Building of Physical and Human Infrastructure for Job Creation and Poverty Eradication, Budget (2005). *Building of Physical and Human Infrastructure for Job Creation and Poverty Eradication. Budget 2005.*

Federal Ministry of Internal Affairs of Nigeria (2004), *Handbook on Expatriate Quota Administration.* Citizenship and Business Department. 2004 revision.

Gelb S (2006). South–South FDI: an African perspective. Presentation to World Bank/IFC PSD Forum 2006. The Edge Institute, Johannesburg and University of Witerswatersrand. 4 April.

Hodgson S et al. (1999). *Land ownership and foreigners – a comparative analysis of regulatory approaches to the acquisition and use of land by foreigners.* In FAO Legal Papers online No. 6.

IFCTU (2005). Internationally recognized core labour standards in Nigeria. Report for the WTO General Council Review of the Trade Policies of Nigeria. Geneva. May.

IMF (2006). *Nigeria Country Report No. 06/180. First Review under the Policy Support Instrument.* Washington D.C.

IMF (2008). Nigeria country report No. 08/64. February.

International Labour Organization (2000). *Termination of Employment Digest.* Geneva.

ITU (2005) *World Telecommunication Indicators.* Geneva.

Leigland J and Pallson G (2007). Port Reform in Nigeria: Upstream policy reforms kick-start one of the world's largest concession programs. In "Gridlines", note No. 17, March.

Mahmoud D (2004). *Privatization and poverty reduction in Nigeria.* The Nigerian Economic Summit Group. Paper presented at a two-day Overseas Development Institute meeting on pro-poor growth in Nigeria.

Moja T (2000). Nigeria education sector analysis: an analytical synthesis of performance and main issues. Report prepared for the World Bank, January.

National Planning Commission of Nigeria (2004). *Nigerian Economic Empowerment and Development Strategy.*

Nigerian Export Processing Zones Authority (2004). *Investment Procedures, Regulations and Operational Guidelines for Free Zones in Nigeria.*

NIPC, 2004. *Structure, Workplan and Implementation Strategy.* Draft.

Nigerian Investment Promotion Commission (2006). *Report on the Establishment of One-Stop-Shop Service in Nigeria.* Abuja.

OECD (2002). *Tax Incentives and Research and Development: Trends and Issues.* Paris.

Ogbuagu CSA (1983). *The Nigerian indigenization policy: nationalism or pragmatism? African Affairs.* Vol. 82/327.

Ohiorhenuan JFE (1990). *The Industrialization of Very Late Starters: Historical Experience, Prospects and Strategic Options for Nigeria.* Institute of Development Studies. Discussion Paper No. 273.

Okigbo PNC (1989). *National Development Planning in Nigeria 1900–1992*. London.

Okongwu DA (2003). IPRs and the Transfer of Technology – African Case Study. Presentation at the WIPO–WTO Joint Workshop on IPRs and Transfer of Technology. November 2003. Geneva.

Oyewale AA (2003). Evaluations of the interactions among the key components of science and technology and innovation system in Nigeria. Ph.D. Thesis. Obafemi Awolowo University, Nigeria.

Sofowora MO (2003). Legal framework of foreign private investment in Nigeria. In "Foreign Private Investment in Nigeria – Proceedings of the Twelfth Annual Conference of the Regional Research Units". Central Bank of Nigeria.

Soludo C (2005). *Towards a new monetary authority and financial system: interim progress report*. Central Bank of Nigeria. December.

South African Institute of International Affairs (2004). Games, D., *An Oil Giant Reforms*.

Tsikata YM (2000). *Globalization, Poverty and Inequality in Sub-Saharan Africa: A Political Economy Appraisal*. OECD Development Centre.

UNCTAD (2000a). TNC–SME linkages for development, issues–experiences–best practices. Proceedings of the Special Round Table on TNCs, SMEs and Development. UNCTAD X. 15 February 2000. Bangkok.

UNCTAD (2000b). *Investment Policy Review of Uganda*. New York and Geneva.

UNCTAD (2004). *World Investment Report: The Shift Towards Services*. New York and Geneva.

UNCTAD (2005a). *International Practice in Regulating the Entry of Foreigners to the Workforce*. Report to the Government of Botswana, May.

UNCTAD (2005b), *Investment Policy Review of Kenya*. New York and Geneva.

UNCTAD (2005c). *The Locations Most Favoured by the Largest TNCs*. UNCTAD Investment Brief, No. 4. New York and Geneva.

UNCTAD (2005d). *World Investment Report 2005: Transnational Corporations and the Internationalization of R&D*. New York and Geneva.

UNCTAD (2006). *Globalization of R&D and Developing Countries*. New York and Geneva.

UNCTAD (2007). *World Investment Report: Transnational Corporation, Extractive Industries and Development*. New York and Geneva.

UNIDO and Federal Ministry of Industry, FRN (2003). *Sector-Wide Assessment Study to Develop a Blueprint for the Improvement of the Textile and Clothing Industry in Nigeria*. November.

The United States Commercial Service (2005). *Report on Nigeria*.

World Bank (1974). *Nigeria Options for Long-Term Development*. Baltimore and London.

World Bank (1996). Restoring urban infrastructure and services in Nigeria. In "Findings". Africa Region No. 62, May.

World Bank (2002), *An Assessment of the Private Sector in Nigeria*. Pilot Investment Climate Assessment.

World Bank, FIAS (2004a). *Free Zones: Performance, Lessons Learned and Implications for Zone Development.* Washington DC. September.

World Bank, AATIC (2004b). *Patterns of Africa–Asia Trade and Investment, Potential for Ownership and Partnership.*

World Bank (2005). *Doing Business in 2005: Removing Obstacles to Growth.* New York.

World Bank (2008). *Doing Business in 2008.* New York.

World Bank, FIAS (2000). *Nigeria: Joining the Race for Non-Oil Foreign Investment.*

World Economic Forum (2006). *Global Competitiveness Report 2005–2006.* Oxford University Press.

WTO (2005) *Trade Policy Review of Nigeria.* Geneva.

SELECTED UNCTAD PUBLICATIONS ON TRANSNATIONAL CORPORATIONS AND FDI

A. Serial publications

World Investment Reports
http://www.unctad.org/wir

UNCTAD, World Investment Report 2008. Transnational Corporations and the Infrastructure Challenge (New York and Geneva, 2008). 294 pages. Sales No. E.08.II.D.23.

UNCTAD, World Investment Report 2007. Transnational Corporations, Extractive Industries and Development (New York and Geneva, 2007). 294 pages. Sales No. E.07.II.D.9.

UNCTAD, World Investment Report 2007. Transnational Corporations, Extractive Industries and Development. Overview. 50 pages (A, C, E, F, R, S). Document symbol: UNCTAD/WIR/2007 (Overview). Available free of charge.

UNCTAD, World Investment Report 2006. FDI from Developing and Transition Economies: Implications for Development (New York and Geneva, 2006). 340 pages. Sales No. E.06.II.D.11.

UNCTAD, World Investment Report 2006. FDI from Developing and Transition Economies: Implications for Development. Overview. 50 pages (A, C, E, F, R, S). Document symbol: UNCTAD/WIR/2006 (Overview). Available free of charge.

UNCTAD, World Investment Report 2005. Transnational Corporations and the Internationalization of R&D (New York and Geneva, 2005). 332 pages. Sales No. E.05.II.D.10.

UNCTAD, World Investment Report 2005. Transnational Corporations and the Internationalization of R&D. Overview. 44 pages (A, C, E, F, R, S). Document symbol: UNCTAD/WIR/2005 (Overview). Available free of charge.

UNCTAD, World Investment Report 2004. The Shift Towards Services (New York and Geneva, 2004). 468 pages. Sales No. E.04.II.D.36.

UNCTAD, World Investment Report 2004. The Shift Towards Services. Overview. 54 pages (A, C, E, F, R, S). Document symbol: UNCTAD/WIR/2004 (Overview). Available free to charge.

UNCTAD, World Investment Report 2003. FDI Policies for Development: National and International Perspectives (New York and Geneva, 2003). 303 pages. Sales No. E.03.II.D.8.

UNCTAD, World Investment Report 2003. FDI Policies for Development: National and International Perspectives. Overview. 42 pages (A, C, E, F, R, S). Document symbol: UNCTAD/WIR/2003 (Overview). Available free to charge.

UNCTAD, World Investment Report 2002: Transnational Corporations and Export Competitiveness (New York and Geneva, 2002). 350 pages. Sales No. E.02.II.D.4.

UNCTAD, World Investment Report 2002: Transnational Corporations and Export Competitiveness. Overview. 66 pages (A, C, E, F, R, S). Document symbol: UNCTAD/WIR/2002 (Overview). Available free of charge.

UNCTAD, World Investment Report 2001: Promoting Linkages (New York and Geneva, 2001). 354 pages. Sales No. E.01.II.D.12.

UNCTAD, World Investment Report 2001: Promoting Linkages. Overview. 63 pages (A, C, E, F, R, S). Document symbol: UNCTAD/WIR/2001 (Overview). Available free of charge.

UNCTAD, World Investment Report 2000: Cross-border Mergers and Acquisitions and Development (New York and Geneva, 2000). 337 pages. Sales No. E.00.II.D.20.

UNCTAD, World Investment Report 2000: Cross-border Mergers and Acquisitions and Development. Overview. 65 pages (A, C, E, F, R, S). Document symbol: UNCTAD/WIR/2000 (Overview). Available free of charge.

UNCTAD, World Investment Report 1999: Foreign Direct Investment and the Challenge of Development (New York and Geneva, 1999). 541 pages. Sales No. E.99.II.D.3.

UNCTAD, World Investment Report 1999: Foreign Direct Investment and the Challenge of Development. Overview. 75 pages (A, C, E, F, R, S). Document symbol: UNCTAD/WIR/1999 (Overview). Available free of charge.

UNCTAD, World Investment Report 1998: Trends and Determinants (New York and Geneva, 1998). 463 pages. Sales No. E.98.II.D.5.

UNCTAD, World Investment Report 1998: Trends and Determinants. Overview. 72 pages (A, C, E, F, R, S). Document symbol: UNCTAD/WIR/1998 (Overview). Available free of charge.

UNCTAD, World Investment Report 1997: Transnational Corporations, Market Structure and Competition Policy (New York and Geneva, 1997). 416 pages. Sales No. E.97.II.D. 10.

UNCTAD, World Investment Report 1997: Transnational Corporations, Market Structure and Competition Policy. Overview. 76 pages (A, C, E, F, R, S). Document symbol: UNCTAD/ITE/IIT/5 (Overview). Available free of charge.

UNCTAD, World Investment Report 1996: Investment, Trade and International Policy Arrangements (New York and Geneva, 1996). 364 pages. Sales No. E.96.II.A. 14.

UNCTAD, World Investment Report 1996: Investment, Trade and International Policy Arrangements. Overview. 22 pages (A, C, E, F, R, S). Document symbol: UNCTAD/DTCI/32 (Overview). Available free of charge.

UNCTAD, World Investment Report 1995: Transnational Corporations and Competitiveness (New York and Geneva, 1995). 491 pages. Sales No. E.95.II.A.9.

UNCTAD, World Investment Report 1995: Transnational Corporations and Competitiveness. Overview. 68 pages (A, C, E, F, R, S). Document symbol: UNCTAD/DTCI/26 (Overview). Available free of charge.

UNCTAD, World Investment Report 1994: Transnational Corporations, Employment and the Workplace (New York and Geneva, 1994). 482 pages. Sales No.E.94.II.A.14.

UNCTAD, World Investment Report 1994: Transnational Corporations, Employment and the Workplace. An Executive Summary. 34 pages (C, E, also available in Japanese). Document symbol: UNCTAD/DTCI/10 (Overview). Available free of charge.

UNCTAD, World Investment Report 1993: Transnational Corporations and Integrated International Production (New York and Geneva, 1993). 290 pages. Sales No. E.93.II.A.14.

UNCTAD, World Investment Report 1993: Transnational Corporations and Integrated International Production. An Executive Summary. 31 pages (C, E). Document symbol: ST/CTC/159 (Executive Summary). Available free of charge.

DESD/TCMD, World Investment Report 1992: Transnational Corporations as Engines of Growth (New York, 1992). 356 pages. Sales No. E.92.II.A.24.

DESD/TCMD, World Investment Report 1992: Transnational Corporations as Engines of Growth: An Executive Summary. 26 pages. Document symbol: ST/CTC/143 (Executive Summary). Available free of charge.

UNCTC, World Investment Report 1991: The Triad in Foreign Direct Investment (New York, 1991). 108 pages. Sales No. E.9 1.II.A. 12. $25.

World Investment Directories

World Investment Directory: Vol. VIII: Central and Eastern Europe, 2003. 86 p. (Overview)+CD-ROM (country profiles). Sales No. E.03.II.D.12. $25.

World Investment Directory, Vol. VII (Parts I and II): Asia and the Pacific, 1999. 332+638 p. Sales No. E.00. II.D.21. $80.

World Investment Directory, Vol. VI: West Asia, 1996. 138 p. Sales No. E.97.II.A.2. $35.

World Investment Directory, Vol. V: Africa, 1996. 461 p. Sales No. E.97.II.A.1. $75.

World Investment Directory, Vol. IV: Latin America and the Caribbean, 1994. 478 p. Sales No. E.94.II.A.10. $65.

World Investment Directory, Vol. III: Developed Countries, 1992. 532 p. Sales No. E.93.II.A.9. $75.

World Investment Directory, Vol. II: Central and Eastern Europe, 1992. 432 p. Sales No. E.93.II.A.1. $65. (Joint publication with the United Nations Economic Commission for Europe.)

World Investment Directory, Vol. I: Asia and the Pacific, 1992. 356 p. Sales No. E.92.II.A.11. $65.

Investment Policy Reviews
http://www.unctad.org/ipr

UNCTAD, Investment Policy Review of the Dominican Republic (Geneva, 2009). 116 pages. UNCTAD/ITE/IPC/2007/09.

UNCTAD, Investment Policy Review of Vietnam (Geneva, 2008). 158 pages. UNCTAD/ITE/IPC/2007/10.

UNCTAD, Investment Policy Review of Morocco (Geneva, 2008). 142 pages. UNCTAD/ITE/IPC/2006/15.

UNCTAD, Investment Policy Review of Zambia (Geneva, 2007). 76 pages. UNCTAD/ITE/IPC/2006/14.

UNCTAD, Report on the Implementation of the Investment Policy Review of Uganda (Geneva, 2007) 30 pages. UNCTAD/ITE/IPC/2006/15.

UNCTAD, Investment Policy Review of Rwanda (Geneva, 2006). 136 pages. UNCTAD/ITE/IPC/2006/11.

UNCTAD, Investment Policy Review of Colombia (Geneva, 2006). 86 pages. UNCTAD/ITE/IPC/2005/11.

UNCTAD, Report on the Implementation of the Investment Policy Review of Egypt (Geneva, 2005). 18 pages. UNCTAD/ITE/IPC/2005/7.

UNCTAD, Investment Policy Review of Kenya (Geneva, 2005). 114 pages. UNCTAD/ITE/IPC/2005/8.

UNCTAD, Investment Policy Review of Benin (Geneva, 2005). 126 pages. UNCTAD/ITE/IPC/2004/4.

UNCTAD, Investment Policy Review of Algeria (Geneva, 2004). 110 pages. UNCTAD/ITE/IPC/2003/9.

UNCTAD, Investment Policy Review of Sri Lanka (Geneva, 2003). 89 pages.UNCTAD/ITE/IPC/2003/8

UNCTAD, Investment Policy Review of Lesotho (Geneva, 2003). 105 pages. Sales No. E.03.II.D.18.

UNCTAD, Investment Policy Review of Nepal. (Geneva, 2003). 89 pages. Sales No.E.03.II.D.17.

UNCTAD, Investment Policy Review of Ghana (Geneva, 2002). 103 pages. Sales No. E.02.II.D.20.

UNCTAD, Investment Policy Review of Botswana (Geneva, 2003). 107 pages. Sales No. E.03.II.D.1.

UNCTAD, Investment Policy Review of the United Republic of Tanzania (Geneva, 2002). 109 pages. Sales No. E.02.II.D.6. $ 20.

UNCTAD, Investment and Innovation Policy Review of Ethiopia (Geneva, 2001). 130 pages. Sales No. E.01.II.D.5.

UNCTAD, Investment Policy Review of Ecuador. (Geneva, 2001). 136 pages. Sales No. E.01.II.D.31. Also available in Spanish.

UNCTAD, Investment Policy Review of Mauritius (Geneva, 2000). 92 pages. Sales No. E.00.II.D.11.

UNCTAD, Investment Policy Review of Peru (Geneva, 2000). 109 pages. Sales No. E.00.II.D.7.

UNCTAD, Investment Policy Review of Uganda (Geneva, 1999). 71 pages. Sales No. E.99.II.D.24.

UNCTAD, Investment Policy Review of Uzbekistan (Geneva, 1999). 5 pages. UNCTAD/ITE/IIP/Misc.13.

UNCTAD, Investment Policy Review of Egypt (Geneva, 1999). 119 pages. Sales No. E.99.II.D.20.

Blue Books on Best Practice in Investment Promotion and Facilitation

UNCTAD, Blue Book on Best Practice in Investment Promotion and Faciliation: Kenya (Geneva, 2005).

UNCTAD, Blue Book on Best Practice in Investment Promotion and Faciliation: United Republic of Tanzania (Geneva, 2005).

UNCTAD, Blue Book on Best Practice in Investment Promotion and Faciliation: Uganda (Geneva, 2005).

UNCTAD, Blue Book on Best Practice in Investment Promotion and Faciliation: Cambodia (Geneva, 2004).

UNCTAD, Blue Book on Best Practice in Investment Promotion and Faciliation: Lao People's Democratic Republic (Geneva, 2004).

Investment Guides
http://www.unctad.org/investmentguides

UNCTAD. An Investment Guide to Rwanda: Opportunities and Conditions (Geneva, 2006). Document symbol: UNCTAD/ITE/IIA/2006/3. Free of charge.

UNCTAD. An Investment Guide to Mali: Opportunities and Conditions (Geneva, 2006). Document symbol: UNCTAD/ITE/IIA/2006/2. Free of charge.

UNCTAD and ICC. An Investment Guide to East Africa (Geneva, 2005). Document symbol: UNCTAD/IIA/2005/4. Free of charge.

UNCTAD and ICC. An Investment Guide to the United Republic of Tanzania (Geneva, 2005). Document symbol: UNCTAD/IIA/2005/3. Free of charge.

UNCTAD and ICC. An Investment Guide to Kenya (Geneva, 2005). Document symbol: UNCTAD/IIA/2005/2. Free of charge.

UNCTAD and ICC. An Investment Guide to Mauritania (Geneva, 2004). Document symbol: UNCTAD/IIA/2004/4. Free of charge.

UNCTAD and ICC. An Investment Guide to Cambodia (Geneva, 2003). 89 pages. Document symbol: UNCTAD/IIA/2003/6. Free of charge.

UNCTAD and ICC. An Investment Guide to Nepal (Geneva, 2003). 97 pages. Document symbol: UNCTAD/IIA/2003/2. Free of charge.

UNCTAD and ICC. An Investment Guide to Mozambique (Geneva, 2002). 109 pages. Document symbol: UNCTAD/IIA/4. Free of charge.

UNCTAD and ICC. An Investment Guide to Uganda (Geneva, 2001). 76 pages. Document symbol: UNCTAD/ITE/IIT/Misc.30. Publication updated in 2004. New document symbol UNCTAD/ITE/IIA/2004/3. Free of charge.

UNCTAD and ICC. An Investment Guide to Mali (Geneva, 2001). 105 pages. Document symbol: UNCTAD/ITE/IIT/Misc.24. Publication updated in 2004. New document symbol UNCTAD/ITE/IIA/2004/1. Free of charge.

UNCTAD and ICC. An Investment Guide to Ethiopia (Geneva, 2000). 68 pages. Document symbol: UNCTAD/ITE/IIT/Misc.19. Publication updated in 2004. New document symbol UNCTAD/ITE/IIA/2004/2. Free of charge.

 UNCTAD and ICC. An Investment Guide to Bangladesh (Geneva, 2000). 66 pages. Document symbol: UNCTAD/ITE/IIT/Misc.29. Free of charge.

Issues in International Investment Agreements
http://www.unctad.org/iia

UNCTAD. Bilateral Investment Treaties 1995–2006: Trends in Investment Rulemaking (New York and Geneva, 2006).

UNCTAD. Investment Provisions in Economic Integration Agreements (New York and Geneva, 2006).

UNCTAD. Glossary of Key Concepts Used in IIAs. UNCTAD Series on Issues in International Investment Agreements (New York and Geneva, 2003).

UNCTAD. Incentives UNCTAD Series on Issues in International Investment Agreements (New York and Geneva, 2003). Sales No. E.04.II.D.6. $15.

UNCTAD. Transparency. UNCTAD Series on Issues in International Investment Agreements (New York and Geneva, 2003). Sales No. E.03.II.D.7. $15.

UNCTAD. Dispute Settlement: Investor-State. UNCTAD Series on Issues in International Investment Agreements (New York and Geneva, 2003). 128 pages. Sales No. E.03.II.D.5. $15.

UNCTAD. Dispute Settlement: State-State. UNCTAD Series on Issues in International Investment Agreements (New York and Geneva, 2003). 109 pages. Sales No. E.03.II.D.6 $16.

UNCTAD. Transfer of Technology. UNCTAD Series on Issues on International Investment Agreements (New York and Geneva, 2001). 135 pages. Sales No. E.01.II.D.33. $16.

UNCTAD. Illicit Payments. UNCTAD Series on Issues on International Investment Agreements (New York and Geneva, 2001). 112 pages. Sales No. E.01.II.D.20. $13.

UNCTAD. Home Country Measures. UNCTAD Series on Issues on International Investment Agreements (New York and Geneva, 2001). 95 pages. Sales No. E.01.II.D.19. $12.

UNCTAD. Host Country Operational Measures. UNCTAD Series on Issues on International Investment Agreements (New York and Geneva, 2001). 105 pages. Sales No. E.01.II.D.18. $18.

UNCTAD. Social Responsibility. UNCTAD Series on Issues on International Investment Agreements (New York and Geneva, 2001). 87 pages. Sales No. E.01.II.D.4.$15.

UNCTAD. Environment. UNCTAD Series on Issues on International Investment Agreements (New York and Geneva 2001). 106 pages. Sales No. E.01.II.D.3. $15.

UNCTAD. Transfer of Funds. UNCTAD Series on Issues on International Investment Agreements (New York and Geneva 2000). 79 pages. Sales No. E.00.II.D.38. $10.

UNCTAD. Flexibility for Development. UNCTAD Series on Issues on International Investment Agreements (New York and Geneva 2000). 185 pages. Sales No. E.00.II.D.6. $15.

UNCTAD. Employment. UNCTAD Series on Issues on International Investment Agreements (New York and Geneva, 2000). 64 pages. Sales No. E.00.II.D.15. $12.

UNCTAD. Taxation. UNCTAD Series on Issues on International Investment Agreements (New York and Geneva, 2000). 111 pages. Sales No. E.00.II.D.5. $15.
UNCTAD, Taking of Property. UNCTAD Series on Issues on International Investment Agreements (New York and Geneva, 2000). 78 pages. Sales No. E.00.II.D.4. $12.

UNCTAD. Trends in International investment Agreements: An Overview. UNCTAD Series on Issues on International Investment Agreements (New York and Geneva, 1999). 133 pages. Sales No. E.99.II.D.23. $12.

UNCTAD. Lessons from the MAI. UNCTAD Series on Issues on International Investment Agreements (New York and Geneva 1999). 52 pages. Sales No. E.99.II.D.26. $10.

UNCTAD. National Treatment. UNCTAD Series on Issues in International Investment Agreements (New York and Geneva, 1999). 88 pages. Sales No. E.99.II.D. 16. $12.

UNCTAD. Fair and Equitable Treatment. UNCTAD Series on Issues in International Investment Agreements (New York and Geneva, 1999). 80 pages. Sales No. E.99.II.D.15. $12.

UNCTAD. Investment-Related Trade Measures. UNCTAD Series on Issues in International Investment Agreements (New York and Geneva, 1999). 64 pages. Sales No. E.99.II.D.12.$12.

UNCTAD. Most-Favoured-Nation Treatment. UNCTAD Series on Issues in International Investment Agreements (New York and Geneva, 1999). 72 pages. Sales No. E.99.II.D.11. $12.

UNCTAD. Admission and Establishment. UNCTAD Series on Issues in International Investment Agreements (New York and Geneva, 1999). 72 pages. Sales No. E.99.II.D.10. $12.

UNCTAD. Scope and Definition. UNCTAD Series on Issues in International Investment Agreements (New York and Geneva, 1999). 96 pages. Sales No. E.99.II.D.9. $12.

UNCTAD. Transfer Pricing. UNCTAD Series on Issues in International Investment Agreements (New York and Geneva, 1999). 72 pages. Sales No. E.99.II.D.8. $12.

UNCTAD. Foreign Direct Investment and Development. UNCTAD Series on Issues in International Investment Agreements (New York and Geneva, 1999). 88 pages. Sales No. E.98.II.D.15A12.

International Investment Instruments

UNCTAD's Work Programme on International Investment Agreements: From UNCTAD IX to UNCTAD X. Document symbol: UNCTAD/ITE/IIT/Misc.26. Available free of charge.

UNCTAD. Progress Report. Work undertaken within UNCTAD's work programme on International Investment Agreements between the 10th Conference of UNCTAD 10th Conference of UNCTAD, Bangkok, February 2000, and July 2002 (New York and Geneva, 2002). UNCTAD/ITE/Misc.58. Available free of charge.

UNCTAD. Bilateral Investment Treaties in the Mid-1990s (New York and Geneva, 1998). 322 pages. Sales No. E.98.II.D.8. $46.

UNCTAD. Bilateral Investment Treaties: 1959-1999 (Geneva and New York, 2000) Sales No. E.92.II.A.16. $22.

UNCTAD. International Investment Instruments: A Compendium (New York and Geneva, 1996 to 2003). 12 volumes. Vol. I: Sales No. E.96.A.II.A.9. Vol. II: Sales No. E.96.II.A.10. Vol. III: Sales No. E.96.II.A.11. Vol. IV: Sales No. E.00.II.D.13. Vol. V: Sales No. E.00.II.A.14. Vol. VI: Sales No. E.01.II.D.34. Vol. VII: Sales No. E.02.II.D.14. Vol. VIII: Sales No. E.02.II.D.15. Vol. IX: Sales No. E.02.II.D.16. Vol. X: Sales No. E.02.II.D.21. Vol. XI: Sales No. E.04.II.D.9. Vol. XII: Sales No. E.04.II.D.10. $60.

UNCTC and ICC. Bilateral Investment Treaties. A joint publication by the United Nations Centre on Transnational Corporations and the International Chamber of Commerce (New York, 1992). 46 pages. Sales No. E.92.II.A. 16. $22.

UNCTC. The New Code Environment. Current Studies, Series A, No. 16. (New York, 1990). 54 pages. Sales No. E.90.II.A.7. Out of print. Available on microfiche. Paper copy from microfiche: $68.

UNCTC. Key Concepts in International Investment Arrangements and Their Relevance to Negotiations on International Transactions in Services. Current Studies, Series A, No. 13. (New York, 1990). 66 pages. Sales No. E.90.II.A.3. $9.

UNCTC. Bilateral Investment Treaties (New York, 1988). (Also published by Graham and Trotman, London/ Dordrecht/Boston, 1988). 188 pages. Sales No. E.88.II.A. 1. $20.

UNCTC. The United Nations Code of Conduct on Transnational Corporations. Current Studies, Series A, No. 4. (New York, 1986). 80 pages. Sales No. E.86.II.A. 15. Out of print. Available on microfiche. Paper copy from microfiche: $88.

Vagts, Detlev F., The Question of a Reference to International Obligations in the United Nations Code of Conduct on Transnational Corporations: A Different View. Current Studies,

Series A, No. 2. (New York, 1986). 17 pages. Sales No. E.86.II.A.11. Out of print. Available on microfiche. Paper copy from microfiche: $24.

Robinson, Patrick, The Question of a Reference to International Law in the United Nations Code of Conduct on Transnational Corporations. Current Studies, Series A, No.1. (New York, 1986). 22 pages. Sales No. E.86.II.A.5. $4.

UNCTC, Transnational Corporations: Material Relevant to the Formulation of a Code of Conduct (New York, 1977). 114 pages (E, F, S). UN Document Symbol: EX. 10/ 10 and Corr. 1. $7.

UNCTC, Transnational Corporations: Issues Involved in the Formulation of a Code of Conduct (New York, 1976). 41 pages (E, F, R, S). Sales No. E.77.II.A.5. Out of print. Available on microfiche. Paper copy from microfiche: $41.

ASIT Advisory Studies
http://www.unctad.org/asit

No. 17. The World of Investment Promotion at a Glance: A Survey of Investment Promotion Practices. UNCTAD/ITE/IPC/3. Free of charge.

No. 16. Tax Incentives and Foreign Direct Investment: A Global Survey. 180 p. Sales No. E.01.II.D.5.

No. 15. Investment Regimes in the Arab World: Issues and Policies. 232 p. Sales No. E/F.00.II.D.32.

No. 14. Handbook on Outward Investment Promotion Agencies and Institutions. 50 p. Sales No. E.99. II.D.22.

No. 13. Survey of Best Practices in Investment Promotion. 71 p. Sales No. E.97.II.D.11.

B. Individual Studies

UNCTAD. Investment and Technology Policies for Competitiveness: Review of Successful Country Experiences (Geneva, 2003). Document symbol: UNCTAD/ITE/ICP/2003/2.

UNCTAD. The Development Dimension of FDI: Policy and Rule-Making Perspectives (Geneva, 2003). Sales No. E.03.II.D.22. $35.

UNCTAD. FDI and Performance Requirements: New Evidence from Selected Countries (Geneva, 2003). Sales No. E.03.II.D.32. 318 pages. $ 35.

UNCTAD. Measures of the Transnationalization of Economic Activity (New York and Geneva, 2001). Document symbol: UNCTAD/ITE/IIA/1. Sales No. E.01.II.D.2.

UNCTAD. FDI Determinants and TNC Strategies: The Case of Brazil (Geneva, 2000). Sales No. E.00:II.D.2.

UNCTAD. The Competitiveness Challenge: Transnational Corporations and Industrial Restructuring in Developing Countries (Geneva, 2000). Sales No. E.00.II.D.35.

UNCTAD. Foreign Direct Investment in Africa: Performance and Potential (Geneva, 1999). Document symbol: UNCTAD/ITE/IIT/Misc.15. Available free of charge.

UNCTAD. The Financial Crisis in Asia and Foreign Direct Investment An Assessment (Geneva, 1998). 110 pages. Sales No. GV.E.98.0.29. $20.
UNCTAD. Handbook on Foreign Direct Investment by Small and Medium-sized Enterprises: Lessons from Asia (New York and Geneva, 1998). 202 pages. Sales No. E.98.II.D.4. $48.

UNCTAD. Handbook on Foreign Direct Investment by Small and Medium-sized Enterprises: Lessons from Asia. Executive Summary and Report on the Kunming Conference. 70 pages. Document symbol: UNCTAD/ITE/IIT/6 (Summary). Available free of charge.

UNCTAD. Survey of Best Practices in Investment Promotion (New York and Geneva, 1997). 81 pages. Sales No. E.97.II.D.11. $35.

UNCTAD. Incentives and Foreign Direct Investment (New York and Geneva, 1996). Current Studies, Series A, No. 30. 98 pages. Sales No. E.96.II.A.6. $25.

UNCTC. Foreign Direct Investment in the People's Republic of China (New York, 1988). 110 pages. Sales No. E.88.II.A.3. Out of print. Available on microfiche. Paper copy from microfiche: $122.

UNCTAD. Foreign Direct Investment, Trade, Aid and Migration Current Studies, Series A, No. 29. (A joint publication with the International Organization for Migration, Geneva, 1996). 90 pages. Sales No. E.96M.A.8. $25.

UNCTAD. Explaining and Forecasting Regional Flows of Foreign Direct Investment (New York, 1993). Current Studies, Series A, No. 26. 58 pages. Sales No. E.94.II.A.5. $25.

UNCTAD. Small and Medium-sized Transnational Corporations: Role, Impact and Policy Implications (New York and Geneva, 1993). 242 pages. Sales No. E.93.II.A. 15. $35.

UNCTAD. Small and Medium-sized Transnational Corporations: Executive Summary and Report of the Osaka Conference (Geneva, 1994). 60 pages. Available free of charge.

DESD/TCMD. From the Common Market to EC 92: Regional Economic Integration in the European Community and Transnational Corporations (New York, 1993). 134 pages. Sales No. E.93.II.A.2. $25.

DESD/TCMD. Debt-Equity Swaps and Development (New York, 1993). 150 pages. Sales No. E.93.II.A.7. $35.

DESD/TCMD. Transnational Corporations from Developing Countries: Impact on Their Home Countries (New York, 1993). 116 pages. Sales No. E.93.II.A.8. $15.

DESD/TCMD. Foreign Investment and Trade Linkages in Developing Countries (New York, 1993). 108 pages. Sales No. E.93.II.A. 12. Out of print.

UNCTC. Foreign Direct Investment and Industrial Restructuring in Mexico. Current Studies, Series A, No. 18. (New York, 1992). 114 pages. Sales No. E.92.II.A.9. $12.50.

UNCTC. The Determinants of Foreign Direct Investment: A Survey of the Evidence (New York, 1992). 84 pages. Sales No. E.92.II.A.2. $12.50.

UNCTC and UNCTAD. The Impact of Trade-Related Investment Measures on Trade and Development (Geneva and New York, 1991). 104 pages. Sales No. E.91 II.A. 19. $17.50.

UNCTC. The Challenge of Free Economic Zones in Central and Eastern Europe: International Perspective (New York, 1991). 442 pages. Sales No. E.90.II.A.27. $75.

UNCTC. The Role of Free Economic Zones in the USSR and Eastern Europe. Current Studies, Series A, No. 14. (New York, 1990). 84 pages. Sales No. E.90.II.A.5. $10.
+
UNCTC. Foreign Direct Investment, Debt and Home Country Policies. Current Studies, Series A, No. 20. (New York, 1990). 50 pages. Sales No. E.90.II.A. 16. $12.50.

UNCTC. News Issues in the Uruguay Round of Multilateral Trade Negotiations. Current Studies, Series A, No. 19. (New York, 1990). 52 pages. Sales No. E.90.II.A. 15. $12.50.

UNCTC. Regional Economic Integration and Transnational Corporations in the 1990s: Europe 1992, North America, and Developing Countries. Current Studies, Series A, No. 15. (New York, 1990). 52 pages. Sales No. E.90.II.A. 14. $12.50.

UNCTC. Transnational Corporations and International Economic Relations: Recent Developments and Selected Issues. Current Studies, Series A, No. 11. (New York, 1989). 50 pages. Sales No. E.89.II.A.15. Out of print. Available on microfiche. Paper copy from microfiche: $60.

UNCTC. The Process of Transnationalization and Transnational Mergers. Current Studies, Series A, No. 8. (New York, 1989). 91 pages. Sales No. E.89.II.A.4. Out of print. Available on microfiche. Paper copy from microfiche: $106.

UNCTC and ILO. Economic and Social Effects of Multinational Enterprises in Export Processing Zones (Geneva, International Labour Office, 1988). 169 pages. ISBN: 92-2106194-9. S1727.50.

UNCTC. Measures Strengthening the Negotiating Capacity of Governments in Their Relations with Transnational Corporations: Regional Integration cum/versus Corporate Integration. A Technical Paper (New York, 1982). 63 pages. Sales No. E..82.II.A.6. Out of print. Available on microfiche. Paper copy from microfiche: $71.

C. Journals

Transnational Corporations Journal (formerly The CTC Reporter). Published three times a year. Annual subscription price: $45; individual issues $20.
http://www.unctad.org/tnc

READERSHIP SURVEY

Investment Policy Review of the Nigeria

In order to improve the quality and relevance of the work of the UNCTAD Division on Investment, Technology and Enterprise Development, it would be useful to receive the views of readers on this and other similar publications. It would therefore be greatly appreciated if you could complete the following question-naire and return it to:

Readership Survey

UNCTAD, *Division on Investment, Technology and Enterprise Development*
Palais des Nations
Room E-10074
CH-1211 Geneva 10
Switzerland
Or by Fax to: 41-22-9170197

> This questionnaire is also
> available to be filled out
> on line at:
> **www.unctad.org/ipr**

1. Name and professional address of respondent (optional):

_____

_____

2. Which of the following best describes your area of work?

Government	◯	Public enterprise	◯
Private enterprise institution	◯	Academic or research	◯
International organization	◯	Media	◯
Not-for-profit organization	◯	Other (specify)	◯

3. In which country do you work?

4. What is your assessment of the contents of this publication?

Excellent	◯	Adequate	◯
Good	◯	Poor	◯

5. How useful is this publication to your work?

Very useful ◯   Of some use ◯   Irrelevant ◯

6. Please indicate the three things you liked best about this publication and are useful to your work:

_____

_____

_____

_____

7. Please indicate the three things you liked least about this publication:

_____

_____

_____

8. If you have read more than the present publication of the UNCTAD Division on Investment, Enterprise Development and Technology, what is your overall assessment of them?

Consistently good ◯   Usually good, but with some exceptions ◯

Generally mediocre ◯   Poor ◯

9. On the average, how useful are these publications to you in your work?

Irrelevant ◯   Of some use ◯   Very useful ◯

10. Are you a regular recipient of Transnational Corporations (formerly The CTC Reporter), the Division's tri-annual refereed journal?

No ◯   Yes ◯

If not, please check here if you would like to receive a sample copy sent to the name and address you have given above. Other titles you would like to receive instead (see list of publications).

_____

_____

_____

11. How or where did you get this publication:

I bought it ◯   In a seminar/workshop ◯

I requested a courtesy copy ◯   Direct mailing ◯

Other ◯

12. Would you like to receive information on the work of UNCTAD in the area of Investment Technology and Enterprise Development through e-mail ? If yes, please write your e-mail address below:

...ay be obtained from bookstores and distributors ...Please consult your bookstore or write to:

...or **Africa and Europe** to:

Sales Section
...ted Nations Office at Geneva
Palais des Nations
CH-1211 Geneva 10
Switzerland
Tel: (41-22) 917-1234
Fax: (41-22) 917-0123
E-mail: unpubli@unog.ch

...**Caribbean, Latin America and North America** to:
Sales Section
Room DC2-0853
...United Nations Secretariat
New York, NY 10017
United States
Tel: (1-212) 963-8302 or (800) 253-9646
Fax: (1-212) 963-3489
E-mail: publications@un.org
All prices are quoted in United States dollars.

For further information on the work of the Division on Investment and Enterprise, UNCTAD, please address inquiries to:
United Nations Conference on Trade and Development
Division on Investment and Enterprise
Palais des Nations, Room E-10054
CH-1211 Geneva 10, Switzerland
Telephone: (41-22) 917-5534
Fax: (41-22) 917-0498
E-mail: alexandre.dabbou@unctad.org
http://www.unctad.org